Diplomatic Divorce:
Why America Should End Its Love Affair
with the United Nations

Stroud & Hall Publishers
P.O. Box 27210
Macon, GA 31221
www.stroudhall.com

The paper used in this publication meets the minimum requirements
of American National Standard for Information Sciences—
Permanence of Paper for Printed Library Materials.
ANSI Z39.48–1984. (alk. paper)

Library of Congress Cataloging-in-Publication Data

Kilgannon, Thomas P., 1966-
Diplomatic divorce / by Thomas P. Kilgannon.
p. cm.
ISBN 0-9745376-6-7 (hardcover : alk. paper)
1. United States—Foreign relations—21st century.
2. International relations.
 I. Title.

JZ1480.K55 2006
327.73--dc22

2006002518

Diplomatic Divorce

Why America Should End Its Love Affair

with the United Nations

THOMAS P. KILGANNON

For Meg

Table of Contents

Foreword

By LtCol Oliver L. North USMC (Ret.)

After the devastating terrorist attacks of 9/11/01, Tom Kilgannon, my friend and colleague at Freedom Alliance, and I remarked to each other that winning the war on terror would require decisive action in two arenas: on the battlefield and within the international community. Since Tom has young children at home, we agreed that I would cover the military side of this campaign while he followed the diplomatic front. It really wasn't a fair division of labor. I got to hang around with heroes in Iraq and Afghanistan while poor Kilgannon was forced to chart the "progress" at the United Nations with the likes of Kofi Annan and his corrupt cronies.

Tom Kilgannon rose to the challenge of this onerous task. He understands the inner workings and hidden mechanisms of the United Nations like few others. Tom knows the aristocratic, liberal elites who are the pandering enablers and apologists for this corrupt, sovereignty-snatching, global bureaucracy. And because Kilgannon attends and monitors UN conferences around the world, he has been an eyewitness to the efforts of Bush-bashing, America haters who carry diplomatic passports and undermine U.S. efforts in the War on Terror, propping up dictators like Robert Mugabe and arming tyrants. In the pages that follow, Tom Kilgannon exposes the scandals, corruption, and conspiracies that the planetary potentates in the Big Blue Building on Turtle Bay try to keep hidden from the American public.

In March 2003, prior to the commencement of Operation Iraqi Freedom, I reported from Kuwait that "senior U.S. military officials were concerned that Saddam Hussein was using cash from the UN Oil-for-Food program to buy votes in the Security Council." The charge was immediately trashed and UN officials claimed the allegation was "preposterous" and "unfounded."

Now we know better. Since that initial report, we have learned that cash from the Oil-for-Food program—administered by one of Kofi Annan's most trusted aides, Benon Sevan—was used by Saddam Hussein for everything *but* food. The Iraqi dictator utilized UN-provided funds to build palaces, buy weapons, finance terror, enrich Communist Party officials, subsidize the P.L.O., and bribe anti-American political figures in France, Libya, Syria, Indonesia, Great Britain, and Russia. Even Kofi's son, Kojo Annan, has been implicated in the scandal.

Annan's ten-year tenure as the head of the United Nations is the most corrupt in the sixty-year history of the organization. During his reign, UN peacekeepers have been accused of child rape in the Congo, killing unarmed civilians in Haiti, and doing nothing to prevent countless murders from East Timor to Bosnia. Ruud Lubbers, the UN High Commissioner for Refugees, was forced to resign under a cloud of scandal that rivals the sexual excesses and escapades of the Clinton White House. And through it all, the self-policed, unaccountable secretary-general sees and hears nothing while being lauded by those around the world who hate America.

As Tom Kilgannon points out in the pages that follow, waste, fraud, and abuse at the United Nations didn't begin with the Oil-for-Food scandal and it doesn't end there. The entire UN establishment—including its Security Council, Human Rights Commission, International Atomic Energy Agency, and peacekeeping operations are rife with incompetence, deceit, and deception. Yet, this powerful globe-spanning bureaucracy, swathed in secrecy and cloaked in diplomatic doublespeak defies efforts at reform while extracting billions of dollars from American taxpayers who foot 22 percent of UN dues, more than any other nation.

Now, with Iranian mullahs acquiring nuclear weapons and the means of launching them, the UN secretary-general purports to lecture the United States not to "escalate" tensions and to wait patiently for the United Nations to act. Before accepting the premise that we should place the safety and security of the American people in the hands of the UN, our leaders should pay attention to this book, *Diplomatic Divorce,* and heed its advice. Tom Kilgannon has exposed the noble, utopian folly of this experiment in "World Government." It's time to send Kofi Annan a "Dear John" letter; pack our bags; leave no forwarding address; get out while the getting's good. As Kilgannon correctly notes, it is time for America to end her love affair with the United Nations.

Oliver L. North
Bluemont, Virginia

Introduction

"Know your enemy," Sun Tzu taught us. It is sound and timely advice if the United States is to remain a great nation, for America finds herself engaged in two great battles.

The first is the war against radical Islamic jihadism that has been foisted upon us by a brutal enemy. The primary theatres are in Iraq and Afghanistan, and the casualties are sadly evident. In this war, our president is fully engaged, leading the charge authorized by the people's representatives.

The second is a war for America's destiny. In it, our political leadership is nonexistent. America's sons and daughters did not invite it, and we do not want it. But fight it we must, and to do so, we have to identify our enemy.

They are the apostles of universal law, adherents of an ideology that would subordinate the Republic to international government. They are globalists who assemble under what Henry Cabot Lodge called the "mongrel banner" of utopian ideals. They are Ivory Tower elites and tambourine tappers from the hippie generation who've joined forces to chant evils against Uncle Sam. They preach a false dogma of international equality and have hung our Constitution on the discount rack.

Our enemy believes in global government. Their faith is vested in the United Nations. Their catechism is the UN Charter. Their Maharishi is Kofi Annan.

Here at home, they have captured the Democratic Party and are making in-roads in the GOP. They are forcing the United States to answer to a higher earthly authority. From trade to national security to tax policy to the Internet, advocates of universal government want to make the decisions that will chart America's future. In some cases, they already are.

Whether we like it or not, we are in a war for America's destiny.

In this war, Kofi Annan is an enemy combatant. He dons not the fatigues of a soldier, but the war paint of a diplomat. His fancy suits and genteel ways have seduced the American Left—and even some on the

Right—into believing that he is an honest broker among nations. *He is not.* As the titular head of the World Federalists, he is committed to bringing the United States into the fold of one-world government.

"If you know your enemy and know yourself," Sun Tzu continued, "you need not fear the result of a hundred battles." But, he warned, "If you know yourself but not the enemy, for every victory gained you will also suffer a defeat."

This is where we are today. Though the warning signs abound, our political leadership fails to identify and engage the enemy. As a result, America's inherent greatness is being discounted to an institution that practices moral relativism, is hopelessly corrupt, inherently flawed, and anti-American to the core.

As a member of Congress from Georgia, Bob Barr recognized the threat and tried to rally a largely ambivalent Republican party. Today he laments that America, despite her wealth and power, is being bullied into abandoning the principles that made this country great. He explained:

> Efforts to destroy the American experiment persist, and our Constitution continues to come under attack from those abroad. Sadly, most Americans are not even aware of these threats. Though not international terrorists, those threatening our freedoms do share a common disdain for America's freedom and strength. I speak of those individuals and governments that have hijacked the United Nations apparatus, in an effort to impose a one-world government at odds with our democratic system.[1]

Pat Buchanan was among the first to identify and articulate the threat. During the 2000 presidential campaign, as the nominee of the Reform Party, Buchanan described this struggle in a speech he delivered to the Boston World Affairs Council.

> This then is the millennial struggle that succeeds the Cold War. It is the struggle of patriots . . . against a world government where all nations yield up their sovereignty and fade away. It is the struggle of nationalism against globalism, and it will be fought out, not only among nations, but within nations. And the old question Dean Rusk asked in the Vietnam era is relevant now: *Whose side are you on?*[2]

It is a question that must be asked—especially of our candidates for public office.

The January 17, 2000, cover story in *The New Republic* magazine declared, "America is surrendering its sovereignty to a world government. Hooray." Author Robert Wright declared that the "argument isn't about whether to have a form of world government, but about what form of it to have."[3]

In fact, the foundation of international government has already been laid and continues to take shape.

American troops serve under UN command and are targets for international prosecutors. Al Gore, while he was vice president, praised U.S. troops who "died in the service of the United Nations." Kofi Annan declared actions taken in the name of America's national security "illegal." He said permission for the United States to neutralize threats can only be granted by the UN. "Agreed," say Democrats in Congress.

Today, Congress's ability to "regulate commerce with foreign nations" is laughable. That power belongs to the World Trade Organization (WTO). One adverse ruling from the WTO sends members of Congress sprinting to their respective chambers to rewrite our laws and regulations. The "Greatest Deliberative Body in the World" has become a toy for the UN's dominatrix of global trade.

Kofi Annan's International Criminal Court is issuing arrest warrants, and Democrats argue that Americans must submit to its will. France, Brazil, and Spain are launching test programs for international taxation of air travel. Through its Millennium Development Goals, the United Nations has laid claim to $80 billion in annual payments from the American taxpayer. Jimmy Carter is all for it.

Meantime, the UN runs the most efficient anti-America propaganda machine on earth. International terrorists travel to Turtle Bay to play "This is Your Life" with their friendly hosts. The General Assembly—a habitat for inhumanity—puts on display those who call the United States a terrorist nation, denigrate our president, and spit on our values. Democrats take it in stride, but hold up the nomination of John Bolton because he might embarrass us at the UN.

Walter Cronkite, once called "the most trusted man in America," openly advocates world government. Strobe Talbott, a friend of Bill and Hillary, says nationhood is "obsolete." Columbia University professor Jeffrey Sachs travels the world as Kofi Annan's bag man and rarely misses an opportunity to speak ill of his homeland. Jimmy Carter, Bill Clinton, John Kerry, and the Democratic Party they continue to lead have signed on to much of the global agenda, abandoning their faith in America for the empty promises of a global cult.

The United Nations has captured a fifth column inside our own country. They brought this war to us, and they fight it daily in big ways and small. They never cede an inch.

For me, the point was hammered home in a small but significant way when I attended Kofi Annan's press briefing in Johannesburg, South Africa, in September 2002 and witnessed the disdain the secretary-general held for the United States.

The official reason for holding the UN World Summit on Sustainable Development in Johannesburg, South Africa, was to discuss world poverty and the environment. But, like most other UN gatherings, the real motivation for the delegates was to deliver a diplomatic kick in the teeth to the United States.

For ten days, more than 60,000 delegates from the United Nations, the world media, and representatives from non-governmental organizations (NGOs) spent $55 million on a global jamboree to protest U.S. policies and criticize the Bush administration. Before it was over, Kofi Annan would feed at the trough of anti-Americanism.

We were assembled in the media room awaiting Annan's entrance. It was September 4, 2002, nearly one year to the day when nineteen terrorists boarded planes in the United States and executed the most damaging terrorist strikes on American soil since Pearl Harbor.

The attacks were devastating: 2,996 Americans were murdered on that Tuesday morning. While UN delegates openly criticized the United States, American citizens prepared to commemorate the first anniversary of those attacks. In the year following the terrorist strikes, the UN's hostility toward the United States grew and was on open display for those of us assembled in Johannesburg.

I sat in the front row of the media room at the UN's convention headquarters along with hundreds of journalists from across the globe. High on the agenda of this World Summit was the issue of poverty. Ironically, UN delegates and NGOs met in Johannesburg's posh Sandton City area to discuss the fate of the world's poor. Impoverished people the world over had their fate decided by those who slept in silk-sheeted luxury hotels, who were driven in police-escorted Mercedes motorcades, and who feasted on relaxed dinners of expensive hors d'oeuvres and exotic game.

For the U.S. delegation, it was a contentious, unwelcoming event. Anti-Americanism was rampant. Fliers denouncing President George W. Bush were distributed freely. Hostile sentiments were posted throughout the conference center, and the media were duly assembled to hear criticisms of all things American. At one entrance to the conference center there was displayed an open threat—a placard that read, "Bush, New York will be No Exception." Inside, delegates and NGOs criticized President Bush for sending Secretary of State Colin Powell in his stead.

Entering the pressroom, Kofi Annan was escorted by his throng of security and staff. The secretary-general stepped to the microphone and was center stage. A staff assistant stood behind him and to his left with her own microphone. His assistant announced, "His Excellency, Mr. Kofi Annan, Secretary-General of the United Nations, will make a brief statement and take a few questions."

She then went on to explain that dignity and decorum were mandatory when His Excellency is present. No shouting. One question only. No follow-ups. Reporters were required to step to their designated microphones and wait patiently until Mr. Annan's assistant, not His Excellency himself, called on reporters.

The secretary-general declared the summit a "success" that had "mobilized people around the world." The throng of news media, not known for their manners, sat silent and attentive. His Excellency demanded nothing less.

Then came time for Q&A. After a few questions, Kofi Annan's assistant called on an American reporter who had patiently waited his turn. "Mr. Secretary-General," he inquired, "do you have any comment on the behavior of the delegates toward Secretary of State Colin Powell? Will you renounce their actions and apologize to Secretary Powell for the way he was treated here?"

What, exactly, was the behavior of the delegates toward Mr. Powell? As CNN reported, Powell faced a "stormy reception" and "was repeatedly forced to halt his speech to delegates as he was booed and heckled."[4] He was shouted down, was called names, and was met with so much hostility that a number of people had to be forcibly removed from the room. They shouted in loud voices and pounded their fists on the tables to drown him out and force him to stop his speech.

Laying the groundwork for the hostile reception was former South African president Nelson Mandela. On the morning Powell arrived in Johannesburg, the papers carried a stinging criticism from the African icon. "We are really appalled by any country . . . that goes outside the UN and attacks independent countries,"[5] Mandela said, referring to U.S. retaliation against al Qaeda in Taliban-controlled Afghanistan.

Powell brushed aside Mandela's criticism and offered African nations more than $15 billion in financial assistance to help them build schools, provide clean drinking water, combat the AIDS epidemic, and supply food for those ravaged by famine. But the UN miscreants neither acknowledged nor appreciated it. This generosity was offered despite the fact that the American economy was devastated by the deadly attacks of September 11.

So, the American reporter wanted to know from Kofi Annan, would he apologize to Powell on behalf of the United Nations?

Annan had no apology. As the question was being asked, he slowly turned to glare at his assistant. "How dare you allow such a question to be asked of me," the anger in his eyes seemed to say to his underling. Noting his disapproval, Annan's assistant cut the reporter off, announced that there would be no more questions, and thanked us all for coming out.

Though he demanded decorum for himself, Kofi Annan refused to condemn the hostility shown to America's top diplomat. He would not apologize to Colin Powell and said nothing to discourage future trash talking about Americans.

Qui tacet consentiret. Silence gives consent.

Though his staff denied it afterward, Kofi Annan heard the question. He acknowledged the reporter as he began his query. Kofi Annan approved the attack on Powell and his country. In diplomatic terms, it was a sucker punch. This example is indicative of the constant hostility with which the United States and our values are met at the United Nations.

The UN cannot be reformed because it is inherently flawed. We do not want, nor should we seek, a "more effective" United Nations, for its goals are not our own. It has stolen significant portions of our sovereignty and is gunning for more. It has rewritten portions of our Constitution and undermined American authority. It has injured our national pride.

America takes her place on the same Human Rights Commission that seats terrorists. We send our troops to defend the people of Iraq while Saddam Hussein bribes UN officials. We invite to our shores those who denigrate us from the podium at Turtle Bay. We receive no help from the UN in our struggle against terrorism. But we will provide the United Nations with an interest-free $1.5 billion loan to finance its new headquarters and perpetuate this hostility.

We can no longer wait while diplomatic dangers gather. We cannot wait for the final evidence that comes in the form of lost sovereignty. Our leaders must come to realize that Kofi Annan is no friend of the American people, and the United Nations is no ally of the United States.

For sixty years, we have tolerated the UN's abusive behavior. The United States is the battered wife in this illegitimate marriage. Diplomatically, but decisively, it is time for America to end her love affair with the United Nations.

In the Security Council We Trust

As baseball analogies go, it was a pitch Senator John Kerry wished he could have back. The sound bite within his winded answer would become one of the defining moments in the 2004 campaign for president. And though the liberal Massachusetts senator believed what he said, it was a rhetorical blunder he would come to regret. It would reside next to "Senator, you're no Jack Kennedy" as one of the more memorable lines in presidential debate history. Kerry's sin? Patriotic apostasy.

It was a time when America was at war; U.S. troops were fighting overseas; the world was being divided into good guys versus bad; and John Kerry sided with the bad guys—the United Nations. It was the evening of September 30, 2004—the first of three presidential debates between Kerry and President George W. Bush. They met at the Convocation Center on the campus of the University of Miami in Coral Gables, Florida.

Because this was the first presidential campaign since the devastating terrorist attacks of September 11, 2001, the two camps agreed that it would focus exclusively on foreign policy and homeland security—issues that had taken on more importance than in previous presidential contests. In order to win, Kerry needed to prove his credentials as a leader who could traverse the challenges of a newly complicated world. In just three years, the American public saw the horrors of terrorism on our shores, the Taliban regime ousted in Afghanistan, a war in Iraq, and a protracted debate in the United Nations Security Council that increased the public's skepticism about the world body.

Even television and radio talk shows, which normally shunned discussion of serious issues, were debating national security. The American people wanted to know: as president, how would either of these men protect them and their families?

For John Kerry it would not be easy. At every stop, he had to tell voters that he served in Vietnam. He paraded his Swift Boat friends on stage at the Democrat convention, and his campaign incessantly reminded audiences that their guy was a "war hero." Polls showed that the American public wanted a candidate who would protect America against future acts of terrorism. That leader needed to be strong, decisive, and confident. And that's where John Kerry blew it.

The Global Test

Long before the debates began, the bipartisanship that reared its head in the wake of the 2001 terrorist attacks had dissipated. Throughout the campaign, John Kerry made a pathetic effort to play both sides of the national defense issue. He tried to appease his core constituency by adopting the pacifist rhetoric of the party's liberal base, but voted in favor of the war in Iraq. His public explanation for the war included so many rationalizations, exceptions, clauses, hypotheticals, parentheticals, semi-colons, ifs, buts, and nuances that even professional linguists were at a loss to understand his position.

Some analysts believed the Democrats erred in agreeing to confine the first debate to the issue of foreign policy and homeland security—topics in which the president excelled and his poll numbers were strong. But Kerry was performing well in this particular debate; he was aggressive and was keeping his answers under the time limit—a challenge for Kerry, who was long-winded even by senatorial standards.

But about two-thirds of the way through the debate, the moderator— PBS's Jim Lehrer—asked Senator Kerry his about his position on "the whole concept of preemptive war."[1] Kerry explained to Lehrer and some 65 million Americans watching on television that as commander in chief, he would tackle threats to America's national security by taking preemptive action only "in a way that passes the test, that passes the global test."[2]

Top members of the president's reelection team were watching the debate on television in a nearby building on the University of Miami campus. When he heard Kerry's answer, Karl Rove, the president's chief political advisor, shouted "Oh, my God."[3] He knew the dynamics of the campaign had just changed dramatically.

On stage, Mr. Bush jumped on the comment. The president understood how Democrats coveted the approval of the United Nations. He had spent the last two years listening to them carp and complain that his administration was not giving the United Nations its due. So when he heard Kerry submit U.S. policy to the approval of the UN, the president reacted:

I'm not exactly sure what you mean, passes the global test. You take pre-emptive action if you pass a global test? My attitude is you take preemptive action in order to protect the American people, that you act in order to make this country secure.[4]

American pride was at stake, and the president understood it. The next day on the stump, in the working-class town of Allentown, Pennsylvania, Mr. Bush mocked Kerry with glee and made the campaign a choice between the United States and the United Nations.

Senator Kerry last night said that America has to pass some sort of global test before we can use American troops to defend ourselves. He wants our national security decisions subject to the approval of a foreign government. Listen, I'll continue to work with our allies and the international community—but I will never submit America's national security to an international test. The use of troops to defend America must never be subject to a veto by countries like France. The President's job is not to take an international poll—the President's job is to defend America.[5]

Political campaigns are often about the friends the candidate keeps. George W. Bush was aligning himself with the American public, while John Kerry was standing shoulder to shoulder with Kofi Annan. Kerry's affection for the United Nations became a regular theme in the president's stump speeches. Within two days, the Bush campaign was running television ads scornful of the senator's remarks.

Narrator: He said he'd attack terrorists who threaten America. But at the debate, John Kerry said America must pass a "global test" before we protect ourselves.

The Kerry doctrine: A global test. So we must seek permission from foreign governments before protecting America? A global test? So America will be forced to wait while threats gather? President Bush believes decisions about protecting America should be made in the Oval Office, not foreign capitals.[6]

A self-described "internationalist," John Kerry had long believed that the United Nations needed to play a larger role in American foreign and military policy. During his first campaign for office in 1970, Kerry told the *Harvard*

Crimson, "I'd like to see our troops dispersed through the world only at the directive of the United Nations."[7]

More than thirty years later, his viewpoint had not changed at all. As the Senate began debate on the issue of war in Iraq, Kerry called for global bureaucracies to take the lead in defending Americans. "It is a time," he said, when "international institutions must rise to the occasion and seek new authority."[8] He wanted the war in Iraq to be authorized and administered by the United Nations.

Kerry mused about what Saddam might do with weapons of mass destruction. He stated his belief that "a deadly arsenal of weapons of mass destruction in his hands is a threat, and a grave threat, to our security and that of our allies in the Persian Gulf region."[9] At the time Senator Kerry voted on the war, he believed that the Iraqi dictator was in possession of weapons of mass destruction that posed a "grave threat" to the United States.

"Can we afford to ignore the possibility," Kerry asked, "that Saddam Hussein might accidentally, as well as purposely, allow those weapons to slide off to one group or other in a region where weapons are the currency of trade? How do we leave that to chance?"[10]

In fact, we shouldn't. Kerry said such a threat should be eliminated—but only by the United Nations. "That is why," he explained, "the enforcement mechanism through the United Nations . . . is so critical to achieve the protection of . . . the United States."[11] Kerry completed his remarks on the Senate floor with the summation that he would vote for the war because he, as a United States senator, "will not permit the United Nations . . . to simply be ignored by this dictator."[12]

John Kerry was voting to send Americans to war because the United Nations had been insulted. His remark was made in the same spirit as that of Vice President Al Gore, who, in 1994, told the families of American service members killed in Iraq that they could be proud their sons "died in the service of the United Nations."

This, then, is the gospel of the Left: There is no greater responsibility than to defend the UN; there is no greater honor than to die for its cause.

In the first presidential debate, Kerry complained that in Iraq, Americans had suffered "90 percent of the casualties" and the U.S. bore "90 percent of the cost." And yet he was fighting to entrust that financial investment and, more importantly, the memories of those dead Americans to the United Nations.

Kerry and his running mate, North Carolina senator John Edwards, ignored George Washington's admonition to "put none but Americans on guard tonight" when they urged that the governance of Iraq be turned over to an "international High Commissioner." This person, they said, would serve as the "senior international representative" in charge of "overseeing elections . . . drafting a constitution, and coordinating reconstruction."[13]

Kerry was speaking for his party, which overwhelmingly wanted the UN to act before they would commit. The American public was appalled. Since 2001, they had come to know the United Nations better than at any time in its history, and they didn't like what they saw—that the UN was stacked against the United States.

News reports revealed that Russia and France—two permanent members of the Security Council—were the two top recipients of Iraqi oil under the UN's corrupted Oil-for-Food program. Prominent politicians in both countries were illegally accepting oil vouchers from Saddam Hussein. Bill Gertz of the *Washington Times* reported that just over a week before the start of the war in Iraq, two Russian generals were photographed in Baghdad receiving awards from Saddam Hussein.[14] China, another permanent member, was becoming increasingly reliant on oil from Iraq and other Middle East countries.

The debate on Iraq began in the Security Council in 2002. Of the fifteen members of the council at that time, only three countries—other than the United States and United Kingdom—became members of the U.S.-led coalition against Iraq.

In 2003, the membership on the Security Council changed, and debate over Iraq intensified. Support for the U.S. position was reduced even further—only Bulgaria and Spain were official partners in the coalition. The following year, Spain would withdraw its troops after al-Qaeda terrorists coordinated the explosion of ten bombs on four commuter trains in Madrid, killing 191 people and injuring more than 1,500 on the morning of March 11, 2004—exactly 30 months after the attacks in Washington, D.C., New York, and Pennsylvania.

Four days later, Prime Minister Jose Maria Aznar—a strong ally of the United States in the war on terror—was swept out of office, and his opponent, Jose Luis Zapetero—who pledged to withdraw Spain's 1,300 troops from Iraq—was in.

Other UN Security Council members to whom Kerry was entrusting the safety and security of Americas were as follows:

• *Angola.* This country had just come off a twenty-seven-year civil war that ravaged the country and left its infrastructure weak. The Angolan government receives $188 million in aid from the United States for such things as repatriating refugees to providing clean water. The State Department classifies Angola's human rights record as "poor."

As of April 2005, Angola was party to only three of twelve international treaties against terrorism. The treaties date from 1963 to 1999 and are considered a measurement of each nation's commitment to curbing terrorism. The treaties target issues ranging from the financing of terrorism to the protection of nuclear materials to the taking of hostages to hijacking aircraft.

In 2003, Angola voted with the United States only 17.7 percent of the time in the General Assembly.

• *Cameroon.* Cameroon, which enjoys close political, economic, and military ties with France, adopted the French position when it came to Iraq, arguing that the UN inspectors needed more time. After congratulating the French ambassador, Dominique de Villepin, on his "particularly dynamic and productive presidency" of the Security Council the month before, Ambassador Francois-Xavier Ngoubeyou of Cameroon thanked Colin Powell for his hour-and-a-half presentation of just declassified information and wondered aloud if it would not "be appropriate to give the inspectors more time to make use of this information?"[15] He went on to suggest that because "peace hangs in the balance," it might be a good idea to send Kofi Annan to Baghdad to meet personally with Saddam Hussein.[16]

In the General Assembly, Cameroon votes against the United States regularly. It voted with the United States only 27.6 percent of the time in 2002 and 18.1 percent of the time in 2003. On votes that the State Department classifies as "important issues," Cameroon voted with the U.S. on 2 out of 14 in 2002 and on 3 out of 15 in 2003.

• *Communist China.* China is a permanent member of the Security Council. Since 2003, China has opposed a U.S. proposal to set up a military hotline between the Pentagon and the Chinese Defense Ministry to help avoid crises. In April 2001, China took twenty-three U.S. military crew members of the EP-3 surveillance plane hostage after the crew made an emergency landing on Hainan Island after a mid-air collision with a Chinese fighter jet over international waters. National defense experts have become increasingly concerned in recent years about its military buildup, its tougher stance toward Taiwan, and its espionage in the United States.

In 2003, China voted with the United States only 13.2 percent of the time in the General Assembly.

• *Mexico.* America's neighbor to the south has encouraged its citizens to make their way north into the United States to find jobs and send money back home. In 2004, the U.S. Border Patrol nabbed 1.1 million Mexicans trying to enter the United States illegally. But millions more are eluding the patrols. The Department of Homeland Security has identified the border as a prime target of exploitation by al-Qaeda. Far from trying to help the U.S., the Mexican government has directed the assault. Representative J. D. Hayworth (R-AZ) has dubbed the Mexican policy "state-sponsored illegal immigration."[17] President Vincente Fox's government has printed and distributed thousands of "how to" guides for illegally crossing the U.S.-Mexican border and exploiting U.S. resources and benefits once inside the United States. In October 2005, Mexico became the 100th country to ratify the International Criminal Court treaty, which the U.S. strongly opposes.

In 2003, Mexico voted with the United States 20.7 percent of the time in the General Assembly.

• *Syria.* Syria is a state sponsor of terrorism and has been classified by the State Department as such since 1979. Syria's support for Palestinian terrorist organizations, its pursuit of weapons of mass destruction, and its military occupation of Lebanon led to President Bush's signing of the Syria Accountability Act in December 2003, which forced the U.S. to place sanctions on the authoritarian regime.

At the time John Kerry proposed that the UN Security Council administer a global test, Syria had opened its borders, allowing a wave of jihadists into Iraq to fight against U.S. troops. Late in 2005, Syria came under fire when a UN report implicated top associates of Syrian president Bashar Assad in the assassination of Lebanese prime minister Rafik Hariri.

In 2003, when Syria was on the Security Council, it voted with the United States 9.6 percent of the time in the General Assembly.

Why would Democrats trust the opinions of such nations whose interests conflict with our own?

As he watched the U.S. presidential debate on television and saw John Kerry explain the tenets of UN superiority, UN secretary-general Kofi Annan must have been excited. Here was a United States senator—who might just be the next president of the United States—explaining to his fellow Americans what Kofi Annan had been trying to get across to them for years: that the United States needed to take its orders from the United Nations.

On the first commemoration of the September 11 terrorist attacks, Kofi Annan took the unprecedented step of releasing the text of his own remarks to the press before President Bush came to the podium. Annan proclaimed the Kofi Doctrine: "there is no substitute for the unique legitimacy of the United Nations."[18]

Its lesson is that nation states may not take military action they deem to be in their own interest without the express written consent of the United Nations Security Council and the secretary-general. To do otherwise would put any nation in violation of international law and would make its leaders eligible for a VIP pass to The Hague and star billing before Kofi's International Criminal Court.

Faith in the UN

Most U.S. Presidents, after reflecting upon their time in the Oval Office, say their most difficult decisions had to do with sending young Americans to war. It is a solemn responsibility, more than any one individual should have, so our Founders entrusted the decision to representatives of the people.

This is why it is so disturbing that when it came time for Congress to debate the issue of going to war in Iraq, many members of the Democratic Party looked to the United Nations for advice and consent. Getting the support of the UN, said Senator Tom Daschle, "will be a central factor in how quickly Congress acts. If the international community supports it . . . then I think we can move to a [Senate] resolution."[19] And when they did offer a resolution, it asked the United Nations to diagnose and treat that which imperiled their constituents.

Dubbed the "Multilateral Use of Force Authorization Act of 2002," the Democrats' measure acknowledged that "Iraq continues to develop weapons of mass destruction," and those weapons are "a threat to the United States."[20] But Democrats put the responsibility for neutralizing that threat in the hands of the UN. Their amendment urged "the United Nations Security Council to . . . authorize the use of necessary and appropriate military force by member states of the United Nations."[21]

It further stated that "the President is authorized to use the Armed Forces of the United States" to destroy Iraq's weapons of mass destruction but only "pursuant to a resolution of the United Nations Security Council."[22] Michigan senator Carl Levin explained the Democrat substitute this way:

I believe if Saddam Hussein continues to refuse to meet his obligation to destroy his weapons of mass destruction and his prohibited missile delivery systems, *that the United Nations should authorize member states to use military force* to destroy those weapons and systems and that the United States Armed Forces should participate in and lead a United Nations authorized force . . . .

If we act wisely, authorizing the use of our forces *pursuant to a UN resolution authorizing member states to use force*, we will not only unite the Congress, ultimately we will unite the world community . . . [and] that is where our focus should be, uniting the world.[23] [emphasis added]

Wrong, Senator. The responsibility of Congress is to determine what is, or what is not, in the national security interests of the United States and to take responsibility for its actions.

Responsibility and accountability are cornerstones of democracy. U.S. trade policy should not have been outsourced to the World Trade Organization because Americans should have a representative in Washington who can respond to their grievances. "Taxation without representation" is one reason why the UN should never have the authority to impose levies on the American people. And when flag-draped coffins are pulled from aircraft at Dover Air Force Base, families have a right either to blame or be consoled by those whose responsibility it was to send those young people to America's defense.

On March 13, 2003, Teddy Kennedy took to the Senate floor and, invoking saints Augustine and Thomas Aquinas, tried to square the administration's policies with their six points of a "just war." One of those points, Kennedy intoned, is that a just war must be declared by a "legitimate authority acting on behalf of the people."[24] True enough. So why then did Kennedy advocate transferring that decision from an institution acting on behalf of the American public to an unaccountable world body?

In trying to justify himself, Kennedy regretted that when Congress voted six months earlier to go to war in Iraq, "most members believed that the use of force by America would have United Nations backing," and declared that America is "divided" on the question of war "without United Nations approval."[25]

Kerry, Kennedy, Durbin and other Democrats were consulting the UN Charter, which states in Article 24 that as a member of the United Nations, the U.S. "confer(s) on the Security Council primary responsibility for the maintenance of international peace and security." Article 39 professes that only "the Security Council shall determine the existence of any threat to the peace, breach of the peace, or act of aggression," and the Security Council will "decide what measures shall be taken" to restore that peace.

"I was wrong."[26] That is how Senator John Edwards began his *mea culpa* in the *Washington Post* three years after he voted take America to war in Iraq. Actually, it was less a mea culpa and more of a hit piece on the president, accusing the Bush administration of manipulating pre-war intelligence for political purposes.

Nonetheless, Edwards's confession is instructive. Here is part of what he wrote:

> It was a mistake to vote for this war in 2002. I take responsibility for that mistake. It has been hard to say these words because those who didn't make a mistake—the men and women of our armed forces and their families— have performed heroically and paid a dear price.[27]

If the Democrats had had their way and young Americans were sent to war under the authority of the United Nations, who, exactly, would take responsibility if that war turned out to be a mistake?

A few years later, Democrats would look back with the luxury of hindsight and argue that no weapons of mass destruction were found in Iraq, and, therefore, soliciting the opinion of the UN was appropriate. But Iraq did have weapons of mass destruction as far as the Democrats were concerned at the time.

"There is no question," said Senator Chris Dodd, "that Iraq possesses biological and chemical weapons and that [Saddam Hussein] seeks to acquire additional weapons of mass destruction, including nuclear weapons. That is not in debate," he said, and went on to call Saddam Hussein a "threat to peace."[28]

Senator Barbara Mikulski of Maryland believed Saddam had WMDs. She also placed her trust in Kofi Annan over President George W. Bush. Mikulski explained herself this way:

> But make no mistake, I firmly believe that Saddam Hussein is duplicitous, deceptive, and dangerous. I despise him. Saddam is a brutal, totalitarian dictator and history shows us how dangerous Iraq is under his rule. He invaded Kuwait and used chemical weapons against his own people. I do believe he has developed chemical and biological weapons, and I also believe he is pursuing nuclear weapons, defying the will of the

international community and also denying the agreement that he made at the end of the Gulf War.

I also really do not believe that Saddam is going to change. The question then is, what does this mean for the future? I think Iraq does have the grim and ghoulish means to carry out its evil plans. I think if we look at declassified CIA reports and the British white paper, we can see that Iraq does continue to develop and produce and stockpile chemical and biological weapons, and is trying to get the technology and materials to produce nuclear weapons. So these threats cannot and must not be ignored.[29]

After stating so emphatically the danger posed by Iraq, Mikulski voted for the Levin amendment, which would "authoriz[e] the use of force only if authorized by the UN Security Council."[30]

In the House of Representatives it was no better. One after another, members rose to defend the United Nations against what they felt was abuse by the Bush administration. Tossing aside the consideration of America's security interests, they were more interested in defending their beloved UN.

Barbara Lee of California complained that "President Bush's doctrine of preemption violates international law [and] the United Nations Charter."[31] James Oberstar of Michigan reasoned that the president should ask Congress for approval to wage war against Iraq only after he "obtain[ed] a Security Council authorization of force."[32]

Jim McDermott of Washington took to the House floor to lodge his protest over what he deemed to be U.S. abuse of his beloved United Nations.

Our government has a history of undermining the United Nations and has been particularly bad regarding Iraq. In 1990, we bribed and threatened and punished the Security Council to force a vote endorsing our war. We bribed poor countries with cheap Saudi oil. We bribed China with diplomatic rehabilitation and new development aid.

And we told Yemen, the only Arab country on the council, that its vote against our war would be "the most expensive vote you ever cast." And then we punished Yemen, the poorest country in the Arab world, with a cutoff of our entire $70 million aid package.

And we try to impose our war again on a reluctant United Nations. I fear that the Yemen precedent is being recalled at the UN today. I hope that our friends and our allies who might be considering a different approach in the UN will not be intimidated by our unilateral abuse of this multilateral institution.[33]

It was a speech that was better suited to *Oprah* than a place where serious business is discussed.

Chaka Fattah, a liberal Democrat from Pennsylvania, showed how Democrats were perfectly willing to transfer their authority under the Constitution. In his reasoning, both Congress and the UN have the same authority to authorize American troops to war. The Democrats' resolution, he explained, "calls on the president to seek authorization from Congress in the absence of a UN Security Council resolution."[34] Fattah continued,

> If we go to war with Iraq, we must do so with the approval of the UN Security Council, and the general cooperation and support of the United Nations. We risk damaging the UN Security Council's legitimacy as an authoritative body in international law if the United States acts unilaterally.[35]

Silvestre Reyes of Texas said, "If the Iraqis defy the inspectors and the U.N. will not authorize force, this Congress will expedite a vote for a new resolution to authorize that force."[36] Congressman Ed Markey of Massachusetts demanded that "the President has an obligation to go to the United Nations first."[37]

At least fifteen times in our nation's history, the president has authorized the use of preemptive force to protect Americans or otherwise act in America's national defense dating back to 1901. The debate over the use of preemptive force is an argument that Americans alone must have amongst themselves.

The fact that some Democrats argued against going to war in Iraq was not wrong, nor was it unpatriotic. What Democrats did that was inexcusable was to hide their opposition to the war under the blanket of the United Nations. Any member of Congress who had doubts about the Iraq campaign should have debated the president, voted against him, and stood proudly on the merits of his or her convictions. Instead, many of them obfuscated the matter by claiming that the United Nations could somehow legitimize that which they believed to be inherently wrong.

If Saddam Hussein was the threat that Democrats admitted him to be, then it was a gross dereliction of duty for them to pass the buck to Kofi Annan. By the same token, if the Bush administration had the luxury to go again and again to the UN Security Council over the course of six months, then Iraq must not have been the danger it was claimed to be.

The Bush administration made a mistake investing so much hope in the Security Council. For months, our troops sat in the desert, at risk of chemical or biological attacks, waiting for the French and the Russians to digest Hans Blix's every utterance. As Jed Babbin explained to me, "We spent six months at the UN fiddling and diddling . . . and in those six months, much of the insurgency was planned and organized and readied."

The UN Security Council is a danger, in part, because it is dividing Americans on the most important issue that faces a country. If we are to go to war, let us go together, as one people, with a common purpose—for the defense of the Republic. No other reason will suffice—and to hell with the international community who think otherwise.

Senator James Inhofe of Oklahoma asked the right question: "Why do those who oppose the President's resolution trust the United Nations more than they trust the President of the United States?"[38] Some might view Inhofe's query as a partisan jab. It's not. It is a profoundly important question that speaks to our values as a nation and our ability to remain a free people. For if we as a nation have reached the point where our elected leaders value the advice of foreigners over their own president, then divisions have run too deep. Such irreconcilable differences have exposed the fault lines of the Republic. We are a house divided that cannot stand.

It is a question that should be posed to Teddy Kennedy who, when faced with a life or death decision, said, "I'm waiting for the final recommendation of the Security Council before I'm going to say how I'm going to vote."[39] A profile in courage.

The Powell Presentation

The Bush administration pushed hard to win UN approval before taking military action against Iraq. Though the president did not seek a permission slip from the United Nations, he did hope for the organization's blessing. But he did it "because Tony Blair could not take Britain to war with us unless we got the UN's approval," Jed Babbin said.

So the administration sent Secretary of State Colin Powell to New York to make the case before the UN. The media predicted it would be a replay of Adalai Stevenson's 1962 showdown in the Security Council when he unveiled photos of Soviet weapons in Cuba.

Powell took with him UN ambassador John Negroponte and CIA director George Tenet. Tenet was key. So much so that Powell didn't even want to enter the building without him, *Newsweek* reported.[40] Having the CIA director on his arm said to the world that Powell was the messenger—and the evidence he was presenting came out of Tenet's shop.

It served the secretary of state well when he was forced to admit a year later that some of the content in his UN presentation was sub par. "It turned out that the sourcing was inaccurate and wrong and, in some cases, deliberately misleading," Powell said. "And for that, I am disappointed and I regret it."[41]

But at the time, Powell's show-and-tell presentation did not disappoint. He was showered with praise from both Republicans and Democrats who said he made a powerful case. Even some who were skeptical about the need to go into Iraq were persuaded by the drama of his diplomatic aria.

But was it necessary? The president was convinced that Iraq was a threat to be neutralized. His advisors agreed. Congress approved. Even many of the most outspoken Democrats admitted that Saddam Hussein had weapons and posed a threat. There was unanimity across the American spectrum.

But U.S. national security was being held at bay by the Doubting Thomases of Turtle Bay. To get them on board—which was highly unlikely—America needed to expose information that, but for the Powell presentation, might still be classified today.

Powell went to the UN to "share . . . what the United States knows about Iraq's weapons of mass destruction."[42] But many intelligence analysts believe he shared too much. During the course of his presentation on live television, Powell showed evidence of intercepted telephone conversations, satellite photos, and information collected by intelligence agents and defectors.

The next day, Dana Priest of the *Washington Post* put it this way: "Never had the U.S. government disclosed as much sensitive, recent intelligence as Secretary of State Colin L. Powell did yesterday when he released surreptitiously intercepted calls between Iraqi officials and information supplied by Iraqi informants apparently close to Saddam Hussein."[43] Pat Roberts, chairman of the Senate Intelligence Committee, told the *Washington Post*, "They frankly revealed more intelligence capabilities and assessment and sources and methods than I've ever seen."[44]

In fact, the use of the intelligence and what to declassify was hotly debated at the CIA and within the administration. Before Powell made his presentation, "U.S. intelligence officers [were] putting up fierce internal resistance to declassifying the Iraqi evidence,"[45] wrote Fred Kaplan in *Slate*, the on-line magazine. "Their big concern," he continued, "is that the United States will blow a lot of highly sensitive intelligence data—the sort of sources and methods that are rarely even discussed, never deliberately revealed—and the cache still won't be persuasive enough, especially not to the layman, to justify war."[46]

Bill Nichols, writing in *USA Today*, reported, "U.S. intelligence officials had been reluctant to divulge evidence behind their claims that Iraq was engaged in an active campaign to deceive UN weapons inspectors. They feared it would compromise spy sources and methods."[47]

In fall 2005, Democrats in Washington were demanding the scalps of Republicans who had allegedly leaked the name of a covert CIA operative who posed for a photo spread in *Vanity Fair* magazine. It was a serious matter, they said—the identities of operatives must be protected. No doubt.

At about the same time, the Bush administration and Republican leaders in Congress became incensed about a leak that revealed secret CIA prisons overseas. They considered, and had not resolved before this writing, launching an investigation into a matter that serious.

Yet, when the United States gave a wholesale presentation of classified information—some which was de-classified only days before—few seemed to care because it was done to appease the United Nations.

There is no doubt that Security Council members like the communist Chinese, whose spies toured our nuclear laboratories during the Clinton administration, were grateful to the United States for revealing its latest espionage capabilities. So too, must have been Russian agents who treated Madeleine Albright's State Department like it was Disneyland. Of course, any of America's enemies could have popped over to the Security Council that day to see America's eavesdropping capabilities. Or, even more convenient, they could have just hit the "Record" button on their VCRs and saved the presentation for future reference.

In his book *Chatter: Dispatches from the Secret World of Global Eavesdropping*, Patrick Keefe explains the dismay of many in the intelligence community at Powell's presentation:

> As Powell rolled out his case, with Director of Central Intelligence George Tenet sitting just behind him, those in attendance were awed by the apparent clairvoyance of the American espionage establishment. But another group of people listening was shocked. For anyone familiar with SIGINT and secrecy, the public unveiling of intercepts so fresh that they had been gathered in the last few weeks was virtually unheard of. One former high-ranking NSA employee who watched the presentation said, "I can only assume that everyone else had the same sense of shock when they actually heard it—a sense of that great sucking sound as all the business goes south."[48]

Powell's slide show included excerpts from transcripts of telephone conversations captured from U.S. satellites. The first was a telephone conversation between two Iraqi military officers on November 26, 2002, the day before the UN weapons inspectors were slated to resume inspections in Iraq. According to Powell, one officer is a colonel, the other a brigadier general, and both belong to Saddam's Republican Guard, an elite unit of Saddam's former military.

The colonel speaks to the general and expresses concern that Mohamed El Baradei, director of the International Atomic Energy Agency (IAEA), will be visiting the next day and the colonel has in his possession a "modified vehicle." The colonel asks the general, "What do we say if one of them sees it?" The conversation continues and the colonel says the modified vehicle comes from the al-Kindi Company, revealing that "we evacuated everything. We don't have anything left."[49]

There is no doubt that what Powell played was dramatic and informative. But was it necessary to divulge what American intelligence knew to an audience that was not about to change its mind?

What Powell did, as Greg Miller of the *Los Angeles Times* described it, was to "lift the cloak on a cloak-and-dagger world . . . providing a rare glimpse of the array of intelligence resources it aims at it adversaries."[50]

Powell played a second conversation that was recorded by satellites. This one took place between two Iraqi officers—one stationed at Republican Guard headquarters and the other in the field. The conversation goes as follows:

> Headquarters: Sir . . .
> Field: Yes.
> HQ: There is a directive of the [Republican] Guard chief of staff at the conference today . . .
> Field: Yes.
> HQ: They are inspecting the ammunition you have . . .
> Field: Yes.
> HQ: . . . for the possibility there are forbidden ammo.
> Field: Yes?
> HQ: For the possibility there is by chance, forbidden ammo.
> Field: Yes.
> HQ: And we sent you a message to inspect the scrap areas and the abandoned areas.
> Field: Yes.
> HQ: After you have carried out what is contained in the message . . . destroy the message.

Field: Yes.

HQ: Because I don't want anyone to see this message.

Field: Okay. Okay.[51]

Even to an amateur with no training in the field of intelligence, this conversation revealed to the Iraqis and to the world—on the eve of war—several things. It revealed to the enemy that the United States has the ability to monitor telephone conversations in Iraq. By extension, that ability probably applies to telephone conversations in Iran, Syria, and numerous other countries around the world. It served as a reminder to al Qaeda operatives to stay off their cell phones. And if phones must be used, America's enemies should be more careful and develop codes to disguise their voices and the meaning of their messages.

After learning about the breach of their security, Iraqi officials no doubt moved to correct the mistake, depriving the U.S. of a potential source of additional information.

"I have great certainty that those guys are either dead or not in their former jobs,"[52] Dan Goure, a former Pentagon official told the *Times of London* about the breach. Tim Ried of the *Times* wrote that CIA officials were "particularly anxious about playing intercepts because alerting Iraqi officials to which conversations had been recorded is particularly risky on the eve of a war."[53]

In his book *The French Betrayal of America*, Kenneth Timmerman discusses the debate held within the intelligence community over how much to reveal.

> All that night, a team of officials from the CIA, the National Security Council (NSC), and Powell's own staff argued over intelligence information Powell could safely reveal in his February 5, 2003, presentation to the UN Security Council. There were heated discussions of whether Powell should play the actual tape of an intercepted conversation from an Iraqi colonel, who was instructing a subordinate to eliminate all references to the term nerve gas in his official communications, in case UN inspectors came looking for evidence. Making the tape public, National Security Agency (NSA) analysts argued, would reveal the extent of their electronic eavesdropping capabilities in Iraq and perhaps give the Iraqis key tips on how to avoid surveillance in the future.[54]

The CIA and the U.S. intelligence community have taken a beating since September 11. They've been criticized for failing to stop the attacks of

9/11 and for getting wrong some of the intelligence that was relied upon to go to war in Iraq. One of the criticisms of the CIA by analysts is that they've come to rely too heavily on technology—satellites, imagery, and eavesdropping—at the expense of human intelligence. After Powell's presentation to the UN, America's technological spying capabilities took a major hit.

There is no way America's intelligence gathering ability was helped by the U.S. presentation to the Security Council on February 5, 2003. It changed no minds and changed no votes in the Security Council. It was made to an institution that the administration had spent months ridiculing. The only conclusion that can be reached is that it was a grave mistake and a colossal failure. And rest assured that the next time the U.S. is in a similar position, the UN will demand that the United States follow the precedent it set in 2003 and put the evidence on the table.

There's a New Sheriff in Town

"At present," British foreign secretary Robin Cook stated with regret, "there is no permanent international body to which the Pol Pots and Milosevics of this world would be answerable." And so, on October 4, 2001, the British government surrendered to international law enforcement administered by the United Nations when it ratified the Rome Statute on the International Criminal Court (ICC).

Four years later, while genocide continued in other parts of the world, three members of Her Majesty's armed forces were indicted for "war crimes" under Britain's International Criminal Court Bill for actions taken during Operation Iraqi Freedom. These men are hardly "the Pol Pots and Milosevics of the world" whom Mr. Cook intended to hold accountable. Fear of having their citizens paraded before the UN's international tribunal forced the Brits to haul these soldiers into their own domestic courts before the UN could get to them. The decision has created open revolt and dissension in the British military.

Sir John Keegan, a military historian and columnist for the *Daily Telegraph*, wrote that these events show "the Americans may have been wise to withhold their consent"[1] from the International Criminal Court.

Let Britain's example be a lesson. If the Democratic Party in the United States had its way, numerous American soldiers would be playing harmonicas in European cell blocks, awaiting prosecution for war crimes by chaps wearing powdered wigs.

The Democratic Party has hitched its wagon to the asses of the internationalists. Their agenda includes the denigration of America's armed forces and its leaders. The Waterloo of the World Federalists will be the sight of an American military officer sitting in The Hague being questioned by the prosecutor of the International Criminal Court. Unfortunately, some elected officials in the United States are laying the groundwork for that very event to occur.

In June 2005, Senator Dick Durbin of Illinois took to the Senate floor and accused U.S. military personnel supervising the detainees at Guantanamo Bay of war crimes. The "atrocities" being perpetrated there, Durbin noted, included playing "extremely loud rap music" and were tantamount to those crimes carried out "by Nazis, Soviets in their gulags, or some mad regime—Pol Pot or others—that had no concern for human beings."[2]

It was a vicious attack. Comparing honorable Americans to dictatorial regimes that committed genocide, mass murder, and torture of the most unspeakable kind only emboldens America's enemies—many of whom work at the United Nations. But Durbin never apologized for his remarks, though they gave comfort to the enemy and armed professional antagonists of the United States with more ammunition.

When asked if the senator would say he was sorry for the remarks, Durbin's spokesman said it was the Bush administration that "should apologize to the American people for abandoning the Geneva Conventions and authorizing torture techniques."[3] *Al Jazeera* lapped it up.

This is the illogic of the domestic and international Left. Blame America first, last, and always. If the so-called plight of detained terrorists can be exploited to score political points, so be it.

But the danger is that these unfounded accusations of American atrocities are not limited to talking points conveyed to the media for political advantage. They are "action items" that are vigorously pursued by an international coalition of courtroom crusaders for the strategic purpose of increasing the authority of the United Nations and diluting the influence and independence of the United States at the same time.

Yes, America is being attacked—not only by al Qaeda, but by warriors of a different kind. They are the briefcase-bearing bulldogs of international institutions, and Kofi Annan is their senior partner. Their weapons are subpoenas, depositions, accusations, and indictments. Their battlefield is the courtroom.

Their latest creation—the International Criminal Court—is a milieu in which these international penal potentates hold a decided strategic advantage. We must never engage them on this turf.

The Creation of he International Criminal Court

"Before the century ends," President William Jefferson Clinton declared before the UN General Assembly in September 1997, "we should establish a permanent international court to prosecute the most serious violations of humanitarian law."

Ironically, many of those to whom Clinton spoke were responsible for the very crimes the court was ostensibly being created to prevent. Mr. Clinton would have been much more effective if, instead of distributing advance copies of his speech, he handed out arrest warrants. Instead, Mr. Clinton opted to help create an institution of international law enforcement that, with time, will target American, British, and Israeli peacekeepers in the same way it targets mass murderers.

A permanent global tribunal with the ability to indict and prosecute individuals has been on the UN's wish list since shortly after President Franklin Roosevelt and his secretary of state Cordell Hull conceived the United Nations. In December 1948, after adopting the Convention on the Prevention and Punishment of the Crime of Genocide, the General Assembly tasked the International Law Commission (ILC) with the responsibility of investigating how an "international judicial organ" could be established to prosecute individuals charged with genocide.

Like any bureaucracy, the ILC saw merit in the idea of making the United Nations bigger and referred the issue back to the General Assembly with its recommendations. The General Assembly then authored a draft statute in 1951 and revised it two years later. However, further consideration of the proposal was postponed until it could define the term "aggression." Fifty years later, the absence of an understanding or definition of the crime of aggression would not deter the ICC's architects.

In 1989, before the General Assembly, the tiny nation of Trinidad and Tobago argued that it was not able to bring drug runners to justice and urged the creation of an international criminal court to which traffickers of illegal narcotics could be referred for prosecution. Then, in the mid-1990s, with violence erupting in the former Yugoslavia, the UN Security Council established the International Criminal Tribunal for the former Yugoslavia to punish those responsible for ethnic cleansing. With that action, the used-car salesmen of the international law movement sensed opportunity and sprung to action.

In July 1998, and with the help of the Clinton administration, the UN convened the "Diplomatic Conference of Plenipotentiaries on the Establishment of an International Criminal Court" in Rome. Their goal: to create a permanent international tribunal to try individuals for "the most serious offenses of global concern." The fact that it could try individuals is what would distinguish it from the International Court of Justice or "World Court," which was created to adjudicate disputes between nations.

After two years of negotiations with the UN, time was running out for the Clinton administration. The United Nations had set a 1999 year-end deadline for signatures on the treaty, and Mr. Clinton was in the evening of his presidency. His successor, George W. Bush, viewed the ICC less favorably and, in Mr. Clinton's view, could not be trusted to do the "right" thing.

Throughout his presidency, Bill Clinton was in constant search of overseas accolades, and he wanted one last round of favorable headlines from London, Paris, and Prague. So from Camp David in the late hours of New Year's Eve, President Clinton affixed his signature to the Rome Statute for the International Criminal Court despite what he called "significant flaws" in the treaty. Clinton's accession to rogue justice won him praise from the well-dressed diplomats. UN secretary-general Kofi Annan praised Clinton's "courage." Richard Dicker, an official with Human Rights Watch, said Clinton "made history" by joining the court.

But others, like Senator Jesse Helms, said that Clinton's move was "as outrageous as it is inexplicable."[4] Helms was a fierce opponent of the court, calling the Rome Statute a "brazen assault on the sovereignty of the American people [and] . . . without precedent in the annals of international treaty law."[5] Among all the treaties that have come before the Senate in Helms's thirty-year history, none of them, he said, were "as genuinely dangerous and un-American as the International Criminal Court."[6]

One of the things that makes the court dangerous is the precedent it sets in allowing the United Nations to impose its will on the rest of the world. The court claims jurisdiction over citizens of nations that have not even consented to it—a move that flies in the face of all precedent in international law.

The way in which the court was established is also disconcerting. The court was born with the agreement of only 60 nations—less than one-third of the UN's 192 member states. Among those opposed to it were the United States, Russia, and China—three of the biggest and most populous countries on earth. They are also three of the five permanent members of the UN Security Council.

"Other opponents of the treaty," explained Freedom Alliance analyst and former State Department official Fred Gedrich, include "India, the world's largest democracy, and Japan, the world's second wealthiest country." "In fact," Gedrich noted, "two-thirds of all of the world's governments, representing about five-sixths of the world's six billion people,"[7] refused to support the International Criminal Court when it claimed authority over all those people.

Gedrich and I were on hand at the United Nations celebration on April 11, 2002—the day the court was inaugurated. We watched as representatives of ten nations—Bosnia-Herzegovina, Bulgaria, Cambodia, Congo, Ireland, Jordan, Mongolia, Niger, Romania, and Slovakia—all ratified the treaty simultaneously, bringing the delegates to their feet cheering. "A dream of world federalists for over fifty years was realized as the International Criminal Court was born,"[8] declared John Anderson, president of the World Federalist Association—an organization that openly advocates global government. But among those sixty countries whose ratifications made Anderson's dream come true were some of the smallest, least influential nations in the world. Most of them do not have a military force that would be affected by the agreement. Many of them do not even have an embassy in the United States.

For example, among the nations that helped to give the UN the sixty ratifications necessary to create the International Criminal Court were the following:

- *Andorra:* a European nation with a population of 70,000 people. The country is ruled under a "co-principality" agreement with its two neighbors—France and Spain—thus making French president Jacques Chirac one of the two co-princes of Andorra.
- *Dominica:* a Caribbean nation with a population of 69,000 and whose economy is heavily reliant on its banana industry.
- *Marshall Islands:* a tiny island in the northern Pacific Ocean about halfway between Hawaii and Australia, with a population of 56,000. The number one sector of the Marshall Islands' economy is foreign aid from the United States.
- *Liechtenstein:* a small European nation with a population of 33,000 and an area smaller than the size of Washington, D.C.
- *San Marino:* behind the Vatican and Monaco, San Marino is the third smallest country in Europe with a land area of approximately 38 square miles and a population of 28,000.
- *Nauru:* with a population of a whopping 13,048, it is a phosphate rock in the South Pacific Ocean measuring 13 square miles. It has no official capital, a legislature with 18 members, and a government that is bankrupt.

The population of the largest of the above countries doesn't even exceed that of an average attendance at a National Football League game. Of the first 60 nations to ratify the treaty, fully one-third of them have populations of 2 million people or fewer. It is the folly of the United Nations' one-country, one-vote system that junior varsity nation-states—with little or nothing to offer in terms of international peace and security—can create an institution that jeopardizes American citizens.

By ratifying the Rome Statute, many of those same nations put their national sovereignty on the chopping block. As an example, in Slovenia, which ratified the treaty on December 31, 2001, the government was forced to amend its constitution, change its penal code, and rewrite its criminal procedure code before it could become a party to the ICC.

Canada, Estonia, Peru, and Slovakia are among the many nations that had to adopt new criminal justice laws to appease the ICC. Portugal was forced to amend its constitution, which had a prohibition on life imprisonment. Likewise, Germany amended its constitution to allow for the extradition of German nationals to the ICC and other European Union countries. It was a grand concession German pols were only too happy to make. "There can be no exceptions to the Rome Statute,"[9] declared Hans-Peter Kaul, who headed the German delegation on the Rome Statute and was later elected a judge at the ICC.

America's Bill of Rights will see dramatic rewrites if our next president leads us into the brave new world of the International Criminal Court.

The Problems with the ICC

The problems with the International Criminal Court are numerous. As outlined above, the court was created largely by a group of nations that will never be affected by its jurisdiction. Such a problem points to the danger of having a UN-friendly president in the Oval Office. Had it chosen to, the Clinton administration could have squashed this court at the early stages before it got off the ground and gained momentum. Instead, Bill Clinton chose to act as a Lamaze partner for this bastard child of international law.

Since the court was created, it has already forced changes in U.S. foreign policy, and as time goes on, it will infringe on our ability to defend our shores. The ICC supplants the authority of the UN Security Council and the veto power held by the United States in that chamber. And, very simply, there is no way to reconcile the ICC with the United States Constitution.

A look at some of the specific provisions of the Rome Statute of the International Criminal Court reveals disturbing claims of authority to which Americans may eventually be subjected:

(1) The International Criminal Court claims jurisdiction over all individuals. In Article 1, the ICC says it may exercise authority over "persons" for the crimes of genocide, crimes against humanity, war crimes, and the crime of aggression. No limitations are placed on which "persons" it claims as subjects. Article 4.2 makes clear that the court always has authority "on the territory of any State Party," and in other cases, "on the territory of any other State,"—even countries that have not ratified the treaty.

The International Criminal Court claims authority over individuals despite the fact that it does not have the "Consent of the Governed." If the ICC were to take custody of a U.S. citizen, that person's Fourth and Fifth Amendment protections against unlawful searches and seizures and due process would be violated.

In our political system, those who run the government are accountable to the people. Our criminal justice system is no different. Prosecutors are accountable to people over whom they claim jurisdiction. Not so with the ICC. One reason the Bush administration cited for rejecting the ICC was that it "purports to have jurisdiction . . . for enumerated crimes alleged against U.S. nationals, including U.S. service members, in the territory of a party, even though the U.S. is not a party"[10] to the ICC.

The United States, or any of its citizens, must never be governed by foreign powers. In testimony before the House International Relations Committee, John Bolton, before he was appointed to the UN, said this provision was "unacceptable; unacceptable, not compromisable; unacceptable, for the United States to be bound by a treaty that it is not a party to."[11]

In June 2005, the Ethical Funds Company—a Canadian firm—issued a report warning that dozens of Canadian energy and mining firms operating in seventeen countries around the world are in danger of having their employees brought before the International Criminal Court if they are found to have committed human rights violations. Corporate officers, directors, and employees, as individuals, "are now exposed to criminal prosecution under the Rome Statute of the International Criminal Court," the report explained.[12]

(2) The ICC claims prosecutorial powers over elected U.S. officials. Under Article 27 of the Rome Statute, no "Head of State or Government . . . elected representative or a government official shall [be] exempt . . . from criminal responsibility under this Statute." Clearly, this provision conflicts with Article I, Section 2 of the Constitution, which gives the "sole Power of Impeachment" to the House of Representatives, and Article I, Section 3, which says those impeachments will be tried by the United States Senate, and in the case of the president, the chief justice of the Supreme Court will preside. On the matter of trying officials of the U.S. government, the ICC also conflicts with Article III, Section 2 of the Constitution, which gives "original jurisdiction" to the Supreme Court for "all Cases affecting Ambassadors, [and] other public Ministers and Consuls."

In addition to the president and members of Congress, the ICC also targets military officials, ambassadors, and members of the president's Cabinet and other high-ranking U.S. government officials. These are the individuals who are responsible for formulating policies to defend U.S. interests.

This claimed authority of the ICC gave the Bush administration most pause. While serving as undersecretary for Arms Control and International Security, John Bolton outlined the administration's concern on this point:

> Our principal concern is for our country's top civilian and military leaders, those responsible for our defense and foreign policy. They are the ones potentially at risk at the hands of the ICC's politically unaccountable Prosecutor, as part of an agenda to restrain American discretion, even when our actions are legitimated by the operation of our own constitutional system.[13]

(3) The ICC is a foreign court in a foreign land. "The seat of the Court shall be established at The Hague in the Netherlands," says Article 3.1 of the Rome Statute. But Americans dragged to the Netherlands will be stripped of their Sixth Amendment right to "a speedy and public trial, by an impartial jury of the State and district wherein the crime shall have been committed."

(4) ICC procedures violate provisions of the Bill of Rights. While it is true that the Rome Statute does build in certain protections for the accused, they are not the constitutional safeguards we know here in the United States. The accused has no right to be judged by a jury as provided in the Constitution's 6th Amendment.

One of the foundations of American criminal law is found in the 5th Amendment, which states, "nor shall any person be subject for the same offence to be twice put in jeopardy of life or limb," otherwise known as "double jeopardy." The ICC gives lip service to this principle, but in Article 20 it retains the right to review U.S. court decisions and re-try individuals if the ICC determines decisions "were not conducted independently or impartially."

Though the ICC allows for defendants to be aided by an attorney, it fails to guarantee "the assistance of counsel for his defence" as provided in the Constitution's 6th Amendment. Only "where the interests of justice so require" will the ICC provide legal counsel to defendants who cannot provide their own. The ICC has also created a preferred list of lawyers who may work for defendants. Further, the evidence that the ICC allows to be presented against a defendant amounts to hearsay and generally is much more lenient than would be permitted in any American courtroom. The prosecutor at the ICC, unlike in the U.S. justice system, may rely on anonymous witnesses.

(5) The office of the prosecutor is contrary to constitutional checks and balances.
The ICC's office of the prosecutor has tremendous authority within the court and is a part of the court itself. Under the U.S. system of justice, the prosecutor is basically a political office that is accountable to political pressures and constituencies. Prosecutors bring cases to the courts, but the two entities are independent of each other. In the International Criminal Court, the prosecutor and the court are one and the same. Thus, the ICC prosecutor is unaccountable, except to a minimal degree, to other offices of the ICC.

If the prosecutor reported to or was otherwise accountable to the UN Security Council, it would reduce some of the concern, but he is not. In fact, in early negotiations, the idea that only the Security Council could refer cases to the court was rejected. It also violates provisions of Chapter 7 of the UN Charter, which states that the Security Council is in charge of international peace and security.

Beyond the constitutional concerns, the claims of jurisdiction made by the ICC create new worries for policymakers charged with America's national defense and foreign policy. This is one of the "significant flaws" to which President Bill Clinton referred even as he was signing the treaty. The administration's concession on this point was described by Clinton's chief negotiator, Ambassador David Scheffer:

The treaty purports to establish an arrangement whereby United States armed forces operating overseas could conceivably be prosecuted by the International Criminal Court even if the United States has not agreed to be bound by the treaty. Not only is this contrary to the most fundamental principles of treaty law, it could inhibit the ability of the United States to use its military to meet alliance obligations and participate in multinational operations, including humanitarian interventions to save civilian lives.[14]

The case of U.S. military personnel serving in UN peacekeeping missions was one that demanded a great deal of attention from the Security Council. As far back as summer 2000, even before Bill Clinton signed on to the International Criminal Court, the United States was trying to win immunity for Americans serving in peacekeeping missions.

The International Criminal Court entered into force on July 1, 2002. At the same time, the Security Council was trying to extend the UN peacekeeping mission in Bosnia and Herzegovina. With dozens of Americans serving in that operation, the United States urged the Security Council to grant immunity from ICC prosecution to U.S. peacekeepers in UN missions. U.S. delegates were simply asking that Article 16 of the Rome Statute be implemented in that it prevents the court from beginning an investigation or prosecution if the Security Council adopts a resolution requesting such.

Other Security Council members and UN honchos were livid. In a letter to Secretary of State Colin Powell, UN secretary-general Kofi Annan said he was "seriously concerned" at the U.S. request. He tried to reassure Powell that the likelihood that a U.S. peacekeeper would be prosecuted was "highly improbable," and, as a consequence of U.S. requests, "the whole system of United Nations peacekeeping operations is being put at risk."[15]

Eventually, and for the next two years, American officials were able to win such immunity. In 2002, the Security Council adopted Resolution 1422, which stated that for a period of twelve months, the International Criminal Court could not proceed with an investigation against personnel in a UN peacekeeping mission who are nationals of a country "not a Party to the Rome Statute"—thus protecting Americans. The same language was adopted in 2003 in Resolution 1487.

But the following year, at about the same time the United States was handing over sovereignty to the Iraqi people, the UN Security Council informed the United States that Resolutions 1422 and 1487 could not be renewed. Incessant news coverage of the Abu Ghraib prison mishap gave Kofi Annan the opening he needed. It "would be unfortunate for one to press for such an exemption given the prisoner abuse in Iraq,"[16] Mr. Annan said, attempting to wrap himself in the mantle of human rights.

Knowing that their attempts to adopt a similar resolution would be defeated, the United States dropped the matter. But given that the U.S. had won specific exemption two years running and they no longer have it, the Security Council sees Americans who serve in UN peacekeeping missions as fair game for the ICC.

The Pentagon saw it the same way and began withdrawing U.S. peacekeepers in Africa and Kosovo and vowed to reassess all other missions so that our soldiers would not have to worry about being targeted by international ambulance chasers with political vendettas. But hundreds of Americans continue to serve in UN peacekeeping operations in military or police capacities in Kosovo and Liberia, while others are stationed in Sierra Leone, East Timor, Georgia, and the Middle East.

Military recruiters have had their challenges over the past fifteen years, and they will only continue as more young Americans come to understand the implications of the ICC. High school and college-aged students inclined to serve in the armed forces are likely to think twice about joining if they could be hauled before a foreign court.

Finally, one other problem with the International Criminal Court is the way in which it claims jurisdiction over others but carves out generous immunities for itself. The "Agreement on the Privileges and Immunities of the International Criminal Court"—ratified with the assent of only ten nations—states that the ICC will enjoy immunity from "every form of legal process." The "property, funds and assets" of the ICC "shall be immune from search, seizure, requisition, confiscation, expropriation and any other form of interference whether by executive, administrative, judicial or legislative action."

Article 8 of the Agreement on Privileges and Immunities makes clear that the ICC is not to be taxed in any way. "The Court, its assets, income and other property and its operations and transactions shall be exempt from all direct taxes" to include "income tax, capital tax, and corporation tax, as well as direct taxes levied by local and provincial authorities." It also exempts itself from having to pay customs duties of any kind.

The court and its members demand to be treated in the same way the highest-ranking diplomats are treated, and they want the same privileges enjoyed by diplomats, including favorable exchange rates, the right to send or receive items via diplomatic pouch, and special mailing privileges.

Members of the ICC have declared themselves immune from "personal arrest or detention"; "legal process of every kind"; and "immigration restrictions." In addition, the "salaries, emoluments and allowances" of the judges, prosecutor, deputy prosecutor, and the registrar of the ICC are exempt from taxation and national service obligations and having to contribute to Social Security programs.

Those who negotiated and worked to create the ICC now enjoy these cushy positions as members of the court. They are demanding to be treated like royalty with no obligations to anyone or any nation, nor do they accept responsibility for their actions, yet they are sitting in judgment of, quite literally, every person in the world.

The Court's Impact on National Security and Foreign Policy

The Pentagon, in its 2005 National Defense Strategy, says "our strength as a nation state will continue to be challenged by those who employ a strategy of the weak using international fora, judicial processes, and terrorism."[17] In an editorial, the *Washington Times* dubbed it "lawfare"—the "ill-intentioned use of international law and the courts to harm American interests."[18] As part of the U.S. defense strategy, the Pentagon explained, it is taking precautions to ensure "protections against transfers of U.S. personnel to the International Criminal Court."[19]

They are forced to do so because international legal groups are in heated competition to be the first to be able to claim responsibility for the trial of an American in the International Criminal Court. And being skilled in their profession, these leftist attorneys understand they cannot simply inundate the ICC with briefs against Americans and hope they will get lucky. Instead, they are building—step by step—a body of legal opinions and precedent in lower courts, in international tribunals, and in international institutions that will one day be the foundation for the ultimate prize they seek.

Doug Feith, undersecretary of Defense for Policy, told the *Associated Press* that this is an effort to "criminalize foreign policy and bring prosecutions where there is no proper basis for jurisdiction under international law as a way of trying to pressure American officials."[20]

Among the legal actions that have been urged or brought against American leaders or our allies are the following:

• *The Center for Constitutional Rights (CCR).* The center is a New York-based leftist organization. In November 2004, under the so-called doctrine of universal jurisdiction, the CCR filed suit in a German court against Secretary of Defense Don Rumsfeld, CIA Director George Tenet, and eight other high-ranking U.S. military and civilian personnel. Citing the isolated abuses at Abu Ghraib prison in Iraq, the group charged these individuals with "torture and other grave violations of humanitarian law," which was, it claimed, "widespread among the US military" and taking place elsewhere around the globe.[21]

• *Amnesty International.* With the release of its 2005 Annual Report, Amnesty charged the United States with a "blatant disregard for international human rights and humanitarian law."[22] The United States, the group said, committed "war crimes in Iraq" and was responsible for "the torture and ill-treatment of detainees in US custody in other countries." They were referring to those accused or suspected of terrorist activities being held at Guantanamo Bay, which Irene Khan, Amnesty's executive director, called a "gulag."[23] Once Amnesty charged the United States with these horrific crimes, it said "all states have a responsibility to investigate and prosecute people responsible for these crimes,"[24] and called on other nations to "exercise universal jurisdiction over persons accused of grave breaches of the Geneva Conventions and torture or to extradite the suspects to a country that will."[25] Among those Amnesty believes should be prosecuted are President George W. Bush, Secretary of Defense Don Rumsfeld, Attorney General Alberto Gonzalez, and CIA Director George Tenet.

• *Dutch activists charged President George W. Bush with "numerous grave violations of the Geneva Conventions."*[26] In May 2005, just days before the president visited Maastricht for a World War II sixtieth anniversary event, a judge turned down the request of the activists to have the American president arrested. Stating the obvious, the court ruled that to have allowed the president's arrest "could have far-reaching consequences for U.S.-Dutch relations."[27]

• *Belgium targets General Tommy Franks.* After the initial phase of the war in Iraq in 2003, anti-war activists filed suit in Belgium against U.S. general Tommy Franks, the commander of coalition forces in Iraq and Afghanistan.

One of "Rumsfeld's Rules,"—a compilation of observations the defense secretary has made over forty years in politics, government, and business—is the rule to "be precise." Rumsfeld applied that rule to this case and simply pointed out that Belgium is the host country of NATO and it would be impractical for U.S. officials to travel there if they have been indicted by the nation's courts. "Belgium has turned its legal system into a platform for divisive politicized lawsuits against her NATO allies," Rumsfeld said, and cautioned that the United States may have to "oppose all further spending for a NATO headquarters in Brussels until we know with certainty Belgium intends to be a hospitable place."[28]

• *Tony Blair declared a war criminal.* In July 2003, the Athens Bar Association filed charges with the International Criminal Court against British prime minister Tony Blair for war crimes in Iraq. The complaint contained a list of twenty-two specific charges and asserted that British participation in the Iraq war violated the UN Charter and the Geneva Conventions. Also named in the suit were Defense Secretary Geoff Hoon and Foreign Secretary Jack Straw.

• *The investigation by Carla del Ponte.* In 1999, Carla del Ponte, prosecutor for the International Criminal Tribunal for the former Yugoslavia, conducted a six-month investigation into the conduct of American pilots and NATO commanders during the seventy-eight-day air war over Serbia. Mrs. del Ponte was forced to drop the investigation only after objections from the White House. Despite this warning sign, President Clinton signed the International Criminal Court treaty.

America's soldiers, sailors, airmen, and Marines are well trained and are confident warriors on the battlefield. But it is precisely these kinds of "sue-first-and-ask-questions-later" legal actions that give them pause.

So when speaking to the soldiers of the 10th Mountain Division at Fort Drum in July 2002, President George W. Bush promised the uniformed warriors that, "we will not submit American troops to prosecutors and judges whose jurisdiction we do not accept."[29]

With the court having been inaugurated only weeks before and the Bush administration actively planning to go to war in Iraq, the idea of American citizens being tried in a foreign court for war crimes was no longer an academic theory—it was one more thing about which deploying soldiers and their families would now have to worry.

Trying to allay concerns of the soldiers, the president assured them that those "who serve under the American flag will answer to his or her own superiors, and to military law, not to the rulings of an unaccountable international criminal court."[30]

Bush was reinforcing action his administration had taken only three months prior. On May 6, 2002, the State Department dispatched a letter to

UN secretary-general Kofi Annan stating the U.S. government's position with respect to the International Criminal Court. The letter was signed by the man who would go on to become the United States' permanent representative to the UN, John Bolton. "Dear Mr. Secretary-General," the notification began,

> This is to inform you, in connection with the Rome Statute of the International Criminal Court adopted on July 17, 1998, that the United States does not intend to become a party to the treaty. Accordingly, the United States has no legal obligations arising from its signature on December 31, 2000.

When Bolton's letter landed on Kofi Annan's desk, the thud resounded throughout the halls of the UN and the U.S. Congress.

Senator Russ Feingold said Bush's actions "call into question our country's credibility in all multilateral endeavors."[31] His colleague, Senator Chris Dodd, said the United States aligned itself with "a handful of rogue nations that are frightened to death of the International Criminal Court."[32]

Even before the official notification was sent, U.S. newspapers warned that the ICC's critics had won the president's heart. According to the *New York Times*, the Bush administration expressed "unreasonable fears" about Americans being brought before the court. The *St. Louis Post-Dispatch* called such concerns "farfetched fearmongering."

The *Milwaukee Journal* said it was a "childish, petulant act, an insult not only to the UN, but to the [other] countries . . . that have signed the treaty."[33] Rejecting the treaty, the paper opined, "would also be a sop to isolationists . . . who have a reflexive and irrational fear of any loss of U.S. sovereignty."[34]

Ivory Tower editorialists don't face the same dangers as do U.S. soldiers, sailors, airmen, and Marines, and so it is understandable that they don't fear the ICC. But such critics, whose deepest battle scars are paper cuts, ought to walk a mile in the boots of young people who are forced to make split-second decisions about "friend or foe"; "life or death." Then they ought to think about what those kinds of decisions mean in the context of an increasingly litigious world.

Administrative officials like John Bolton thought long and hard about such issues, so it is easy to understand why Bolton said sending his letter to Kofi Annan was "the happiest moment of my government service."[35] The Bush administration showed great courage in standing up to relentless pressure from NGOs and their allies in Congress. It was a bold and long overdue move that had to be carried out over the objections of career diplomats in the State Department.

While the administration's action was anything but symbolic, it was not absolute either. Despite the widespread characterization that the administration "unsigned" the treaty, it simply informed the UN that the United States "does not intend" to ratify the treaty. Pierre Prosper, U.S. ambassador for war crimes issues, called it a "rare . . . but not unprecedented action."[36] In a briefing with reporters, State Department spokesman Richard Boucher was asked about the use of the term "unsigned." He said he would not use the term "because that's not what we did."[37]

Nonetheless, what they did do was send a wake-up call to Turtle Bay that the new administration would not tolerate the institution's imposition on American sovereignty or dismiss those actions as black helicopter conspiracy theories as did Secretary of State Madeleine Albright during the Clinton administration.

And to the credit of the Bush administration, they were not about to let Bolton's letter become an American Maginot Line—they stayed on the offensive. In August 2002, the president signed legislation that included the American Servicemembers' Protection Act (ASPA), introduced in Congress by Senator Jesse Helms and Representative Tom DeLay. DeLay said he introduced the bill because while he "firmly supports efforts to hold tyrants, dictators, and war criminals accountable for their crimes,"[38] he believes the ICC is an "unchecked power that poses a real threat to our men and women fighting the war against terror."[39]

Among other provisions, ASPA prohibits official U.S. cooperation with the ICC including the taxpayer funding and sharing of classified information. It also restricts U.S. involvement in UN peacekeeping missions and prohibits military aide to nations that are a party to the ICC.

The administration has also been engaged in an intensive effort to enter into what are known as "Article 98 Agreements"—bilateral non-extradition accords provided for in Article 98 of the Rome Statute. Any country that signs one of these promises not to surrender an American citizen in their custody to the International Criminal Court. The stated goal of the Bush administration is to enter into an Article 98 Agreement with every country on earth. On May 2, 2005, the United States signed its 100th such agreement with Angola.

Signing these agreements has not been without challenge. In August 2002, after Romania entered into a pact, Romano Prodi, president of the

European Commission, ordered other European Union nations not to enter into such agreements. His comments were especially directed at nations that were hoping to become members of the EU. One month later the EU adopted a common position to reject Article 98 Agreements with the United States on the ground that they are inconsistent with international law, although the Rome Statute specifically allows for them.

In Nigeria, the Senate has asked President Olusegun Obasanjo to rescind the country's agreement with the United States. International NGOs have been urging governments to reject U.S. requests for cooperation and have urged the interim government in Iraq to join the International Criminal Court, which would endanger more than 100,000 American troops.

The Case of the British

For years leading up to the creation of the International Criminal Court, its proponents assured skeptics that responsible nations had nothing to fear from the ICC. The court was being created to prosecute "real" war criminals like Saddam Hussein, Slobodan Milosevic, and the like. Only the modern-day Adolf Hitlers, they said, would find themselves in UN-issued leg irons. As an added bonus, they explained, brutal dictators who would otherwise commit genocide, torture, and repress their own people would be deterred by the prospect of standing before eighteen judges in powdered wigs.

Place your trust in the International Criminal Court and the world will be a safer place, advocates of the ICC argued. The British government bought into it hook, line, and sinker. In announcing the introduction of the domestic International Criminal Court Bill, British Foreign Secretary Robin Cook said, "The International Criminal Court will always be there to call the world's tyrants to account."[40] With the signing of the bill, Cook said, we will "send a clear message to the world's tyrants that Britain wants them to face international justice."[41] But today, millions of Britons deeply regret Her Majesty's decision to subject her subjects to the jurisdiction of the International Criminal Court and its global sheriff, Kofi Annan.

In July 2005, Attorney General Peter Goldsmith announced that three British veterans of Operation Iraqi Freedom were the first to be charged by the Crown with committing "war crimes" under Article 8(2)(a)(ii) of Britain's International Criminal Court Act. Corporal Donald Payne, Lance Corporal Wayne Crowcroft, and Private Darren Fallon, each with the Queen's Lancashire Regiment, were accused of "inhuman treatment" of an Iraqi prisoner—Baha Musa—who died in their custody while they were serving in Basra in September 2003. The statute, however, does not define or explain what constitutes "inhuman treatment."

Nobody is arguing that British soldiers should be able to act with impunity, but citizens are concerned that the charges against the men are politicized and they are being tried in order to appease the ICC. The charges filed against these men also contradict the assurances given by advocates of the ICC, like U.S. Senator Patrick Leahy who said, "The court would only prosecute the most atrocious international crimes such as genocide and crimes against humanity."[42]

Britain's International Criminal Court Act 2001 serves as a legal shell game imposed by globalist sympathizers within the government, allowing them to feign concern for national sovereignty by insisting British citizens will never be brought before the ICC in The Hague. The act writes into British law the elements of the Rome Statute of the International Criminal Court—essentially importing the ICC to London.

In the case of the three soldiers of the Queen's Lancashire Regiment, it is a political show trial in which the government is forced to prosecute or face the prospect of its citizens being tried in The Hague before the ICC. Because the ICC "has the authority to bring individuals to trial without needing permission from any individual or government,"[43] politicians in countries like Britain are forced to prosecute individuals domestically for crimes for which they might not otherwise be charged. In other cases, they might be charged with more serious crimes than are warranted to keep the global sheriff off their backs.

The affection average Britons have for their military personnel is no different than Americans have for their soldiers, sailors, airmen, and Marines. So when the news was announced that their men and women in service were being tried under the International Criminal Court Act, the sparks began to fly.

"By exposing our troops to the procedures of the International Criminal Court," wrote Bruce Anderson in the *Sunday Scotsman*, the Blair government "is dishonouring them and undermining their morale."[44] The *Daily Telegraph* agreed, arguing that the spirit of the British military is being challenged by a cadre of "tank-chasing human rights lawyers, who can be expected to pursue allegations of misconduct long after hostilities have ended."[45]

The *Telegraph* argues that the soldiers "will now fall prey to a shabby political game in which they are made scapegoats to appease the still-vociferous opponents of the war."[46] It is the anti-war activists who have the most influence with prosecutors and judges at the International Criminal Court. And, even in its infancy, argues Edwin Bramall, who has had a long and distinguished career in the British armed forces, the ICC has impacted British law to the point that

> [t]here is considerable disquiet among some members of the forces and concern that, even when doing their perceived duty in an operational situation, they may become vulnerable to prosecution and will not always be backed up higher up the chain of command, where it may be claimed that the matter has been taken out of their hands.[47]

Ben Wallace, a conservative elected to Parliament in May 2005, believes the political games have already begun and suggests that "if we are charging some of these men with neglect of their duties, then we must recognise that the chain of command does not stop with commanding officers but goes right to the door of Number 10."[48]

Britons know their uniformed countrymen serve honorably and represent the values of a civilized and responsible people. Like Americans, they take pride in the manner in which their military personnel conduct themselves under conditions of hardship and stress.

They take great pride in soldiers like Colonel Tim Collins who are not only willing to take on the dangerous work required by today's military, but do so with grace and honor. On March 19, 2003, the night before they went into battle, Tim Collins addressed the men of the 1st Battalion of the Royal Irish Regiment. It was one of the most moving military speeches since MacArthur bid farewell to the Long Gray Line, and it shows the sentiments with which British soldiers are sent into battle. In part, Collins told his men,

> We go to liberate, not to conquer. We will not fly our flags in their country. We are entering Iraq to free a people and the only flag which will be flown in that ancient land is their own. Show respect for them . . . if you are ferocious in battle, remember to be magnanimous in victory . . . . You will have to go a long way to find a more decent, generous and upright people than the Iraqis. You will be embarrassed by their hospitality even though they have nothing. Don't treat them as refugees, for they are in their own country . . . . If there are casualties of war then remember that when they woke up and got dressed in the morning they did not plan to die this day. Allow them dignity in death. Bury them properly and mark their graves . . . . If you harm the regiment or its history by over-enthusiasm in killing or in cowardice, know it is your family who will suffer. You will be shunned

unless your conduct is of the highest order. . . . We will bring shame on neither our uniform or our nation.[49]

Such words are not the sentiments of war criminals. Yet Tim Collins was himself charged with war crimes before being acquitted.

But when the infrequent occasion arises in which a member of their military is accused of wrongdoing, proud Britons consider themselves quite capable of policing their own and need not the advice of UN desk jockeys who long to refer cases to the ICC. "Perfectly adequate laws already existed," the *Daily Telegraph* wrote, "enforced by courts martial long before the [International Criminal Court Act] came into force."[50] Peter Inge, former chief of the Defence Staff, said "that if a soldier on operational service has broken the law, he should be tried by his own nation and not subject to the humiliation of going to the International Criminal Court."[51]

That sentiment was echoed by MP Lindsay Hoyle, who worried that the highly decorated Colonel Jorge Mendonca may find himself in The Hague. Mendonca was the commander of the Queen's Lanchashire Regiment at the time of the alleged crimes, but, by all accounts, was twenty miles away from the location in which the incident is said to have occurred. But under Britain's International Criminal Court Act, Mendonca could still be held responsible for the actions of others. Section 65 of the act states in part,

> A military commander . . . is responsible for offences committed by forces under his effective command and control . . . as a result of his failure to exercise control properly over such forces where . . . he either knew . . . should have known that the forces were committing or about to commit such offences, and . . . he failed to take all necessary and reasonable measures within his power to prevent or repress their commission.

Lindsay Hoyle worries that a high-ranking distinguished officer could be paraded before the ICC in The Hague and the implications that would have for troop morale and the reputation of the British armed forces. In the House of Lords, Hoyle argued,

> What is now hanging over [Colonel Mendonca] and other soldiers is that the case may be referred to the International Criminal Court. That court was not set up for that purpose. It was set up to deal with cases of genocide and with war criminals. That that gallant officer could be in the same dock as that in which Milosevic has appeared must be wrong in itself . . . . If they charge the colonel or other soldiers under the International Criminal

Court, they will destroy the morale of all the soldiers, not just the Queen's Lancashire Regiment but soldiers serving in Iraq, Afghanistan or any other theatre of war.[52]

The impact of Mendonca's prosecution on "the bonds of loyalty and trust," says MP Julian Brazier, are the very reason "why many of us were deeply concerned that Parliament should have subjected the armed forces to a legal framework that is alien to British law and enforceable by foreign judges who are wholly ignorant of the British military way—and, in many cases, of war itself."[53]

Brazier goes one step further and points out that because the United Kingdom signed on to the International Criminal Court, "even if the charges against [Colonel Mendonca] are dropped, the International Criminal Court is free to pursue him as it, and it alone, is the judge of whether any investigation in this country was adequate."[54]

The prosecutions of military personnel under the International Criminal Court Act has caused uncertainty among the troops, and some commanders still serving in Iraq, warned Colonel Tim Collins, are becoming "cautious, some even over-cautious,"[55] for fear of prosecution. The foundations of trust in the British military are being destroyed; lives are being put in danger; and the country's national security is being put at risk. It is all a result of putting their faith in the United Nations.

Democratic Support for the Court

The problems facing the British military could easily occur here in the United States.

"I think if we have a Democrat President in January of 2009," explained Jed Babbin, former deputy undersecretary of defense in the first Bush administration, "by the end of 2010, you will have American soldiers in front of the International Criminal Court."[56]

Babbin, who recently had published his own book on the United Nations, told me that "Democrats are totally devoted to the United Nations and they do not see the problem with us sacrificing our constitutional rights or the sovereignty of our nation to this false idol they bless and pray to."

Babbin is right, and had the results of the 2004 election been different, U.S. military personnel might already find themselves in The Hague. It was a weakness of John Kerry's that President Bush was eager to point out during their first debate. Said Bush,

My opponent talks about me not signing certain treaties. But let me tell you one thing I didn't sign—and I think it shows a difference of our opinion . . . and that is I wouldn't join the International Criminal Court. This is a body based in The Hague where unaccountable judges and prosecutors could pull our troops, our diplomats up for trial. And I wouldn't join it. And I understand that in certain capitals around the world that that wasn't a popular move. But it's the right move, not to join a foreign court . . . where our people could be prosecuted. My opponent is for joining the International Criminal Court.

Indeed he was. Kerry and his running mate, North Carolina senator John Edwards, both expressed their support for the court. Furthermore, Kerry had to appease a liberal constituency that is four square behind the International Criminal Court, including the American Bar Association, Moveon.org, Amnesty International, Human Rights Watch, and a host of other powerful liberal lobbying organizations funded by the likes of George Soros, Ted Turner, and the Hollywood Left.

Other contenders for the Democratic nomination in 2004 were also in favor of the ICC. Speaking with Wolf Blitzer on CNN's *Late Edition* in July 2002, former NATO commander General Wesley Clark explained that it really isn't a big deal if Americans are dragged before international tribunals. "I was subjected to a war crimes investigation in my role as NATO commander," Clark said, "it didn't bother me a bit."[57] Though he fully understands that under the ICC, "American soldiers could be subject to whimsical or politically motivated charges . . . we've got to find a way to work with this court."[58]

Senator Joe Lieberman, a 2004 presidential candidate and the Democratic Party's vice-presidential nominee in 2000, explained in the *Hartford Courant* on November 25, 2002, that in order for the Bush administration to win the heart of European nations, he must "demonstrate understanding and compromise on issues of great importance" to them—such as the International Criminal Court.

For more than a decade, Senate Democrats were helping globalists to build the foundation of an international jail cell that would house Americans who strayed from the tenets of the new world order. In 1994, under Democratic control, the Senate voted 55-45 to "encourage the establishment of an international criminal court within the United Nations system."[59] At that time, Senator Joe Biden, a possible presidential contender in 2008, called it a "positive development."[60] Senator Claiborne Pell, a leader in shaping the Democrats' foreign policy, called it the "logical next step in efforts to strengthen international institutions."[61]

As President Bill Clinton was considering the International Criminal Court in December 2000, eighteen senators and thirty-two members of the House—mostly liberal Democrats—wrote to him to urge him to sign the Rome Statute. One of those House members was Congressman Dennis Kucinich, who was also a candidate for president in 2004 and appealed to the extreme liberal base of the Democratic Party. Kucinich believes that nearly every facet of American policy should be subordinated to the United Nations. He attends UN gatherings to berate his own country; has vehemently protested American policy in Iraq; and openly advocates bringing American officials before the International Criminal Court to try them for war crimes, which he outlined in a December 9, 2004, column:

> In the wake of the attack on Iraq, questions have been made regarding the responsibility of members of the Administration and their contractors, for authorizing torture, for the destruction and appropriation of property, unlawful confinement, attacks on civilians, attacks on civilian objects, exacting excessive incidental death, injury or damage, destroying or seizing the enemy's property, employing poisoned weapons, and outrages upon personal dignity, all of which constitute war crimes or crimes against humanity under the International Criminal Court statute. . . . Given the public record of its conduct in Iraq, is it any wonder that the Administration, in order to avoid accountability under the ICC for the results of its own directives, would go to extraordinary efforts to weaken and even destroy the ICC . . . . It is more likely that those whose protection the administrators seek wear not the uniform of our nation, but the business suits of top civilian government officials who wrap themselves in the flag and hide behind the troops while insisting upon impunity for the deadly consequences of their own political decisions.[62]

As the 2008 presidential campaign approaches, there will be others whose beliefs are similar to those of Mr. Kucinich—they just won't express them as clearly.

Leading contenders for the Democrat nomination in 2008, like senators Joe Biden and Russ Feingold, speak favorably of the ICC. The most anticipated candidate—Hillary Rodham Clinton—favors U.S. participation as well. In a February 2005 speech to the German Media Prize Dinner, Clinton acknowledged that the United States is "more vulnerable to the misuse of an international criminal court because of the international role we play and the resentments that flow from that ubiquitous presence around the world." But she argued, "that does not mean . . . that the United States should walk out of the International Criminal Court."

If elected, there is no doubt that Mrs. Clinton will work hand-in-glove with the United Nations. She believes the UN is "an indispensable organization" that should be made bigger, stronger, and more authoritative. Hillary describes her participation in the UN Conference on Women held in Beijing as "one of the highlights of my own life."[63]

Another possible contender is New Mexico governor Bill Richardson, who served as U.S. ambassador to the United Nations in the Clinton administration. On October 24, 2004—known to the globalists as "United Nations Day"—Governor Richardson signed an executive proclamation declaring United Nations Day in his state and extolling the virtues of the global tribunal.

Even some on the Republican side have voiced approval for the ICC. One of the media darlings is Senator John McCain of Arizona, who gave George W. Bush a run for his money in the 2000 primary season. McCain is a leading powerbroker in the Senate and is openly considering another run for the White House in 2008. Even if McCain chooses not to run, his views on the ICC will influence the media and other Republicans who look to him for leadership on defense and foreign policy matters.

In a March 2004 interview on *Fox News Sunday*, McCain told anchor Chris Wallace, "I think we should open a dialogue on a variety of issues that the Europeans care about: climate change, international criminal court."[64] A year later, he was even more emphatic: "I want us in the ICC,"[65] he said during a debate at the World Economic Forum in Davos, Switzerland, in January 2005.

America's submission to the International Criminal Court must be a major point of scrutiny in the candidates' records in 2008. Most candidates will try to walk a fine line in which they say we should join the court, but carve out exemptions for U.S. troops. For all the reasons outlined, that will not suffice. Not only must we completely disavow the International Criminal Court—beyond even the efforts of the Bush administration—but we must dismantle it. The day an American is brought before the International Criminal Court, our Constitution will cease to have meaning.

Don't Ask Me, I Just Work Here

"No ruling of the World Trade Organization," fumed Mickey Kantor, the U.S. trade representative under President Bill Clinton, "mandatorily requires us to do anything in the United States, at any level of government with any regard, any law or regulation, or any other ruling."[1]

It was January 1996, and Kantor was putting on a brave face, trying to explain the implications of the very first decision issued by the World Trade Organization (WTO)—a ruling against the United States. Clinton and Kantor were the chief pompom shakers for the WTO, insisting that U.S. membership in the global trade body was essential to American interests.

Only one year after the WTO had hung out its shingle, it delivered an ignominious blow to the country that created it, ruling that the United States was "discriminating" against Venezuelan and Brazilian gasoline products. But the two countries were trying to sell products to the U.S. that failed to meet environmental and safety standards required by the Clean Air Act.

The bureaucrats in Geneva had no interest in America's desire to improve air quality or protect the health and safety of its citizens. Either the U.S. would allow sub-par gasoline products from Venezuela and Brazil into the country, or it would face fines imposed by the world trade body. Fix the problem, the WTO ordered the Clinton administration.

Surely the United States would not bow to such a brazen and unprecedented attack on our national sovereignty. As Mickey Kantor assured us, no WTO ruling can force the U.S. to change even a comma in any law, rule, or regulation.

So how did the Clinton administration react? It fell to its knees, shouted mea culpa, begged forgiveness, and changed the Environmental Protection Agency's (EPA) standards in order to bring the EPA's regulations into compliance with WTO demands.

What Mr. Clinton should have done was told World Trade Organization bureaucrats to go to hell. After that, he could have politely explained that

Venezuela and Brazil were welcome to sell the United States as much oil as they would like, provided their products met the consumer safety requirements enacted into U.S. law by the legitimately elected representatives of the people of these United States.

It would have been a great lesson in republican governance and a directive that would have won Mr. Clinton kudos from both his conservative critics and his friends in the environmental movement. Such a move would have been a terrific defense of American sovereignty and her national pride. But, oh, what could have been.

Instead, Mr. Clinton enlisted the United States in a global game of "Mother, May I?" And today, the business plans of American companies, which dare to practice commerce overseas, must first comply with the whims of un-elected, unaccountable trade czars in the posh Geneva headquarters of the World Trade Organization. His actions ensured the irrelevance of Congress on trade matters and carved off a large piece of American sovereignty on which international vultures continue to feed.

But as satisfying as it would be to lay the blame for this debacle at the feet of William Jefferson Clinton, it is not his doing alone. The outsourcing of American trade policy was, and remains, a bipartisan affair. In 1994 when the WTO was being created, Clinton was aided every step of the way by Republican leaders in Congress.

By day, Newt Gingrich was the architect of the Republican Revolution—writing the Contract with America and overthrowing a corrupt Democratic establishment that had ruled for more than forty years in the House. By night, he was pulling strings for the White House to engineer support for the WTO.

For Bob Dole, the Republican leader in the Senate, creating a new institution of government—be it domestic or international—was an idea with which he was perfectly comfortable. Dole helped Gingrich and Clinton create the WTO, then—in an effort to burnish his conservative credentials—tried to use it as a whipping boy during his 1996 run for the presidency. Dole went down in flames as his conservative base of supporters relied on Shakespeare's advice to "trust not him that hath once broken faith."

The views of the public that had just elected the historic freshman class of 1994 were ignored as the Old Guard of the Republican and Democratic parties marched Americans lock step into the brave new world of WTO-controlled commerce. Contrary to Mr. Kantor's reassurances, it is a world in which the laws, regulations, and policies of the United States are rewritten according to WTO dictates. In this Constitution-free environment in which we find ourselves, the Founders' insistence that Congress "regulate Commerce with foreign Nations" no longer applies. When the World Trade Organization says "jump," U.S. government officials ask "how high?"

Advocates tend to view America's participation in the WTO as strictly a matter of dollars and cents. They adhere to Calvin Coolidge's motto that "the business of America is business" and believe that if WTO intervention can help reduce the price of U.S. consumers goods, that is all that really matters. After all, it is the entrance of the neighborhood Wal-Mart, not the factory gate, where today's political candidates meet their constituents.

But trade is about so much more than the price of socks and DVD players. International trade is an instrument of foreign policy and a component of national defense. It can even be used as a catalyst to improve human rights. Environmental concerns, labor regulations, consumer safety standards, and protection of intellectual property are all impacted by trade-related decisions. Before handing it to the WTO, America's trade policy was once a component of domestic politics—giving a voice to the producer and consumer alike and forcing elected officials to balance what are often competing interests. How the American public is impacted by each of these policy areas is now the responsibility of the World Trade Organization.

By joining the WTO, the United States has not only sacrificed a piece of her sovereignty, but we have issued a gold-plated invitation to the United Nations to take even more of it in the future.

The WTO is the model for a second Bretton Woods. To accompany the World Bank and the IMF, which were established in the first Bretton Woods conference, globalists are clamoring for an International Finance Facility to force nations pay their "fair share" of contributions to a UN-run global welfare scheme. An International Tax Office (ITO)—barely defeated in Monterrey, Mexico, in 2002—is still on the UN's "to do" list. An ITO would have the authority to regulate the tax policies of national governments to keep rates artificially high and prevent competition for investment dollars among nations. And French president Jacques Chirac simply won't rest until he gets the World Environmental Organization of which he has long dreamed.

Proponents of each of these institutions have studied the blueprints of the World Trade Organization. Any new international institution they build from here on out will be in the WTO image: limit the voting power and influence of the United States, and have the authority to force change in the policies of national governments.

In creating the WTO, American leaders insisted it was necessary because only an international organization could act as a fair arbiter for an issue that affects all nations. But that only bolsters the argument in favor of U.S. participation in a World Environmental Organization that could enforce global environmental rules. Under such logic, any policy portfolio that transcends borders should be the responsibility of the UN. The exploration of outer space, the use of the seas, and governance of the Internet are all ripe for UN intervention because of the creation of the WTO. Under this expansion of global governance, even immigration and certain health matters are policy issues that could come under the management of anti-American bureaucrats in Turtle Bay or Geneva or The Hague.

Unfortunately, there are many in Congress who would welcome such "advancements." While there are exceptions, most members of Congress are a craven lot. Just as the WTO lifts their burden of having to decide between competing constituencies without ever having to accept responsibility for the outcome, so too would new global institutions allow them to empathize equally with all sides without having to accept the responsibility for making a decision. All the tough choices will be left to the WTO or some other UN body that does not have to answer to the American public.

Creation of the World Trade Organization

Like the International Criminal Court, the World Trade Organization can trace its roots to the early days of the United Nations. The globalists long wanted an international organization to police world commerce. So even before the United Nations was officially inaugurated, its institutions were being built. In 1944, representatives from forty-four countries met in Bretton Woods, New Hampshire, at the United Nations Monetary and Financial Conference to draw up the blueprints for a new international financial order.

Three institutions were planned to regulate international trade and finance. First was the International Monetary Fund, which would act as a sort of central bank for the world's governments. The International Bank for Reconstruction and Development (World Bank) was to be, before the implementation of the Marshall Plan, the institution that rebuilt Europe. The first action taken by the World Bank was a $250 million loan to France—a move that helps explain France's continued devotion to world government.

Finally, in order to regulate a host of issues related to global commerce, an International Trade Organization (ITO) was planned. But the Bretton

Woods conference would have to settle for two out of three on their wish list. Objections from the U.S. Congress forced negotiators to set aside their hope for a permanent trade institution. But three years later, they revisited the idea, and in 1948 adopted the General Agreement on Tariffs and Trade (GATT). Though it was not as expansive or authoritative as the ITO would have been, the GATT was nonetheless the set of rules that would govern world trade for the next forty-seven years.

In the GATT's first five negotiating sessions—or "Rounds" as they are known—the topics were limited to tariffs and only two to three dozen countries participated. But the Kennedy and Tokyo Rounds in the mid-1960s drew more participation and included debate on issues such as dumping and non-tariff trade barriers. Already, the trend had begun in which the GATT expanded its authority over more national trade policies.

The Uruguay Round—which took place between 1986 and 1994—was the most comprehensive set of trade negotiations. With the help of the newly elected Clinton administration and its trade czar Mickey Kantor, it gave internationalists what they had worked decades for—the World Trade Organization. While the GATT dealt mostly with international trade in products, the WTO's mandate was expanded to include authority over intellectual property and services. Some want the WTO to expand its portfolio further to include arbitration on disputes such as the environment and labor issues.

Located in Geneva, Switzerland, the World Trade Organization has 630 employees and a hefty annual budget of $167 million—more than three times the size of the U.S. trade representative's office. The United States pays the largest percentage to the World Trade Organization—about 16 percent of the WTO budget, or $26.5 million annually—twice as much as any other country ponies up.

However, when it comes to voting, the United States is put on a par with the smallest countries in the world like Liechtenstein and Fiji. Despite its generosity, the U.S. gets no veto in the WTO as it does in the UN Security Council, and many of the organization's member countries are the same nations that consistently vote against U.S. interests in the General Assembly.

A closer look at the inequity of the WTO's financial structure reveals the following:

- There are 148 member countries in the WTO. The United States pays more than the combined membership dues of 122 other countries—82 percent of WTO members.
- There are 97 countries in the WTO that contribute only 1 percent or less of what the United States pays in membership dues, yet they are treated as equals with the U.S.
- There are 42 countries that pay less than *1/10* of 1 percent of what the United States pays.
- Brazil and India each pay about 17 times less in membership dues than the U.S., but they have brought 8 and 6 complaints against the United States, respectively.
- While the U.S. contributes 16 percent of the WTO budget, only 4.2 percent of WTO employees are American. By contrast, Great Britain contributes 5.7 percent to annual operations, but 13 percent of WTO employees are British. France contributes only 5.1 percent to the trade body, but dominates its workforce as French nationals make up 26.1 percent of all WTO employees.

Uncle Sam has not only built the asylum, but he is allowing the inmates to run it.

Another problem with the World Trade Organization is the lack of transparency with which it operates. Even Mickey Kantor called the WTO "one of the most secret organizations in the world."[2]

Walter Jones, congressman from North Carolina, explains that "trade disputes are decided by international panels that are hand-picked by the WTO. The identities of panel members are kept secret, and deliberations are kept confidential."[3]

As the Uruguay Round agreement was being pushed through Congress in September 1994, more than four dozen journalists and First Amendment advocates sent a letter to President Bill Clinton protesting the secrecy with which the WTO makes decisions—calling it "an affront to the democratic traditions of this nation." The letter went on to say that the WTO's "unprecedented secrecy is particularly offensive, given the vast powers to punish and penalize that this body will hold, not over just the federal government, but state and local ones, too." The group asked that the press and public be allowed to monitor WTO deliberations; they wanted public access to WTO documents and public disclosure by WTO officials of potential conflicts of interest.[4]

These are all reasonable requests because they are all embedded in the American tradition of openness in government. But freedom and transparency in government is a secondary consideration to organizations like the WTO, and ten years later, WTO proceedings remain closed to public and media scrutiny.

Before the WTO was created, Congress had already transferred much of its authority on international trade to the executive branch. But with approval of the WTO, there is no longer even a pretense that Congress has a say in matters of trade policy. Even one of the World Trade Organization's most vocal advocates, Congressman Newt Gingrich, recognized the wholesale transfer of constitutional authority to an international body. Before the WTO was approved by a lame-duck session of Congress in 1994, Gingrich conceded the significance of what was about to take place:

> I am just saying that we need to be honest about the fact that we are transferring from the United States at a practical level significant authority to a new organization. This is a transformational moment. I would feel better if the people who favor this would be honest about the scale of change. This is not just another trade agreement. This is adopting something which twice, once in the 1940's and once in the 1950's, the U.S. Congress rejected. I am not even saying that we should reject it. I, in fact, lean toward it. But I think we have to be very careful, because it is a huge transfer of power.[5]

The WTO's Impact on National and State Sovereignty

While dead wrong in his vote, Gingrich's analysis was spot on. The creation of the WTO was a huge transfer of power to an unaccountable body. Clinton and Congress severed their allegiance to the Constitution and placed the fate of much of America's economic policy in the hands of international pen pushers. This "transformational moment" of which Gingrich spoke paved the way for others. Less than ten years after the birth of the WTO, Democrats were advocating American membership in the UN's International Criminal Court, and arguing that the U.S. needed approval from the UN Security Council before defending our national interests.

California congressman Dana Rohrabacher lamented the loss of national confidence his colleagues were displaying by placing their trust, and the fate of their constituents, in the hands of supra-national authorities.

We are living in a time when a significant number of Americans are rushing forward to support any effort to transfer sovereignty from elected officials in the United States to unelected officials elsewhere at a global level who will exercise power and control, mandate policies, and shape our lives; yet they are not elected by the people of the United States of America, as if we should expect them in the WTO or even the United Nations to watch out for our interests. It is our job to watch out for the interests of the American people. We are elected to do so. Transferring our sovereignty and decision-making power to the WTO, to the United Nations, or any other international body is not in the long-term interests of our people.[6]

What Dana Rohrabacher is concerned about, in part, is the authority the WTO is exercising over policy that is supposed to be the purview of the Congress. Yet, under the Trade Policy Review Mechanism, the World Trade Organization reviews the national trade policies of most member countries every six years. But the United States is held to a different standard. Every two years, foreigners from the WTO examine American trade regulations.

Even today, after the evidence has piled up, there are those who refuse to admit that the decisions of the World Trade Organization adversely impact American sovereignty.

A propaganda sheet from the U.S. trade representative's office claims that the World Trade Organization has "no authority to change U.S. law or to require the United States or any state or local government to change its laws or decisions."[7]

During debate in the House, Congressman Jim Kolbe of Arizona rose to "rebut an all-too-often made allegation . . . that membership [in the WTO] is a violation of U.S. sovereignty." He explained that "WTO dispute panels cannot overturn or change U.S. Federal, State, or local laws . . . only the Federal or State governments can change a Federal or State law."[8]

But what the U.S. trade representative (USTR) and Mr. Kolbe fail to explain is that every time the World Trade Organization rules against the United States, the U.S. is given a Hobson's choice—either change the law or regulation in question or pay massive fines imposed by the WTO. These are not the options of a sovereign, free, or independent country. And like the Stepford Nation we have become, the United States has—time and again—obediently bowed to the demands of foreigners who operate in secret at the WTO.

William Hawkins, a senior fellow at the U.S. Business and Industrial Council, says fear of running afoul of the WTO has so pervaded Capitol Hill that "legislators fall all over themselves trying to placate WTO opinion."[9] How the global trade body may rule is even influencing the way Congress writes legislation. "Too many of our elected lawmakers," Hawkins explained, "act as if the WTO has a preemptive veto over Congress, and will not even draft language that Geneva may not like."[10]

Congresswoman Ileana Ros-Lehtinen of Florida worries about the impact the WTO is having on American sovereignty. "The WTO," she explained, "is selectively challenging our local, State, and Federal laws, saying that they are infringements on free trade," and warned that "no U.S. laws or regulations are safe from the reaches of the World Trade Organization."[11]

One need only read the lead paragraphs of newspapers' trade stories over the past several years to see her point. Following are just a few examples of the ways in which reporters at home and abroad have chronicled America's submission to WTO demands:

• Greg Wright, *Gannett News Service*: "The United States must stop giving millions to help steel, ball-bearing, pasta and other companies that claim imports are choking business, the World Trade Organization ruled yesterday. The Bush administration said it would comply with the order."[12]

• John Skorburg, *Budget & Tax News*: "On June 17, the U.S. House of Representatives passed HR 4520, the American Jobs Creation Act of 2004, which repeals export subsidies found to be in violation of World Trade Organization (WTO) agreements."[13]

• Jeffrey Sparshott, *Washington Times*: "Congress spent two years repealing an export subsidy in order to comply with a World Trade Organization ruling. The WTO said yesterday that Congress didn't finish the job. A panel of WTO judges said that despite Congress' effort the United States continues to break global trade rules . . . . The European Union, which first challenged U.S. tax laws at the WTO in 1998, said the decision would allow it to punish U.S. firms with trade sanctions unless Congress repeals the illegal tax provisions."[14]

• Alan Beattie, *Financial Times*: "Congress last year also passed a bill ending the so-called foreign sales corporation (FSC) scheme, a $4 billion-a-year tax break for US exporters that had been ruled illegal by the WTO in a case brought by the EU. The legislation . . . was striking because it was passed solely in order to comply with WTO rules."[15]

• Peter Ford, *Christian Science Monitor*: "European leaders hailed President Bush's retreat from import tariffs on steel . . . welcoming it as a sign that Washington is ready to abide by international rules despite the US administration's reputation abroad for 'America First' policies."[16]

There is no argument—the World Trade Organization is dictating American policy.

Each change in U.S. policy is the result of a complaint being lodged against the United States in the WTO. As critics predicted, more suits have been filed against the United States in the World Trade Organization than against any other country. As of September 2005, a total of eighty-nine complaints have been lodged against the U.S.—five times more than any other country. America's most prolific antagonists are the European Union, twenty-nine cases; Canada, thirteen cases; Brazil, eight cases; Japan, eight cases; Korea, seven cases; India, six cases; and Mexico, six cases.

To believe that America can send teams of lawyers to Geneva and hold her own against frivolous trade disputes is to divorce oneself from reality. At the WTO, to the aggressors go the spoils. According to Public Citizen, the country that files the challenge has "at least partially prevailed in 102 of 118 completed WTO cases."[17] The group further explains that in 85.7 percent of the complaints against the U.S. (forty-two out of forty-eight cases), the WTO has ruled against the United States on everything from tax policy to environmental standards,[18] a finding that supports Indiana congressman Peter Visclosky's belief that the World Trade Organization is "grossly prejudiced against U.S. interests."[19]

Here is a glance at some of the cases in which the WTO has ruled against U.S. interests, and the United States has taken action to comply with the World Trade Organization.

Reformulated Gas Products

The very first ruling of the World Trade Organization was issued against the United States. It was filed by Venezuela three weeks after the WTO was created and later joined by Brazil. The two countries complained about import restrictions on their gasoline products that were unable to meet environmental standards required by the Clean Air Act. It took the WTO just over a year to issue their ruling and "request" that the U.S. either change a regulation affecting the health and public safety of its citizens, or face $150 million in annual fines.

The Clinton administration caved in to the WTO's demands. Sixteen months after the ruling, the Environmental Protection Agency (EPA) published in the *Federal Register* a "proposed rule [to] revise the requirements for imported gasoline." The rationale for the rule change was stated as follows: "EPA believes the proposed rulemaking would be consistent with . . . the U.S. commitment to ensure that the regulation is consistent with the obligations of the United States under the World Trade Organization."[20]

Representative Phil Crane, a vocal backer of the World Trade Organization, defended the ruling. The WTO's decision, Mr. Crane argued, "has been portrayed by some as an assault on U.S. environmental laws. Nothing could be further from the truth. It should be pointed out," he explained, "that the case involved an EPA regulation, not U.S. law."[21]

Patriots, stand down. Apparently it is now acceptable for unelected judges in a foreign land to overturn U.S. regulations.

Internet Gambling

In March 2003, the tiny country of Antigua and Barbuda—with a population of only 70,000—hauled the United States before the WTO, demanding that U.S. laws be changed to accommodate the Internet gambling haven in the Caribbean. The ruling of the first WTO panel stated that the laws of four different states—Utah, Louisiana, South Dakota, and Massachusetts—along with three federal laws—violated WTO trade regulations. The U.S. appealed and received a slightly more favorable ruling the second time around, but it was not enough.

Mark Mendel, Antigua's attorney, told the *Associated Press* that the April 2005 appellate body ruling for Antigua was "clear cut. We won on all the major points." The WTO decided that "the United States [has] a commitment to grant full market access in gambling and betting services" to other countries.[22] Peter Allgeier, the acting U.S. trade representative, conceded, saying, "this report essentially says that if we clarify U.S. Internet gambling restrictions in certain ways, we'll be fine."[23]

But neither the United States nor any of its fifty states should have to "clarify" any law or regulation for the benefit of Antigua or the World Trade Organization. As Utah attorney general Mark Shurtleff said, "under our constitutional system of federalism, states should continue to have the flexibility and sovereign authority to determine whether—and under what conditions—gambling occurs within their borders, without such decisions being second-guessed by WTO tribunals."[24]

The Byrd Amendment

Perhaps the most visible and hotly contested case in which the WTO has ruled against the United States involves the Continued Dumping and Subsidy Offset Act, otherwise known as the "Byrd Amendment" for its sponsor, Senator Robert Byrd of West Virginia. When companies are found to have illegally dumped their products in the United States, the Byrd Amendment requires that the fines collected be given directly to affected U.S. businesses instead of being deposited into the U.S. Treasury.

In January 2003, a WTO appellate body affirmed an earlier ruling that the Byrd Amendment violated its rules, and as such, the United States had better bring the Byrd Amendment into conformity with its obligations to the WTO. European Union trade commissioner Pascal Lamy delighted in the decision, saying the Byrd Amendment is "WTO-incompatible . . . and must therefore go."[25]

The Bush administration has bowed to the demands of the World Trade Organization, calling for repeal of the law. But this is one of the few cases in which Congress has resisted WTO demands. In February 2003, seventy senators, representing forty-one states, voiced their support of the Byrd Amendment in a letter to President Bush. Meanwhile, the WTO authorized seven countries—Brazil, Chile, India, Japan, Korea, Canada, Mexico—and the European Union to impose millions of dollars in fines against the United States.

Foreign Sales Corporation (FSC) Statute

The FSC is a provision of U.S. tax law that dates to the Reagan administration and is an attempt to equalize the competitive disadvantage faced by American exporters, particularly when selling goods in European countries. It permits U.S. businesses to withhold from taxation a portion of income derived from exports. In 1998, the European Union (EU) complained to the World Trade Organization that, under WTO rules, this provision of tax law was an illegal export subsidy. The WTO agreed and ordered the United States to repeal it.

The WTO authorized up to $4 billion in sanctions against the United States—the most severe injunction ever issued. The ruling was hailed by EU trade commissioner Pascal Lamy, who said the decision "makes the cost of non-compliance with the WTO crystal clear."[26] Congress and the administration buckled under, and in October 2004, President Bush signed the JOBS Act, which repealed the offending provision to appease foreign critics.

After having been forced to change a long-standing provision of U.S. law and pay record fines, Senator Chuck Grassley, chairman of the Senate Finance Committee, inexplicably defended the WTO. "We must not allow this setback to undermine either the World Trade Organization or our support for this vital institution,"[27] he pleaded.

Grassley's statement is reminiscent of that scene in John Belushi's *Animal House* in which pledges to a fraternity are forced to strip to their underwear and take to the floor on all fours. Once in position, they are ignominiously smacked on the fanny with a large wooden paddle. After each whack, fighting back the pain and tears, the pledge is forced to recite the subservient refrain, "Thank you, sir, may I have another?"

In fact, in October 2005, the WTO whacked the United States again on the same case. Not satisfied with $4 billion in payoffs, the EU once again dragged the U.S. before the WTO, arguing that the U.S. was holding back on making all the changes required. Congress must now change the tax code a second time to suit WTO and European Union demands.

Cotton Subsidies

In September 2004, the WTO ruled that U.S. subsidies to cotton farmers violate international trade rules. After being appealed by the United States, the decision was upheld by the WTO's appellate body, which ordered the U.S. to end the subsidies "without delay."

The decision impacts some 25,000 U.S. farmers and was not expected by the Bush administration, which was trying to write laws based on WTO guidelines. U.S. trade representative Robert Zoellick explained, "We believe U.S. farm programs were designed to be, and are, fully consistent with our WTO obligations."[28] Nonetheless, the Bush administration vowed, once again, to comply with WTO demands.

Roberto Azevedo, a legal advisor to the Brazilian government, called the WTO's ruling a "precedent" and said the assault on American trade regulations "is a war that must continue."[29]

Antidumping Act of 1916

American steel makers used this law to sue Japanese and European steel producers who were illegally dumping products in the U.S. to undercut American manufacturers. The Antidumping Act allows U.S. companies that were injured by illegal dumping to collect up to three times the amount by which they were harmed.

The Japanese and Europeans acted aggressively. They took their complaint to the World Trade Organization, which ruled the Antidumping Act a violation of WTO rules. The strategy of the U.S. government was complete and total surrender. "We do not believe this will pose a problem," explained Richard Mills, a USTR spokesman. "If Congress continues to make progress and repeals the 1916 act, this matter will be resolved."[30]

In other words, do exactly what the World Trade Organization tells us to do and we won't have any problems. Because of the WTO ruling, the Antidumping Act was repealed when the president signed the Miscellaneous Tariff Act into law in December 2004.

In case after case, where U.S. interests were on trial in the World Trade Organization, Congress and the White House have capitulated to international demands. The WTO has forced the United States to make changes to laws or regulations in the area of copyright law, trademark law, environmental regulations, health and safety concerns, public morality, tax law, export provisions, and others. A whole slew of American products have been adversely affected by WTO actions to include cotton, steel, underwear, gasoline, intellectual property, lamb, shrimp, lumber, wool, stainless steel, and more.

American independence isn't what it used to be. The U.S. Business and Industry Council concludes that "the vast majority of the decisions rendered by the WTO have harmed American interests and restricted American sovereignty."[31]

And the Republican party—which portrays itself as the more forceful defender of American sovereignty—is split when it comes to the World Trade Organization. Republicans have long criticized activist judges for whimsically overturning federal statutes and setting national policies from their isolated perches in the courts. But WTO Republicans are not only silent on the issue of legislating from the international bench; they endorse it. On numerous provisions they consider "protectionist" or somehow harmful to the theory of "free trade," these Republicans are eager to subvert U.S. trade policy to the dictates of an unaccountable international body, provided that body prescribes the "correct" remedy.

The siren song of the World Trade Organization has forced many to barter constitutionalism for opportunism. WTO rulings that force repeal of nasty tariffs are welcomed in the spirit of "international cooperation" and "respect of our trading partners." Permission slips from the World Trade Organization are a common request in Washington.

What WTO-friendly Americans see as "international cooperation" is viewed by the WTO as obedience to internationalism.

Effect on U.S. Trade

At first glance, observers would say that the U.S. economy fared well in the period since the World Trade Organization was appointed as America's trade czar. The period between 1995 and 2001 gave us a rising stock market, increased exports, and an abundance of cheap consumer products, of which the American people could not get enough.

But a closer look is cause for concern. Recent years have seen Congress and the White House spending like drunken fools. In 2004, just three years after posting a $128 billion surplus, the federal government spent $412 billion more than it took in—a record amount. That deficit was added to the $8 trillion the United States has amassed in debt. In 2005, more than $350 billion of what taxpayers sent to the federal government was used to pay interest on the debt. The United States has been losing its manufacturing base, and the 2005 hurricane season not only caused gasoline prices to skyrocket but once again exposed America's dangerous reliance on foreign oil.

When the United States joined the WTO, our annual trade deficit stood at $95 billion. By 2005, the trade gap soared 550 percent to more than $617 billion.

Annual U.S. Goods & Services Trade Deficit Since Creation of World Trade Organization (In Billions)

Year	U.S. Trade Deficit	Increase From Previous Year
1995	$95.1	n/a
1996	$102.9	8.2%
1997	$107.0	3.9%
1998	$163.2	52.5%
1999	$261.2	60.0%
2000	$375.4	43.7%
2001	$362.7	-3.3%
2002	$421.7	16.2%
2003	$495.5	17.7%
2004	$617.7	24.4%

Source: International Trade Administration[32]

It is true that more American products and services are being sold around the world. In 2004, the United States sold in excess of $1.14 trillion worth of goods and services overseas—a record amount. Unfortunately, it was not the only new milestone the foreign commerce segment of our economy hit in that year. American consumers also purchased a record amount of goods and services from foreign competitors—$1.76 trillion worth—an amount that far exceeded the total of what was sold overseas.

From 2003 to 2004, the U.S. trade deficit increased $122.2 billion—the largest dollar increase in history—and left the annual U.S. trade deficit at $617.7 billion. And though that amount is yet another all-time high, analysts expect it to climb to nearly $800 billion by the end of 2006.

Since the creation of the World Trade Organization, the U.S. trade deficit has exploded. With one exception, as the table above indicates, America's shortfall grew with each passing year. And given that the rate of growth in imports far exceeds the growth rate in exports, there is no credible scenario suggesting this problem will correct itself anytime in the near future. America, a once-proud and self-sufficient example to the world, is increasingly reliant on other countries for the goods that outfit the lifestyles to which we have become accustomed.

The trade gap is not only growing in real terms, but also as a percentage of Gross Domestic Product (GDP). At the birth of the WTO, the U.S. trade deficit stood at 1.5 percent of GDP. By the end of 2004, it had nearly quadrupled to 5.7 percent of GDP and is expected to increase to 6.6 percent by the end of 2005.

U.S. Trade Deficit as a Percentage of Gross Domestic Product

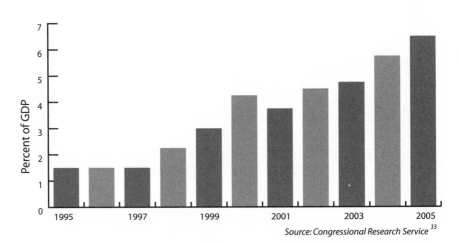

Source: Congressional Research Service [33]

An expanding trade deficit forces Uncle Sam to borrow from other countries, putting taxpayers in debt to foreign interests. As the trade deficit expands, the value of the dollar contracts, making U.S. imports more expensive.

Despite the WTO's impact on the trade deficit, Congressman Jim Kolbe insists that U.S. membership in the global trade body is "essential," and that it is "definitely in our national and our political and our economic interests to continue to be a member."[34] Kolbe values the theory of free trade above all else, and it has blinded him to economic reality. It is important, when trying to create a healthy trade policy, not only to consider the quantity, but the quality of a nation's ability to trade with other countries.

Ten years after the fact, WTO membership has made the United States the flea market to the world. Sidewalk salesmen from across the globe are peddling cheap consumer products in the American market—goods that in some cases are made by slave labor. It is not only clothing and toys that Americans are buying from overseas. Big-ticket items that were once produced in American factories—steel, lumber, autos, electronics, and military hardware and equipment—are increasingly purchased from foreign companies.

America's manufacturing base is eroding. The problem pre-dates the WTO, but certainly U.S. membership in the institution is not helping. As the American Iron and Steel Institute pointed out, U.S. exports have grown only 4.7 percent in the last five years. But in the five-year period before the World Trade Organization was created, U.S. exports had grown 30 percent.

Since the late 1800s—when the fist disposable razor rolled off the assembly line—Americans took immense pride in their manufactured products. U.S. Steel, Henry Ford, Harley-Davidson, Goodyear, General Motors, Gillette, and Kellogg were giants of American industry. Many of them made the products that built roads, bridges, homes, factories, towns, and cities.

When it came to defending our nation, our fathers and their fathers relied on themselves. The greatest generation comprised not only those who wore the uniform; it also included those who donned overalls and turned out the trucks, tanks, and planes that would bring America victory in two world wars.

But too often today, Pentagon procurement officers are sending their purchase orders to factories overseas. My colleague Oliver North, after returning from one of his numerous trips to Iraq, told me that a machine gun made by Fabrique Nationale, a Belgian company, "has now all but replaced the venerable American-made M-60 that was the U.S. weapon of choice from Vietnam to the first Gulf War." The pistols they carry are made by Beretta, an Italian company.

North went on to explain that components for one of the key weapons in the U.S. arsenal—the Joint Direct Attack Munition (JDAM)—are manufactured by Micro Crystal, a Swiss company. But because of Swiss opposition to the Iraq war, the company refused to ship the parts needed, putting America at risk.

Even Marine One—the majestic helicopter that ferries the president to and from the South Lawn of the White House—will now be made by foreigners, the Pentagon announced in 2005.

In the last five years, America has lost three million manufacturing jobs—more than 17 percent of manufacturing employment. Since 1997, more than 250 textile plants have closed. Dozens of communities have been devastated by factories that have been forced to close their doors and move overseas. Many members of Congress understand the problem but are helpless to try to fix it, given the authority the WTO holds over the United States and its trade policy.

Members of Congress want those jobs back because they provide employment for workers with limited or no education. Manufacturing, through its "multiplier effect," creates new jobs and strengthens other sectors of the economy. Manufactured products, for example, not only have to be produced, but they have to be inspected, packaged, loaded, shipped, stored, insured, and sold—creating jobs and investment at every stage of the process. And research and development is studying ways in which to make the process more efficient at each interval. Jobs in the service industry have a much less dynamic multiplier effect.

The problem is so great that the National Association of Manufacturers reports that "if the U.S. manufacturing base continues to shrink at its present rate and the critical mass is lost, the manufacturing innovation process will shift to other global centers. Once that happens, a decline in U.S. living standards in the future is virtually assured."[35]

Is it any wonder that states with some of the largest manufacturing sectors—Ohio, Pennsylvania, Illinois, and Michigan—have become some of the most hotly contested states in the last two presidential elections?

"The fundamental cause of the manufacturing crisis," reports the U.S. Business and Industry Council, "is the cumulative and continuing impact of two decades of misguided, ill-advised, and weak-willed U.S. trade and globalization policies." Those policies, which created the WTO, have also caused our trade deficit to balloon. And by running consistent deficits, we are putting more financial resources in the hands of our economic and political competitors.

The countries that run the largest trade surpluses against the United States are:

- China $162 billion
- Japan $75 billion
- Canada $66 billion
- Germany $46 billion
- Mexico $45 billion
- Venezuela $20 billion

The $162 billion trade deficit the U.S. runs with communist China has many analysts concerned because it is subsidizing the construction of a large, modern military. In recent years, Beijing has significantly added to its arsenal of surface ships, submarines, fighter jets, helicopters, surface-to-air missiles, and other military hardware. At 2.5 million forces, China's military is nearly twice the size of U.S. active duty forces.

U.S. Trade Deficit with China

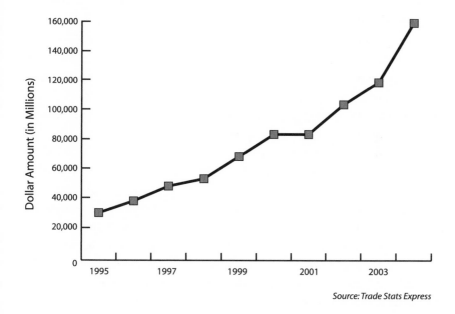

Source: Trade Stats Express

China also boasts an aggressive espionage operation that has set its sights on U.S. industry, military equipment, and nuclear technology. Pat Choate, an economist and Reform Party presidential candidate in 1996, calls China "the global epicenter of pirating and counterfeiting,"[36] and though China was supposed to crack down on its theft of intellectual property when it joined the World Trade Organization, it hasn't—and the United States is doing nothing about it.

"China is pursuing a national development strategy," says Choate, "based on the uncompensated, unapproved stealing of other nations' best ideas and technologies."[37] And yet, he explains, the United States "has not filed a single intellectual property case at the World Trade Organization," against China or any other country.

As a permanent member of the UN Security Council, China can use its veto to influence UN resolutions and build anti-American coalitions in the Security Council. Recently, the Chinese have been conducting joint military operations with the Russians and making inroads in America's backyard, warming up to Cuba's Fidel Castro and Venezuela's Hugo Chavez. The reason for the aggressive military buildup, many believe, is that China's leaders are preparing to take control of Taiwan, which the United States is committed to defend.

Senator Lindsey Graham of South Carolina sees the obvious connection between America's diminished manufacturing base, our trade deficit, and China's aggressive military makeover. "Maybe the greatest cost [of lost manufacturing]," Senator Graham explains, "is to our national security. There is no doubt that the United States was the single greatest military power in the 20th century because of its industrial strength. If we make China the new industrial superpower, will that not translate into China becoming the single greatest military power of the 21st century?"[38]

It very well might. And if the United States continues to submit to the will of the World Trade Organization, we will only accelerate the pace at which that day might arrive.

Democracy works, in part, because citizens have a say in shaping public policy. By granting the WTO authority over U.S. trade policy, Congress has not only shunned its responsibility, it has robbed Americans of their right to participate in the legislative process.

The rulings of the WTO are punishing—as a starting point—the poorest and least educated of our fellow citizens, and those who are further up the economic ladder are not immune. Our participation in the World Trade Organization is resulting in a slow erosion of the American dream.

The Terrorists' Club

Former New York City mayor Ed Koch once called the United Nations "a cesspool." In fact, it is worse than that. The United Nations of today is the world's largest terrorist cell. It is a place where terrorist nations meet, hold membership, and promote their agendas. It is an institution through which they spread hate and encourage violence. This behavior is carried out on American soil and subsidized by American taxpayers.

By providing a forum, the United Nations does for terrorist diplomacy what *Al Jazeera* does for terrorist propaganda. It is a leading dispensary of jihadist poison. The General Assembly of the United Nations is for today's terrorists what the Ravenite Social Club was for John Gotti—a home away from home, a place where business is conducted.

The United States must recognize this fact and put the UN out of business. We must do so because international terrorism aimed at the United States and her citizens is the number one concern for American foreign policy and national security. It will continue to be for many years to come, as it should have been prior to September 11, 2001, when alarm bells rang throughout the 1980s and 1990s.

During that time, the U.S. was the target of major attacks, mostly overseas. The modern terrorist war against America can be traced to the 1979 takeover of the U.S. embassy in Tehran, where 52 American hostages were held for 444 days. In 1983, the U.S. embassy in Beirut was attacked in April, and then in October, 241 Marines were killed during the bombing of the Marine barracks, also in Beirut. Libya carried out terrorist attacks on American citizens in 1986 at a German disco and in 1988 when it blew Pan Am flight 103 out of the sky over Lockerbie, Scotland.

In the 1990s, Americans were targeted in the first attempt on the World Trade Center in February 1993. In 1995 and 1996, there were attacks on U.S. military facilities in Riyadh and at the Khobar Towers in Saudi Arabia. On August 7, 1998, U.S. embassies in Nairobi, Kenya, and Dar es Salaam,

Tanzania, came under attack, killing more than 300 people. In 2000, it was the bombing of the USS *Cole* in Aden, Yemen. Seventeen American sailors lost their lives that day, and another thirty-nine were injured.

But the attacks of September 11, 2001, crystallized the nature of the threat against the United States, and the Bush administration decided to change the way business was done in Washington with respect to fighting terrorism. The FBI's first priority would no longer be to solve terrorist crimes, but to prevent them. The CIA and the FBI were ordered to cooperate with one another. A new Department of Homeland Security was created. The Patriot Act was pushed through Congress and defended over loud criticisms.

Soldiers, sailors, airmen, and Marines would not be the only individuals fighting. The United States was now engaged in a different kind of war that required the help of lawyers, accountants, public relations specialists, linguists, bankers, law enforcement personnel, and many others with special skills. The terrorists were to be engaged—not just in the desert—but anywhere their activity could be disrupted.

Nine days after the 9/11 attack, President Bush spoke to the nation before a joint session of Congress and explained how it would work:

> Our response involves far more than instant retaliation and isolated strikes. Americans should not expect one battle, but a lengthy campaign, unlike any other we have ever seen. It may include dramatic strikes, visible on TV, and covert operations, secret even in success. We will starve terrorists of funding, turn them one against another, drive them from place to place, until there is no refuge or no rest. And we will pursue nations that provide aid or safe haven to terrorism. Every nation, in every region, now has a decision to make. Either you are with us, or you are with the terrorists. From this day forward, any nation that continues to harbor or support terrorism will be regarded by the United States as a hostile regime.[1]

The Bush Doctrine had been defined. But apparently, nobody sent a copy of it to the UN. The United Nations harbors terrorists. It should be treated as a hostile regime.

The UN General Assembly is littered with terrorist governments, human rights abusers, corrupt regimes, dictatorships, and political deviants of all stripes. The United Nations provides them membership and grants them legitimacy; in so doing, it absolves them of their sins.

In turn, the United States treats the UN as a friend, an ally. It is not. The United Nations is an institution that, by virtue of its incompetence, moral relevancy, and desire to acquire political power, is an adversary of the United States.

Washington's policy makers would be well advised to follow Sun Tzu's advice—"know your enemy"—and realize once and for all that Kofi Annan is no friend of the American people, and the United Nations is no ally of the United States.

Coddling Terrorists at the UN

The United States Government—in Title 22, Section 2656f(d), of the U.S. Code—defines terrorism as "premeditated, politically motivated violence perpetrated against noncombatant targets by sub national groups or clandestine agents, usually intended to influence an audience."[2] In simple terms, terrorism is the deliberate torture or killing of innocent men, women, and children for political purposes.

Prior to the U.S. liberation of Iraq, the State Department listed seven countries as "state sponsors of terrorism." They were Iran, Iraq, Syria, North Korea, Cuba, Sudan, and Libya. On October 20, 2004, after its liberation and restoration of sovereignty, Iraq was removed from the list. The other six retain the highest diplomatic condemnation by the U.S. government.

Those six state sponsors of terrorism—the governments that facilitate the deliberate killing of innocent men, women, and children for political purposes—are all members in good standing of the United Nations. They are "peace-loving states" according to the UN Charter. Their leaders are known to Kofi Annan as "Excellencies."

As Kofi Annan sees it, they are members of the global community—the family of nations—and legitimate members of international society. As such, Annan views the leaders of these states as individuals with whom he will meet, discuss, negotiate, and break bread. Representatives from these countries can vote in the General Assembly, introduce resolutions, speak to the UN, sit on committees within the institution, form coalitions, and influence proposals within the United Nations.

Yet, they are state sponsors of terrorism, and they should be recognized and treated for what they are: murderous regimes deserving of expulsion from the institution.

In the immediate aftermath of September 11, there was hope that Kofi Annan might make meaningful changes in the way terrorist regimes are treated at the UN. Writing in the *New York Times* less than two weeks after the attacks, Annan said, "The international community is defined not only by what it is for, but by what and whom it is against. The United Nations must have the courage to recognize that just as there are common aims, there are common enemies."[3]

But the UN could not identify a common enemy. It simply continued its forty-year debate over the definition of terrorism and could not form a conclusion as to the meaning of the word. To Kofi Annan and his friends at the UN, one man's terrorist is another man's freedom fighter.

Nor has Mr. Annan placed the eradication of terrorism high on his priority list. Again and again, he had the opportunity to put the issue before the international media, but failed.

In December 2001, Annan had the opportunity to define terrorism, to condemn it, to offer hope for its defeat and paint a vision of a world in which the use of suicide bombers and other terrorist tactics was no longer tolerated by any government. The occasion was Annan's acceptance of the Nobel Peace Prize in December 2001 in Oslo, Norway. The world was watching and the global media were taking down his words. But the word "terrorism" never appeared in his speech, and he barely condemned the September 11 attacks.

Since September 11, 2001, Kofi Annan has appointed sixty-nine "Special Envoys" or "Personal Representatives" of the secretary-general. These are Annan's cabinet members in the field—the individuals who champion a cause on behalf of the secretary-general who deems it important. None of those sixty-nine special envoys was assigned to deal with the issue of terrorism. Kofi Annan has no "point man" on the subject. But he did find it important to employ, in July 2003, a special advisor for the UN's project to control the Internet. Annan also hired a "Special Adviser to the Secretary-General on Gender Issues and Advancement of Women,"; a "Special Advisor on the Global Compact"; and a "High Representative of the Secretary-General for the Least Developed Countries, Landlocked Developing Countries and Small Island Developing States."

In the months after 9/11, Kofi Annan could have asked a high-profile American to help him in the fight to eradicate terrorism and send a strong message to the world. He did not. He did, however, ask a liberal partisan—Professor Jeffrey Sachs—to be his special adviser on the Millennium Development Goals; and he appointed former president Bill Clinton as his special envoy for Tsunami Recovery. Mr. Clinton's former chief of staff, Erskine Bowles, also joined the effort as Clinton's deputy. But none were appointed to deal with international terrorism.

During his lifetime, Yassir Arafat was the poster child for terrorism. He did as much to encourage and finance death by suicide bombers as anybody ever has. Arafat's political skills can't be denied; but he was a snake, an individual possessed of evil to the core. That made no difference to Kofi Annan. During a trip to the Middle East in March 2005, Annan not only made a visit to Arafat's grave, but he laid a wreath there as a sign of respect and affection. New York congressman Anthony Weiner called it "almost grotesque."[4]

The UN's approach to state sponsors of terrorism and dictatorial regimes is moral relevance of the most dangerous kind. It is "one of the most fundamental defects of the United Nations," explains Jed Babbin. "The UN charter basically says that all nations are created equal—and that is just flat wrong."

Babbin is right. While America is the greatest nation on earth, we certainly don't reflect that prestige when we go slumming with hoodlums at the UN. Instead, the United States should set a new standard and ask other responsible nations to join us. No longer should we hold membership in any international institution that allows state sponsors of terrorism as members.

Without such a bare minimum standard, the United Nations is incapable of reforming itself, and we ought to stop wasting our time trying. No American politician would join the Ku Klux Klan to try to change the system from within. In politics, symbolism is substance, and when America takes her seat next to the most despicable regimes on earth, we do an injustice not only to our own citizens, but to those all over the world who are tortured and repressed and deprived of basic human dignities by their rulers.

The UN's history of granting legitimacy to dictators and terrorists is long and will only continue in the future. Not only do terrorist states hold membership, but their rulers are put on display.

In 1974, Yassir Arafat would make his first of several speeches before the General Assembly. It was a long-winded tirade in which he compared his leadership of a terrorist organization to that of George Washington and Abraham Lincoln. He denounced the United States and Israel and accused both countries of hateful crimes. "The record of Israeli rulers is replete with acts of terror,"[5] Arafat charged. He then demonstrated the danger of legitimizing the United Nations.

Need one remind this assembly of the numerous resolutions adopted by it condemning Israeli aggressions committed against Arab countries, Israeli violations of human rights and the articles of the Geneva Conventions, as well as the resolutions pertaining to the annexation of the city of Jerusalem and its restoration to its former status?[6]

By allowing illegitimate regimes to craft conspiratorial screeds in the General Assembly that the body then approves, it gives thugs like Arafat the ammunition they need to attack America and her allies. Arafat continued while the delegates sat in rapt attention:

The difference between the revolutionary and the terrorist lies in the reason for which each fights. For whoever stands by a just cause and fights for the freedom and liberation of his land from the invaders, the settlers, and the colonialists cannot possibly be called terrorist, otherwise the American people in their struggle for liberation from the British colonialists would have been terrorists; the European resistance against the Nazis would be terrorism, the struggle of the Asian, African, and Latin American peoples would also be terrorism, and many of you who are in this Assembly hall would be considered terrorists.[7]

It's true that many in the assembly hall were terrorists, but not for the reasons Arafat cited.

UN officials wondered how they could possibly top such a performance, so the following year, they brought in Ugandan leader Idi Amin—a brutal dictator who would have upwards of 500,000 of his citizens murdered during his reign. He not only tortured and killed his enemies, but in death he insulted their dignity, reportedly feeding their corpses to crocodiles or storing their heads in his freezer. Known as the Butcher of Uganda, Amin was also rumored to be a cannibal.

Though his eating habits have never been questioned, Cuba's Fidel Castro is as brutal a dictator as there is, and he has seen his share of time at the podium in the General Assembly. His first address to the UN was in 1960, shortly after he came to power in Cuba. Castro's address set a long precedent of using the UN to denounce the United States and make wild accusations against the American government, while casting himself as a victim of American oppression. In his first speech to the General Assembly, Castro called Senator Jack Kennedy an "illiterate and ignorant millionaire," and went on to say,

The Government of the United States considers it has the right to promote and encourage subversion in our country. The Government of the United States is promoting the organization of subversive movements against the

Revolutionary Government of Cuba, and we wish to denounce this fact in this General Assembly.[8]

Jaime Suchlicki, director of the Institute for Cuban and Cuban-American Studies, says that for more than forty years, Fidel Castro has been "the most vocal and active proponent of anti-Americanism throughout the developing world."[9] He explains that many countries believe "that the U.S. is an evil power, guilty for much of the problems and sufferings of the poor nations [which] is owed in great part to the propaganda efforts of Castro and his officials." Much of that propaganda has been spread through the UN General Assembly and UN conferences.

During the most recent UN World Summit, the General Assembly podium was given to Mahmoud Ahmadinejad, leader of Iran's terrorist state, who accused the United States of supporting terrorism; Robert Mugabe, the despot of Zimbabwe who routinely condemns the United States; and Hugo Chavez, the dictator of Venezuela who called President George W. Bush a terrorist.

These are not isolated incidents or diplomatic slips of the tongue. They are part of a deliberate attempt to undermine the reputation of the United States throughout the world. "Only constant repetition will finally succeed in imprinting an idea on the memory of the crowd," Adolf Hitler wrote in *Mein Kampf.* And the idea that the United States is the world's great evil is being imprinted on the minds of millions throughout the world by virtue of the constant repetition provided by UN forums.

The representatives of these and other dictatorial countries speak before UN audiences in New York and around the globe regularly. They call America greedy and stingy. They say the United States is imperialist and an occupying force. They accuse the U.S. of warmongering and terrorist acts. They verbalize these anti-American ideas again and again—in speeches and documents and resolutions and press conferences—all facilitated by the United Nations. And their verbal hate crimes are underwritten by the U.S. government.

Ironically, Congress—lead by senators John McCain and Russ Feingold—has curtailed the ability of American citizens to complain about individual members of Congress and candidates for public office. They did this through the Campaign Finance Reform Act (CFRA), signed by President Bush in March 2002. The CFRA regulates the content of political speech in America and places limits on what voters can say, how they can say it, and how much they can spend in an election season. But at the same time, Congress and the president are flooding the United Nations with unregulated soft money that is used to undermine every part of our Constitution.

It's time for a policy change. The United States should withhold funding of the United Nations and pull the curtain on the Turtle Bay circus. Our message to Robert Mugabe, Hugo Chavez, Fidel Castro, and Kofi Annan should be that their fifteen minutes of American-funded fame is over. For the UN is of no value to the United States as she pursues her most important foreign policy goal.

Over the last thirty years, the United Nations has adopted twelve conventions dealing with international terrorism. But only sixty-eight countries, besides the United States, are a party to each of those treaties that are designed to prevent terrorist bombings, the financing of terrorism, terrorist acts aboard aircraft, and the taking of hostages, for example. Behavior that should be universally condemned is not. There are forty UN member states that are a party to only six or fewer of the agreements. Even many of those states that have ratified the protocols "have not fully implemented them despite becoming parties,"[10] the State Department laments.

With that track record, the UN adopted Resolution 1373, which requires member states to "deny safe haven to those who finance, plan, support, or commit terrorist acts, or provide safe havens." The resolution also called on states to report their efforts to curtail terrorism to the UN. For many of those that did, their reports were more useful to Jay Leno's joke writers than to those committed to saving lives.

Syria, a state sponsor of terrorism, wrote in its report that it "has always condemned terrorism in all its forms" and promised the Security Council that it "does not provide a safe haven for those who finance, support, or commit terrorist acts." Iran claims that it regards terrorism as "a global menace"; and Libya, which sponsored the bombing of Pan Am 103, issued its "unequivocal condemnation of terrorism in all its forms." The United Nations accepted and circulated these reports as if they were worthy of reading.

Underwriting Deviancy

Columnist Arnold Beichman wrote that "UN Secretary-General Kofi Annan and a majority of UN members, many of them dictatorships and enemies of democracy, can only be regarded as enemies of the world's most successful democracy."[11] Beichman's got it right. The United Nations is not the noble cause of its false reputation. It is a culture of deviancy propped up by the U.S. Treasury.

Whereas the United States pays 22 percent of the regular UN budget each year, or roughly $363 million, terrorist states pay only a fraction of that cost. The full benefits, privileges, and legitimacy of UN membership was bestowed on Iran—which the State Department calls "the most active state sponsor of terrorism"—for the bargain price of $3.6 million. During 2003, the "peace-loving" state of Iran "provided Lebanese Hizballah and Palestinian rejectionist groups—notably Hamas, the Palestine Islamic Jihad, and the Popular Front for the Liberation of Palestine . . . with funding, safe haven, training, and weapons,"[12] according to the State Department.

In October 2005, Iran's president Mahmoud Ahmadinejad, while speaking to an estimated 4,000 students at a conference titled "A World without Zionism," called for Israel to be "wiped off the map." Ahmadinejad said he had "no doubt the new wave [of attacks] in Palestine will soon wipe off this disgraceful blot from the face of the Islamic world." He went on to threaten other Arab states, saying, "anybody who recognizes Israel will burn in the fire of the Islamic nation's fury."[13] Two days later, the Iranian president marched in the streets of Tehran with several hundred thousand protestors who were chanting "Death to America" and "Death to Israel" and burning the flags of both countries. A peace-loving state indeed.

Syria not only provides support for terrorist organizations; it has also opened its borders to allow terrorist fighters into Iraq to fight against American and coalition forces. It permits terrorist groups like Hamas and the Popular Front for the Liberation of Palestine to operate from Syrian soil. "Syria also continued to permit Iran to use Damascus as a transshipment point for resupplying Hizballah in Lebanon,"[14] according to the State Department. In 2003, Syria's membership in the UN was enhanced with a prestigious seat on the Security Council. All that for a mere $1 million membership fee.

Syria was also implicated in the February 14, 2005, assassination of Lebanese prime minister Rafik Hariri. Two months after the assassination, the Security Council adopted Resolution 1595, which established an investigative committee that would help the Lebanese identify the culprits. In October, the committee issued preliminary findings that "there is converging evidence pointing at both Lebanese and Syrian involvement in this terrorist act."[15] The report also stated, "it would be difficult to envisage a scenario whereby such a complex assassination plot could have been carried out without [the] knowledge [of] Syrian Military Intelligence."[16]

Other state sponsors of terrorism also get the benefits of UN member-ship for bargain rates. Libya pays only $904,000 in membership dues to the UN; Cuba forks over a mere $405,000; and North Korea, which is threaten-ing the world with nuclear weapons, pays only $121,000 to the UN.[17]

UN membership has its privileges. Syria was seated on the UN Security Council. Cuba, Sudan, and Syria have been members of the UN Human Rights Commission. Libya was nominated to chair the Human Rights Commission in 2003. Representatives from both Syria and Iran have enjoyed membership on the International Law Commission.

The General Assembly is a hotbed of anti-Americanism. The countries there do not share our values and vote against them on a consistent basis. The United States is virtually alone in the United Nations—standing up for peace and security, accountability, free markets, private property, and demo-cratic values. It is important to note just how often U.S. interests conflict with the proposals of other member states in the United Nations.

In 2004, there were ninety recorded votes in the General Assembly. On sixty-two occasions, the United States found other countries' proposals so objectionable that it voted against them. In only seventeen of ninety instances was the U.S. able to vote in favor of a UN resolution. (The U.S. abstained on eleven occasions.)

The United States voted "no" on General Assembly resolutions more than any other country. What better proof is there that the UN—with finan-cial resources provided by the United States—is writing, debating, and implementing policies that are contrary to American values and priorities? The resolutions they propose in the General Assembly are just a small reflec-tion of the anti-American actions these countries take in the hundreds of agencies and commissions that are part of the UN system.

There are only three countries in the General Assembly that vote with the United States more than 75 percent of the time—Palau, Israel, and Micronesia. On General Assembly votes, these nations agree with the United States 98.5 percent, 93.2 percent, and 78 percent of the time, respectively. The support of Palau and Micronesia is welcome, but on a practical level it is meaningless. Neither has a military or an economy of which to speak, and with a combined population of 130,000 people, these are not the first two countries to whom Uncle Sam turns when forming a "coalition of the willing."

Of the top ten countries that vote with the United States, half of them are not what international political observers would call powerhouses of the world stage.

Top Ten Countries Voting with United States in UN General Assembly 2004

Country	No. of Votes with U.S.	No. of Votes against U.S.	Abstentions	Absences	% of votes in favor of
Palau	67	1	0	11	98.5%
Israel	55	4	14	6	93.2%
Micronesia	46	13	4	16	78.0%
Marshall Islands	44	28	3	4	61.1%
Australia	34	26	17	2	56.7%
U.K.	38	29	12	0	56.7%
France	33	28	17	1	54.1%
Albania	29	29	15	6	50.0%
Canada	32	32	13	2	50.0%
Latvia	32	36	9	2	47.1%

Source: U.S. State Department[18]

Besides the United States, there are 190 other countries in the UN General Assembly, and as the table above illustrates, only 9 of those countries vote with the United States more than 50 percent of the time. So when the General Assembly votes on issues like UN dues, or human cloning, or banning private ownership of firearms, or global welfare, 181 countries routinely vote against America's position. The United States is outnumbered and underwriting our own demise.

The table is instructive in other ways. It shows—based on their voting records—that Israel is the only country of political substance that can be counted on to agree with the U.S. more than 75 percent of the time. But once again, Israel's support is not of much value in the UN, simply because the General Assembly is so vehemently anti-Semitic that Israel's support does not translate into political leverage for the U.S. It is also true that many of the votes on which the U.S. and Israel find themselves in agreement are resolutions targeted against Israel.

We must also examine the voting records of Australia and the United Kingdom. Both countries are strong allies in the war on terror and can be counted on to fight by America's side. But the votes taken in the General

Assembly are not usually of a military or security nature. The fact that Great Britain and Australia—two strong military allies of the United States—are voting with the United States only 56 percent of the time should be cause for concern.

It means that on issues related to global governance, those governments place a great deal of faith in the United Nations. While they may be with us on the question of Iraq, they are likely to be against us on matters of international law, the environment, the global economy, and the creation of new supranational institutions. Both countries strongly support the International Criminal Court.

A review of the General Assembly voting patterns reveals disturbing findings:

- There are 131 countries in the UN that vote against the United States at least 75 percent of the time.
- The United States provides foreign aid to 144 of the 190 member states of the United Nations, yet, when the voting records of all countries are tallied together, the General Assembly votes in the interests of the U.S. only 23.3 percent of the time.
- There are 45 countries that vote with the United States less than 10 percent of the time.
- On average, the coalition of African nations votes against the United States 87 percent of the time.
- Asian countries oppose the United States on 84 percent of General Assembly resolutions.
- Latin American countries vote against the U.S. position in the General Assembly 82 percent of the time.
- Countries belonging to the Organization of the Islamic Conference vote against the United State 88 percent of the time.

Of those ninety votes in the General Assembly, there were ten that the United States singled out as being "important," i.e., they were votes on major issues in which the U.S. has a security or strong moral interest. One of the "important" votes was on an anti-American resolution condemning the long-standing U.S. economic embargo on Cuba.

On this issue, Fidel Castro's government has manipulated the General Assembly since 1992, when the Cuban delegation first introduced the resolution demanding the U.S. lift its embargo of the communist country. When it was first introduced, 59 countries voted with Castro. But during the

Clinton years, the United States lost ground, and today, 179 countries vote against the United States. The member states of the United Nations choose to stand by the side of a communist dictator, Fidel Castro. Only three countries voted with the United States.

It is precisely this kind of situation that caused Kim Holmes, former assistant secretary of state for International Organizations, to remark that countries like Cuba and Iran have "way too much influence over the outcomes of UN activities."[19]

Other General Assembly votes considered important to the United States included resolutions on the protection of human rights in Sudan and Iran and the protection of religious freedom in all countries. On these votes of major importance, the countries of the UN General Assembly voted with the United States only 35 percent of the time.

The United States gives the UN more than $300 million every year just in regular dues. When U.S. contributions to peacekeeping and the numerous UN agencies created by the General Assembly are tallied, it is closer to $3 billion annually. All that money, just so the General Assembly can oppose the U.S. on nearly seven out of every ten major issues.

On those important votes, only eight countries supported the United States five or more times—and again those include some of the smallest countries in the world. On the big issues—the most important issues facing the American people in the General Assembly—among the few countries that stand shoulder to shoulder with the United States of America are Palau, the Marshall Islands, Micronesia, Nauru, and Grenada. Not exactly a global all-star team.

The United States is being treated like an international doormat in the General Assembly. With the kind of money American taxpayers are pouring into the UN, we should have the right to expect a little more loyalty from our so-called friends. It doesn't have to be what Lyndon Johnson demanded of his aides—"a kiss-my-ass-at-high-noon-in-Macy's-window loyalty,"[20] but for $3 billion a year, it should be more than we are getting.

Human Rights

There is at least one area where an institution like the United Nations could play a useful role. It could, if it wished, choose to be a true partner with the United States to improve the human rights of individuals around the world. Here, the UN has had the opportunity to be a voice of great moral courage; a beacon of hope for the oppressed. But it has failed miserably.

A concerned secretary-general could harness the righteous indignation of caring hearts the world over and stand at an international podium of puissance to proclaim the dignity and rights of all of God's children. Instead, the United Nations cowers before tyrants. It has betrayed its founding and crushed the hopes of enslaved peoples in numerous nations.

The UN Commission was established "to promote and protect human rights." It first met in 1947 to write the Universal Declaration of Human Rights, which proclaims in Article 1 that "All human beings are born free and equal in dignity and rights. They are endowed with reason and conscience and should act towards one another in a spirit of brotherhood."

But today when the commission meets, it looks less like a human rights symposium and more like a casting call for *America's Most Wanted.* The UN Human Rights Commission is infested with the world's worst tyrants.

In a February 2005 cover story, *Parade* magazine asked, "Who is the World's Worst Dictator?" It then listed rulers of twenty countries who are guilty of committing genocide, causing famine and starvation, employing slave labor, and repressing women and minorities. Some of those countries include communist China, Pakistan, Saudi Arabia, Zimbabwe, Swaziland, and Cuba.

What makes these dictatorial regimes unique is that they each enjoy a prestigious membership on the UN Human Rights Commission. In fact, almost half the dictators listed by *Parade* magazine are on the commission, casting judgment on the way in which other governments treat their people. Government-sponsored murder, torture, and oppression are the modus operandi for these rulers.

In addition, when Transparency International conducted its annual survey in 2004 of the most corrupt countries in the world, there was overlap with the membership of the Human Rights Commission. Of the twenty most corrupt nations, eight of them held membership on the commission.

These brutal regimes also show up in the State Department's annual report on Human Rights Practices. It finds that half of the members of the UN Human Rights Commission have a record on the subject that the State Department judges to be "poor" or worse. In Saudi Arabia, "the religious police continued to intimidate, abuse, and detain citizens and foreigners," the report states. In a typical Foggy Bottom understatement, the report called the human rights record in China "disappointing."

Other members of the UN Human Rights Commission with poor records include Congo, Swaziland, and Togo. A 2003 report on Togo from Human Rights Watch says that girls as young as three and four years old are recruited into the domestic labor market to cook and clean and maintain the garden. They are forced to work long hours and generally are not paid.[21]

In Indonesia, according to the State Department, there is wholesale abuse of citizens:

> Security force members murdered, tortured, raped, beat, and arbitrarily detained civilians and members of separatist movements . . . . Some police officers occasionally used excessive and sometimes deadly force in arresting suspects and in attempting to obtain information or a confession. . . . The judicial system was corrupt, which contributed to the failure to provide redress to victims of human rights violations or hold perpetrators accountable . . . the Government jailed some peaceful antigovernment protestors for "insulting the President" or "spreading hatred against the Government."[22]

Yet these countries and others that are committing atrocities are allowed to sit on the UN body established by Eleanor Roosevelt that would set standards to which nations could aspire.

The most egregious corruption of the Human Rights Commission is the membership of Sudan, where, in the Darfur region of that country, a government-sponsored genocide has displaced more than 2,000,000 people and killed upwards of 300,000 by way of starvation and murder.

Brad Phillips is president of the Virginia-based Persecution Project, a Christian ministry dedicated to serving the persecuted and suffering. Phillips first visited Sudan in 1998 and returns there four to five times each year as his organization conducts its relief work. I talked at length with him about the situation in the Sudan and some of the horrors he has learned through his visits.

The suffering of many of the individuals Phillips has met is gut wrenching. He told me about a young girl named Leah whose village was attacked by the Popular Defense Force (PDF). Because she could not see, she was left behind only to be gang raped by members of the militia. The product of that rape is Leah's daughter, who serves as her seeing-eye guide.

"I met another man," Phillips told me, "who was thrown into a fire [and] burned all over his body. I've spoken to all kinds of women who have been raped or members of their family who were raped." He explained that "rape is one of the weapons of genocide." It is used, he said, against African Christians as part of the process of "forced Islamization." Phillips has seen children with their hands cut off—"a common practice in Islam . . . for a violation of Sharia law."

He told me the story of a young man named Joseph who was abducted and sold into slavery. After disobeying his master, Joseph was beaten, tortured, and crucified. Then he was left for dead before being rescued by the master's son. That is the short and polite version of the story. To relate the horrors this young man suffered, as Phillips learned, would make the reader physically ill.

The broader problems of genocide occur when the Janjaweed fighters ride into a Christian village and destroy it by killing or stealing cattle and forcing people from their homes. The refugees then have two choices, Phillips explained: "they can stay scattered in areas that are not under the control of Khartoum; or they can move into garrison towns that are controlled by Khartoum where they can receive help." But if they take refuge in the latter, "they're placing themselves under the administration of Khartoum and . . . they have to subject themselves to Sharia law," he said.

In a nutshell, "that is what the war in Sudan has been about," Phillips said. "It's about the imposition of Sharia law on people that don't want to be under Sharia law . . . just give up your African name or your Christian name and take an Islamic name and then you can be fed." Forced Islamization—Sudan's ticket to the UN Human Rights Commission.

These are the kinds of atrocities that are taking place right under the nose of the United Nations, and Kofi Annan will not use the bully pulpit of his office to denounce such countries. Thomas Jacobson of Focus on the Family has on numerous occasions traveled to Geneva, where the UN's Human Rights Commission is headquartered. He told me that "the UN and the diplomats who represent their countries there, for the most part, lack the courage to take a stand against severe atrocities." The one country that is willing to stand up for the oppressed—the United States—was booted off the commission in 2001. Kofi Annan stood by and let it happen.

Amid these ignominious machinations and the repeated abuse and mockery in the press, Annan was forced to act. He has called for a change the membership standards of the Human Rights Commission as part of the UN's reform agenda and moving from a commission to a Human Rights Council that would have more clout. But the cause of human rights will never be reformed at the UN by changing a few bylaws. It has to begin in the hearts of those who run the institution.

By its own admission, in the 1990s the UN Human Rights Commission shied away from setting standards of universal human rights and "increasingly turned its attention to the needs of States to be provided with advisory services and technical assistance."[23] Not wanting to cause controversy, the commission focused less on human atrocities that were being committed and placed more emphasis on "the promotion of economic, social, and cultural rights, including the right to development and the right to adequate [sic] standard of living."[24]

Such a strategy ignores those who most need the help of human rights advocates or others in society who have already begun to climb the social ladder. In the end, it will fail for all. A just human rights policy cannot advocate a minimum wage for some while slave labor still exists for others. By placing an emphasis on "cultural rights," the UN undermines the struggle for religious freedom.

With its current makeup, the UN Human Rights Commission is at the same time a joke and a travesty. And just as the United Nations needs to search its soul, so too should the United States government.

The United States invested $10 million in 2004 in the Human Rights Commission—nearly double the amount of the second-highest contributor. In contrast, Sudan invested all of $2,500 and Armenia a whopping $1,096 in the Human Rights Commission. They provide this money not because they care about the less fortunate, but to try to improve their image on the world stage, protect their interests, and attack the United States.

When Cuba and Zimbabwe were recently elected to the Human Rights Commission, Tom Casey of the State Department responded,

> The United States believes that countries that routinely and systematically violate the rights of their citizens should not be selected to review the human rights performance of other countries. Despite the inappropriate membership of Cuba and Zimbabwe, we look for the working group to conduct its procedures in a balanced and transparent way.[25]

This is the State Department at its worst. The election of Cuba and Zimbabwe to the Human Rights Commission is not "inappropriate"; it is a travesty. It is cause for soul searching. Instead of hoping that the commission will work in a "balanced and transparent way," the U.S. should have stated the obvious—that the Human Rights Commission is a sham and America wants no part of it. We should have resigned our membership, demanded our money back, and encouraged other countries to do the same.

When these countries are given such a forum, they drive stakes of criticism through the heart of Uncle Sam. For example:

• In June 2005, UN Human Rights investigators accused the United States of stonewalling their efforts to gain access to U.S. facilities in which terrorists are being detained. They claimed they had "allegations of torture" by Americans against individuals who committed acts of "alleged terrorism." Four months later, in October 2005, the Defense Department extended an invitation to three UN human rights inspectors to visit the detention facility at Guantanamo Bay, Cuba.

• Also in June 2005, Manfred Nowak, the UN's special rapporteur on torture, who is appointed by the Human Rights Committee, alleged that the U.S. may be torturing prisoners on the high seas. He told *Agence France-Presse* "there are very, very serious accusations that the United States is maintaining secret camps, notably on ships."[26] Nowak admitted the accusations "are only rumors"[27] but launched an investigation regardless.

• UN Human Rights officials chose the presidential election year of 2000 as a convenient time to raise numerous questions about the death penalty in the United States—and more specifically in the state of Texas, whose governor, George W. Bush, was the Republican nominee for president.

• In November 2001, the UN special rapporteur on the independence of judges and lawyers accused President George W. Bush of "repressive measures" when he signed an order to provide for trials by military commission for non-citizens who have been accused of committing or abetting an act of terrorism.

• In December 2001, the UN's special rapporteur on "the adverse effects of the illicit movement and dumping of toxic and dangerous products and wastes on the enjoyment of human rights" visited the United States to inspect environmental procedures and how they affect human rights. In her report, the special rapporteur told the U.S. it should ratify three international treaties; she "encouraged" the government to change its official classification of certain hazardous products "in order to harmonize [the classification]" with an international treaty the U.S. has not ratified; and she lobbied for more funding of the Environmental Protection Agency "to allow it to implement the recommendations" that she herself was demanding.[28]

• UN Human Rights representatives have also taken the opportunity to criticize the U.S. on such issues as race relations, prison conditions, and police behavior.

Such examples show that the UN's Human Rights apparatus is more than happy to lob political grenades at the U.S. and hope that they can cause some damage. What is inexplicable is why our elected representatives continue to arm these illegitimate regimes with ammunition. Michael Corleone's strategy to "keep your friends close, but your enemies closer" is inoperable when your enemies are so boldly trying to undermine you.

The U.S. policy of accepting illegitimate condemnation has to change. Before abandoning the Human Rights Commission completely, there will be an effort at reform—a policy even Kofi Annan had no choice but to embrace. When Annan issued his "In Larger Freedom" report in March 2005, he admitted that the commission was suffering from a "credibility deficit." The secretary-general explained, "States have sought membership of the Commission not to strengthen human rights but to protect themselves against criticism or to criticize others."[29]

Annan has proposed that a smaller Human Rights Council replace the discredited commission and that membership be decided by a two-thirds vote of the General Assembly. Few aspects of the United Nations are worth saving, but a credible body that can speak with moral clarity and advance the cause of human rights could be one of them. There is now widespread acceptance of the fact that the current human rights body is worthless. Reform of this particular function is worth an investment of time, but not much. If the UN can't fix the problem by the time a new secretary-general takes office in 2007, the United States should walk away from the Human Rights Commission.

An Investment in Failure

Despite the overwhelming evidence of corruption, George W. Bush has hope for the United Nations. He has cast his lot in favor of trying to reform the institution. One of his own reform proposals, which he outlined in his 2004 address to the General Assembly, was the creation of a UN democracy fund to which he has pledged $10 million as an initial donation. The fund, which was officially created on July 4, 2005, will accept voluntary contributions by member states and is run by the UN.

I asked Jed Babbin if the idea of creating and contributing to a democracy fund within the United Nations was like putting lipstick on a pig. "It's a lot worse than that," he told me. "It's like putting lipstick on a snake." Babbin estimates that there are roughly fifty democracies in the United Nations, "so in order to fix the UN, you'd have to take away the votes of the illegitimate governments and they have the votes to prevent that from happening."

The very idea that the United States belongs to an institution in which we have to encourage democracy should tell us something about the composition of the UN. Creating a democracy fund within the UN is like starting an NAACP chapter within the Klan—their memberships are so corrupt as to not be dignified. "I have given up on any hope of reforming the UN," Cliff Kincaid, a long-time UN observer and President of America's Survival, told me. "I think it is a failed institution [which] gives people false hopes."

One of the reasons so many people have given up on the UN is the corruption and scandal within the institution. There have been numerous examples of it in recent years, and often they go uncorrected. In most cases, it is only after relentless pressure that UN officials taken any action at all.

In February 2005, Ruud Lubbers, the UN's high commissioner for refugees, was forced to resign from his post amid charges of sexual harassment of a female colleague. The UN Office of Internal Oversight issued a report on the matter and charged the former prime minister of the Netherlands with a "pattern of sexual harassment."[30] Coming under the heading of "only at the UN," Lubbers held a press briefing and demonstrated how he put his arm around the woman by using one of the male reporters as a prop. Before he left, he had a parting shot for Kofi Annan: "Despite all my loyalty, insult has now been added to injury and therefore I resign as high commissioner."[31]

In April 2005, reports surfaced in the *New York Times* that Michael Wilson, a businessman from Ghana and a figure in the Oil-for-Food scandal, was alleged to have involvement in a $50 million bribery scam at the World Intellectual Property Organization (WIPO). The $50 million contract was for the renovation of a building at the WIPO headquarters. In October 2005, an independent investigator was appointed to look into that charge and other allegations of mismanagement at the organization.

In the first six months of 2003, reported John Zarocostas of the *Washington Times*, the inspector general for the United Nations high commissioner for refugees logged eighty-two complaints—of which 26 percent had to do with sexual exploitation of refugees.[32] In March 2005, Column

Lynch of the *Washington Post* obtained a confidential report "conducted by a Swiss consulting firm" and informed readers that "the UN's top elections official, Carina Perelli, presided over a department whose leadership tolerated sexual harassment, misused office funds, and engaged in favoritism." Working conditions at the UN agency were "abusive" and "offensive" it said.[33]

In October 2005, Zimbabwe's president Robert Mugabe—who has inflicted famine upon his nation with his confiscation of white-owned farms and misguided agriculture policies—was invited to speak to the sixtieth anniversary of the UN's Food and Agriculture Organization. In his speech, Mugabe called President George W. Bush and British prime minister Tony Blair "international terrorists"[34] and compared them to Adolf Hitler and Benito Mussolini. According to the UN's own statistics, at least 4 million citizens of Zimbabwe are in desperate need of food.[35] During my own trip to the northern border of South Africa in 2002, the locals complained that Mugabe's policies had exacerbated the problem of poaching in the game parks, but whereas poachers usually kill the big animals for ivory, in this case they were killing them for food.

The accumulation of scandals at the UN upset two constituencies— those who believe deeply in the institution and those who understand that the scandals are simply more evidence of the organization's inherent corruption. Kofi Annan believed that complaints about these types of scandals, along with the criticism he received as part of the Oil-for-Food investigation, were coming from a "lynch mob"[36] that was out to destroy him.

The movie *The Interpreter*—starring Sean Penn and Nicole Kidman—is the story of a United Nations translator who overhears a murder being planned on the floor of the General Assembly after business hours. When director Sydney Pollack was promoting the movie, he said the General Assembly room was "designed to have an emotional effect on you." Pollack was given special dispensation to film the movie at UN headquarters, something that hadn't been done previously in the organization's history, and when he saw the massive room where the delegates of 191 countries meet, he said, "It looks like a place of high purpose; it looks like a place where very, very important things are going to happen."[37]

If only that were the case. When when the General Assembly is not engaged in scandal, it undertakes the creation of inane holidays and commemorations. On the UN calendar, the organization has identified dozens of days and their purpose for celebration. These are just a few examples:

• *International Mother Language Day (February 21).* In its 2000–2001 Program and Budget, UNESCO called on all UN member states "to formulate and implement language policies designed to ensure linguistic diversity and multilingual education at all levels of education . . . [and] promote the implementation of linguistic rights as an integral part of human rights."[38] So much for English as the official language.

• *World Meteorological Day (March 23).* In 2005, the UN's World Meteorological Organization (WMO) spent thousands of dollars to promote World Meteorological Day and itself as "the authoritative voice of the United Nations system on weather, climate, and water."[39] To commemorate the solemn occasion, Secretary-General Kofi Annan issued a statement and the organization produced a thirty-two-page booklet about "Weather, climate, water, and sustainable development." It also produced a video, brochures, and posters and issued press releases to make sure the world understood the significance of the occasion. The United States gives the WMO roughly $10 million per year. A more accurate forecast of the weather can be obtained for less than $20 from the *Farmer's Almanac.*

• *United Nations Public Service Day (June 23).* The United Nations Division for Public Administration and Development Management (UNDPDM) is a bureaucratic agency of an international government institution widely known for its corruption and inefficiency. When the UNDPDM is not performing its completely worthless mission of "assist[ing] governments in strengthening policy-making and improving the efficiency of their governance systems through disseminating information, delivering technical assistance, and providing an international forum for the exchange of national experiences,"[40] it is giving out awards to national bureaucracies for the UN Public Service Day.

•*International Tolerance Day (November 16).* The United Nations' Declaration on Principles on Tolerance gives us the meaning of the word that is celebrated this day. Tolerance "is not only a moral duty, it is also a political and legal requirement." Conversely, tolerance "also means that one's views are not to be imposed on others."[41] I congratulate readers who can tolerate that level of stupidity.

• *World Television Day (November 21).* Each year, the United Nations devotes an entire day to celebrating the contribution and potential of the television in society. They do this on November 21—the day, in 1877, when Thomas Edison invented the phonograph.

• *International Civil Aviation Day (December 7)*. The United Nations chooses to commemorate the flight industry on December 7—the day in 1941 when more than 350 Japanese aircraft launched strikes on Pearl Harbor that killed at least 2,400 Americans. It was, until September 11, 2001, the worst terrorist attack in American history. As President Franklin Roosevelt said, December 7 is "a day that will live in infamy." It isn't for the United Nations.

• There is also, for the few who are interested, an *International Day for Biological Diversity, International Migrants Day*, and *World Telecommunications Day*—to name a few more asinine projects supported by American tax dollars.

If that weren't bad enough, the United Nations, in many cases, has built in redundancies for its commemorations. For example:

• If you happen to forget the *International Day for the Remembrance of the Slave Trade and Its Abolition* on August 23rd, don't worry, you can celebrate the *International Day for the Abolition of Slavery* on December 2nd.

• Food for thought: Couldn't the UN combine *World Day for Water* on March 22nd with *World Food Day* on October 16th? Just a suggestion.

• For the more erudite UN bureaucrats, there is an abundance of holidays. There is April 23rd, which is *World Book and Copyright Day*, but that is not to be confused with *World Press Freedom Day*, which falls on May 3rd, nor are they to be celebrated at the expense of *International Literacy Day* on September 8th.

• Even the kids get a double holiday: August 12, which is *International Youth Day*, and November 20, which is a more festive *Universal Children's Day*.

All at once, the UN General Assembly serves as a safe haven for terrorists, a forum for undermining American values, and a launching pad for useless innovations in public policy. On any level it is worth neither American time or investment.

You Can't Fight City Hall
(or Global Government)

Only five months after taking the oath of office as the United Nations' new secretary-general, Kofi Annan spoke to the International Women's Forum in New York and outlined his strategic vision for the future of the UN and the role he expected his institution to play in the world. "We have to show," Mr. Annan said, "that this organization deals not in dusty abstractions, but in crucial life-and-death matters affecting the well-being of all women, men, and children, every citizen of this planet."[1]

If similar words were spoken within the context of their defined constituencies by the mayor of a major American city or a governor of any of the fifty states, they would be perfectly appropriate. For it is the responsibility of such elected officials to provide the infrastructure and services needed for the community and its residents to thrive. Rescuing the cat from the tree, turning on the streetlights, and filling the potholes have been, and ought to remain, the responsibility of the sheriff, the alderman, the mayor. Despite Kofi Annan's view of himself as wet nurse to the world, we need not, and ought not, internationalize such duties.

A few months later, at the World Economic Forum in Davos, Switzerland, the secretary-general elaborated. "The United Nations once dealt only with governments," he said. But in today's world, according to Annan, "the business of the United Nations involves the business of the world."[2]

Take note, citizens, for the United Nations has claimed its mandate. Henceforth, there is no great controversy nor petty annoyance on which the United Nations and its vast bureaucracy will not sound its voice. The UN has declared that your problems are theirs and the fate of your family rests in Turtle Bay. Kofi Annan has done Bill Clinton one better: he will not only feel your pain; he will ease it. And if no institution of world government yet exists to manage the crisis de jour, rest easy—it will be created.

For Kofi Annan has proven the wisdom of one of America's original federalists. "It is a favorite maxim of despotic power," explained Fisher Ames, "that mankind are not made to govern themselves."[3]

And that is why the United Nations is such an expansionist force. It neither sees nor sets limitations for itself and its role in the world. It rules not with military might but with the imposition of international apparatus. Specialized agencies, commissions, treaties, agreements, protocols, offices, councils, and bureaucracies of all nature are created and staffed from the ever-expanding roster of one-world policy wonks who then pass judgment, claim authority, and influence national governments. "Institutions are more powerful than men,"[4] Karl Marx said, which is why the United Nations has always built itself on backs of bureaucracy, not personalities. It is all being done, ostensibly, in the name of helping the poor and innocent—to bring hope to "we the peoples." But the accumulation of power is a dangerous thing.

America's Founding Fathers limited the role of the federal government and assured us that "the powers not delegated to the United States by the Constitution" belong to the states and the people. The UN recognizes no such suppressant on its appetite for power.

When the UN was created, it was a forum for the representatives of governments to gather. According to its charter, it was supposed to help "develop friendly relations among nations" and "be a centre for harmonizing the actions of nations." But when Kofi Annan expressed his desire to be intimately involved in solving the day-to-day problems that confront individuals—whether they be in Nantucket or in Nigeria—he violated his own oath and the UN Charter, which states in Article 2, Section 7, that the UN will not "intervene in matters which are essentially within the domestic jurisdiction of any state."

But through the creation of more and more international institutions, the United Nations is interfering in, or adversely influencing, the policies of the United States.

- The UN Security Council delayed in the U.S. liberation of Iraq.
- World Trade Organization decisions force Congress to rewrite U.S. laws.
- The creation of the International Criminal Court required the State Department to expend political capital and strike bilateral agreements with every nation on earth to protect U.S. military personnel.

- The International Court of Justice has forced a delay in the case of a Mexican national convicted of the rape and murder of an American citizen.
- Kofi Annan's Millennium Development Goals spawned the creation of Mr. Bush's Millennium Challenge Account and a spike in U.S. foreign aid.
- UN treaties have influenced decisions of the U.S. Supreme Court.

This is global governance that is hostile to the United States. Even the UN itself admits to this. In a report commissioned by the UN's International Labor Organization, the World Commission on the Social Dimension of Globalization says, "globalization has reduced the power and autonomy of States in various ways."[5]

And yet, in many cases, Americans—led by Democrats—are advocating, building, or legitimizing the institutions that are wreaking havoc on U.S. policy.

Ralph Nader advocates the creation of a World Consumer Protection Organization. During his announcement for the presidency of the United States, Congressman Dick Gephardt called on the World Trade Organization to implement a global minimum wage. Environmental activists are demanding the creation of a World Environmental Organization to act as a global EPA. Such ministries are inconsistent with the infrastructure of a constitutional republic.

As a matter of policy, the institutions of the United Nations are the architecture of an illegitimate regime. As a matter of politics, Republicans would be foolish to allow any more of these agencies to see the light of day, for they act as the supply depots for the UN's assault on conservative values and American sovereignty. Simply put, they are nothing more than international field offices for the Democratic National Committee. But as far as the United Nations is concerned, they have only broken ground and the real construction has yet to begin.

The World Commission on the Social Dimension of Globalization (WCSDG) was created by the United Nations' International Labor Organization. In 2004, it issued a lengthy report in which it spelled out in detail the ambitions of internationalists. And despite the progress they have made, they issued a call to arms, saying, "the issue of global governance now warrants serious attention."[6]

"Better instruments for the governance of globalization"[7] must be built, the commission demanded. As evidenced by the histories of the International Criminal Court and the World Trade Organization, advocates of these global building blocks will work for years, if they must, to see their dreams come to fruition.

But it is unlikely they will have to. The pace of globalist construction has increased of late. Already, some of their wishes have been met and more are being proposed. And while the United Nations has been practicing eminent domain on American public policy, our leaders have largely complied—not realizing the magnitude of the damage being done.

Richard Rahn, a senior fellow at the Discovery Institute, explained the problem this way:

> Over the last 80 years, we have seen the endless drift of government power from local to state and regional to the federal and now increasingly to multinational institutions that have become quasi-governments fulfilling some government functions, particularly on trade, financial, environmental regulation and even criminal justice, given the advent of the International Criminal Court. The drift toward global statism has continued at a relentless but measured pace; so, like the frog in the pot, we don't realize we are being boiled to death.[8]

Not only are we being boiled to death, but we're paying the cook's salary. The U.S. is the primary financier of most of these global institutions, requesting from Congress $3.4 billion to fund the United Nations and its specialized agencies in fiscal year 2006. And while one or more of these proposed international agencies may be opposed by the current administration, they are only a Democrat president away from their grand openings.

International Finance Facility

Now in its third trimester, the International Finance Facility (IFF) is likely to be the next institution to which the United Nations will give birth. It is the brainchild of Gordon Brown, Britain's Chancellor of the Exchequer, who says the IFF will be "nothing less than a modern Marshall Plan for the new world."[9] Brown bristles at the charge that he is creating another global institution, calling the IFF a "temporary" institution that, by his own admission, will have to exist for at least thirty years. At that time, we are led to believe, the bureaucrats running the IFF will sell off the leftover paper clips and voluntarily close the doors. The IFF has already gained the support of many non-governmental organizations (NGOs) and world leaders, and if Mr. Brown succeeds Tony Blair as Britain's next prime minister, as he is expected to, he will have ample opportunity to twist the arms of those who are not yet signed on to his "New Deal for the global economy."

One of the cheerleaders for the IFF is Mark Malloch Brown, who, as the administrator for the United Nations Development Program, called the IFF a "bold proposal . . . one of the most important new ideas to come in a long time."[10] Today, Mark Malloch Brown serves as Kofi Annan's chief of staff. Professor Jeffrey Sachs, one of Kofi Annan's closest advisors, is another fan of building the IFF.

The UN's overwhelming faith in bureaucracy is one of the principal reasons for limiting the role of the United Nations in policy matters. Each time the UN sets out to solve a problem, it creates a new program or institution charged with that particular responsibility. The IFF is a perfect example.

The IFF is a direct response to Kofi Annan's Millennium Development Goals (MDGs). The MDGs are a set of commitments governments pledged at the International Conference for Financing and Development in Monterrey, Mexico, in 2002. The "Monterrey Consensus" included an agreement by participating nations that each would give 0.7 percent of its national income—amounting to tens of billions of dollars—to the UN's Official Development Assistance program to eradicate or reduce certain problems related to disease and poverty.

In formulating these goals, the United States, once again, was singled out for criticism. In a preliminary document leading up to the conference that was commissioned by Kofi Annan, it said, "in the United States of America, the public has little awareness of the moral issues or the dictates of self-interest in alleviating poverty elsewhere in the world."[11] It went on to say that the American people "have little idea of how meagre is the actual record of foreign aid giving"[12] by the United States.

The timetable for the completion of these goals is 2015. So the UN pleaded its case and twisted arms and was able to convince governments to sign on to the Millennium Development Goals. Though the Bush administration disputes that it agreed to give a specific percentage of national income, they nonetheless bowed to UN pressure and vastly increased the amount of aid the United States is giving to Official Development Assistance for the MDGs.

But the accumulation of money, power, and authority never occurs quickly enough for the United Nations and its adherents. "It is not enough to increase development assistance," Kofi Annan said, "that is why we find the International Finance Facility proposed by Chancellor Gordon Brown to be a wonderful proposal."[13]

So they have created this scheme known as the International Finance Facility that will "frontload" billions of dollars of aid pledged by governments in Monterrey and funnel it through yet another layer of bureaucracy before doling it out like welfare payments to third-world nations who have little desire to end their cycle of dependency on American generosity.

IFF backers claim the institution would attract an additional $50 billion per year—or upwards of $500 billion by 2015—in pursuit of their goals. It would do so by issuing bonds that are guaranteed by Congress with pledges that are "legally binding."[14] Democrats in the House have already shown strong support for the International Finance Facility. Representatives Jim McDermott and Charlie Rangel have introduced legislation to increase taxes in order to provide funding for an International Finance Facility.

The reason for investing so heavily in the Millennium Development Goals in the short term is to lift third-world countries out of poverty; get them on their feet. But even the UK's own IFF proposal concedes that "investing in poverty reduction through the IFF *would not remove* the need for continued, substantial development assistance in the medium to long-term"[15] (emphasis added). And much of the money given to these countries will never be seen again. "The bulk of the IFF's funds should be disbursed as grants,"[16] the IFF proposal states, meaning it will never be paid back.

The IFF is nothing more than another component in a never-ending global welfare scheme financed by American taxpayers. It is a scheme Congressman Henry Hyde would like to see end. Writing in London's *Daily Telegraph*, Hyde panned the idea of the IFF and the failed foreign aid policies the United States continues to pursue. In fact, Hyde shows, the IFF would actually result in a net loss of development aid to Africa. Wrote Hyde,

> We must no longer treat Africa as a ward of the developed world. We must no longer espouse the welfarism of patting the continent on the head, muttering "poor Africans" while opening our wallets so we can sleep better at night thinking we've made a difference when we haven't. No nation ever spent its way out of poverty by cashing foreign aid cheques.[17]

Though the IFF is little more than a scheme of robbing Peter to pay Paul—which some UN NGOs admit, they favor it because they believe the International Finance Facility is the path to the Holy Grail of globalism—international taxation. Leading activists have linked the International Finance Facility with the Tobin Tax—a scheme proposed by economist James Tobin to tax international currency transactions.

Analysts from the Tobin Tax Network wrote in a 2003 briefing paper that the International Finance Facility and the Tobin Tax are "extremely complementary."

> It is important that the Tobin Tax Network support HM Treasury in its efforts to secure the IFF. However, it is equally important that this support is met with the acknowledgement that alone the IFF is unlikely to achieve the MDGs and that another powerful income stream such as the Tobin Tax is a necessary, rather than an optional, accompanying initiative.[18]

Since its inception, the United Nations has been financed by assessments placed on member countries. The United States—in addition to providing the UN its home in New York City—pays the greatest amount of the UN's $1.2 billion annual budget—22 percent. Funding for peacekeeping operations, which runs approximately $3 billion to $4 billion annually, is assessed separately, and once again the U.S. pays the lion's share at 27 percent. The United States had to fight in recent years to get its assessments reduced for both regular dues and peacekeeping, which were as high as 25 percent and 31 percent, respectively. The amount the United States pays in regular dues alone has increased 57 percent since fiscal year 2003.

Because UN dues are based on a nation's "ability to pay," most member countries pay next to nothing for the opportunity to rise on the floor of the General Assembly and stick it to the United States. Many countries—forty-eight in fact—pay the minimum assessment—0.001 percent—which amounts to roughly $11,000 per year. The system is so inequitable that six countries—the United States, Japan, Germany, France, Great Britain, and Italy—contribute 69 percent of all UN dues.

Member nations speak of how indispensable the United Nations is and constantly praise the UN and the vital role it plays in the world. But you wouldn't know it from the funding patterns. Many nations, especially those that have to pay very little, often don't pay at all. As such, the UN finds itself in a constant state of having to beg nations to pay their regular assessments. In recent years, the UN has accepted funding from private sources such as Ted Turner, Bill and Melinda Gates, and the Rockefellers. But accepting gifts from charities or corporations is a violation of the UN Charter, which states in Article 17 that "the expenses of the Organization shall be borne by the Members as apportioned by the General Assembly." Allowing these international sugar daddies to bankroll the UN gives them unaccountable access and influence.

That is why the United Nations has long wanted an automatic funding mechanism for the UN—not to replace the system of assessments, but rather to enhance it. Such a system would be a form of taxation that would flow directly into the UN coffers and would relieve the institution of having to be accountable to member governments.

There is a long history of international tax proposals that could be administered by the UN or collected by governments on behalf of the UN. They include:

- taxes on international trade;
- international taxes on aviation fuel;
- taxes on the use of natural resources;
- service fees on the so-called "global commons" such as the oceans;
- taxes on e-mails;
- fees for international postal services;
- a global lottery;
- and a host of other ideas to include taxes on the use of the atmosphere, outer space, tobacco, nuclear energy, and pollution. There has even been a proposal to allow individuals to allocate a portion of their taxes for the UN on their national tax forms.

Some of these proposals never made it past the paper on which they were written. But at least one proposal—the Tobin Tax—has gained a great deal of support and attention over the years. This proposed tax on international financial transactions is named after economist James Tobin and has received the support of thousands of government officials and global activists. Such a levy, supporters conservatively estimate, would raise at least $150 billion to $200 billion every year for the United Nations. Two Democratic members of Congress—Representative Peter DeFazio and the late senator Paul Wellstone—introduced legislation in 2000 to create a Tobin Tax.

The ideas for UN-imposed taxes come mostly from international activists—NGOs who want to see the UN grow in power and influence. Many UN bureaucrats also believe in global taxes but would not allow themselves to be quoted as such. Though there is support for global taxes in European nations and certainly among African nations who would benefit from the largess, the political staff at the United Nations have long understood that to advocate a global tax openly would cripple the organization's relationship with the United States.

In most instances, they have been, and remain, very careful not to cross that line. After all, Secretary-General Boutros Boutros-Ghali's call during his tenure for a UN tax on airline tickets so that the UN "would not be under the daily financial will of member states"[19] cost him a second term and led to legislation in Congress to prevent any kind of UN taxation on the American public.

A few years later, the UN Development Program commissioned the 1999 Human Development Report, which stated in part, "New sources of financing for the global technology revolution could be investigated, to ensure that it is truly global and that its potential for poverty eradication is mobilized." The report held out the possibility of pursuing a "bit tax" on e-mail as a revenue source. Mark Malloch Brown, then the head of UNDP and now Kofi Annan's right-hand man, was forced to shoot down the trial balloon. In a letter to the State Department, Brown wrote, "UNDP does not advocate and will never advocate the establishment of this or any other kind of global tax."[20]

But as Bob Dylan sang, "the times, they are a-changin'." NGOs are becoming more aggressive and the UN is laying the groundwork for tax implementation that might have a chance under a more UN-friendly administration in the White House. The report commissioned by the UN's International Labor Organization did not pull any punches on the issue. It openly and boldly stated that global taxes and tax cooperation are under discussion in several UN agencies:

> An International Tax Dialogue has already been launched by the IMF, OECD, and the World Bank to encourage and facilitate discussion of tax matters among national tax officials and international organizations. There is a strong sense amongst many countries and experts that a comprehensive and accessible basis for international tax cooperation needs to be created and that the United Nations would be the appropriate forum for this. The Secretary-General has recommended that the Ad Hoc Group of Experts on International Cooperation on Tax Matters be upgraded into an intergovernmental body.[21]

The report goes on to concede that the United Nations is not able to collect taxes without the global equivalent of an Internal Revenue Service (IRS) and says that fact needs to be changed.

However, quite apart from the debate over whether or not global taxes are desirable, there are at present insuperable political obstacles to putting them in place. The problem is not so much a question of what or how to tax, since a variety of technically feasible proposals exist. The point is that taxes are collected by governments within countries, and there is no global institutional framework with the necessary political authority to determine tax burdens and decide resource utilization. We believe this is an important issue, on which discussion of possible practical actions should be encouraged.[22]

A 2001 report commissioned by Kofi Annan—the High-level Panel on Financing for Development—was full of new ideas for the expansion of global government. One was to hold a "globalization summit" to plan the new institutions of international government that it believes are needed to manage the world economy. Another idea put forth by the panel was global taxes. The report stated:

> We believe the International Conference on Financing for Development and the Globalization Summit should first discuss whether or not the world should have global, and not only sovereign, imposition of taxes. Next, if global taxation is considered desirable, they should proceed to discuss seriously the pros and cons of two such sources: a currency transactions tax and a carbon tax.[23]

The promotion of global taxation is not being left only to the broken-down bureaucrats who operate from the bowels of UN headquarters. World leaders openly and forcefully advocate international taxation. "*Trouvons de nouvelles sources de financement,*"[24] proclaimed French President Jacques Chirac at the UN's World Summit on Sustainable Development in 2002. "Let us find new sources of financing."

In 2004, just before the opening of the General Assembly, Kofi Annan met with Chirac and several other world leaders once again to address the issue of global taxation. They endorsed a report that outlined several different kinds of taxation and attacked President George W. Bush for not attending the meeting. But Mr. Bush's agriculture secretary, Ann Veneman, attended and said the report placed "too much emphasis on schemes such as global taxes." She called global taxes "inherently undemocratic" and said "implementation is impossible."[25]

But Jacques Chirac had a different take on the matter. On the issue of global taxes, Chirac said, "However strong the Americans may be, you cannot in the long run emerge victorious by opposing an idea that is backed by 100 countries."[26]

As painful as it is to admit, Chirac has a point. And that is why it is not enough that the United States be the voice of discontent at the United Nations. Uncle Sam is no longer strong enough to stop the train of global government that is speeding down the tracks. The United States could not prevent the creation of the International Criminal Court. With all its influence, the U.S. cannot get the UN to focus its attention on terrorism. For decades, the United States has been unable to create any meaningful support for Israel within the UN. International treaties and international institutions that are opposed by America are created without our consent. The only way to prevent this leviathan from getting bigger is to chop off its head. Remove American support for the United Nations and many of these problems will go away.

And let it not be said that Jacques Chirac never put other people's money where his mouth is. Though an ailing Chirac could not make the UN's 2005 World Summit in New York, he showed through his foreign minister, Dominique de Villepin, that he is the tax collector for international government.

Mr. de Villepin joined Brazilian president Lula da Silva and about 300 representatives of the world press corps at a media availability in the basement of the United Nations headquarters. These two leaders, along with the presidents of Spain and Chile, unveiled the Declaration on Innovative Sources of Financing—an initiative to generate new government revenue to be turned over to the United Nations to fight poverty and hunger, a condition President Lula called "the greatest weapon of mass destruction that exists in our world today."

"Creating new financing mechanisms is the ambition we have," said de Villepin, who did not come to New York to speak empty rhetoric. He came to unveil Chirac's plan to implement a global airline tax to fund the UN's poverty program.

One new financing mechanism that "could easily be put into place" according to de Villepin is a "solidarity levy on air tickets," which would make it possible "to garner considerable resources which are stable and long-term." At the direction of President Chirac, France will institute such a proposal in February 2006. The plan is expected to tax passengers on flights departing France and could be as much as 5 euros for economy class and 20 to 25 euros for first-class passengers. Such rates could yield up to 10 billion euros annually, according to French estimates.

President Lagos of Chile announced that beginning January 1, 2006, his administration would institute a two-dollar tax "on all international flights for those leaving Chile to go abroad, whether they are Chilean or foreign nationals." The airline taxes are intended to help France and other countries meet their UN commitment for Official Development Assistance (ODA)— the amount each developed country is expected to provide to the UN to redistribute to poor nations in the name of the Millennium Development Goals. Any American citizen traveling to France will now indirectly pay a global tax to the United Nations. Chirac has stated that his airline tax is only a "pilot program" that he hopes will be taken over by the United Nations, and levies on international air travel will be directly assessed by the UN.

Activists dedicated to global taxation immediately embraced the French initiative. The air ticket levy, said David Hillman of Stamp out Poverty, "should serve as a stepping stone for more ambitious and innovative ways of raising money to fight poverty in the future, such as a currency transaction tax." Jacques Chirac and Dominique de Villepin—the tax collectors for the global welfare state—are on the offensive, and their "ambition for new financing mechanisms" is directly impacting Americans traveling abroad.

International Tax Organization

The United Nations tried to create an International Tax Organization (ITO) in 2002 during the International Conference for Financing and Development in Monterrey, Mexico. Only through the last-minute intervention of conservative watchdogs was the creation of the ITO delayed—not defeated, but delayed. For like other institutions of the United Nations, the ITO will live to see another day, perhaps with a different moniker, but the UN will never give up on an idea it believes has merit.

The proposal for the International Tax Organization was contained in the report of the High-level Panel on Financing for Development, otherwise known as the "Zedillo Report" for its chairman Ernesto Zedillo, former president of Mexico. Kofi Annan praised the panel, which he appointed "to recommend strategies for the mobilization of resources" for the UN and said their report was a "solid piece of work and it has a number of innovative proposals."[27]

The Zedillo Report asked the participants at the International Conference for Financing and Development to "consider the potential benefits of an International Tax Organization." This institution, the report said, would,

- "develop international norms for tax policy and administration";
- "maintain surveillance of tax developments" in member countries;
- "take a lead role in restraining tax competition" among nations;
- "develop procedures for arbitration when frictions develop between countries on tax questions";
- "sponsor a mechanism for multilateral sharing of tax information";
- "develop and secure international agreement on a formula for the unitary taxation of multinationals."[28]

This is the Internal Revenue Service gone global—and it shows just how aggressive the United Nations has become in pushing international taxation. The UN believes it must create an International Tax Organization because taxation is "the principal area of economic policy where international spillover effects are strong but no international organization is yet charged with addressing them."[29] Levying taxes on individuals or corporations could also be accomplished through an ITO, which would be helpful in "securing an adequate international tax source to finance the supply of global public goods,"[30] according to the UN.

Dan Mitchell of the Heritage Foundation argues that the proposed ITO is little more than a way for governments to conspire to keep tax rates artificially high. "By world standards," Mitchell explains, "the U.S. is a low-tax country, and it is clear that an International Tax Organization would undermine our ability to use this advantage to create jobs and growth."[31]

The UN's call for an ITO to conduct tax arbitration between nations shows the danger of the United States joining the World Trade Organization. For the WTO is the model of the global governance apparatus. If nations can put their trust in the WTO to settle grievances on trade matters, why not create an International Tax Organization to arbitrate tax disputes among nations?

When the United States led the charge for the WTO, it failed to see the global forest through the trees. If an International Tax Organization is not created soon, countries like France and others that support the initiative will increase their WTO complaints on tax-related trade issues and argue for a special tax court within the WTO that can then be spun off into its own institution.

The Zedillo Report did not stop at just an International Tax Organization—it also called for an "international agreement on the movement of natural persons,"[32] meaning the UN wants to control America's immigration policies. It also wants to control economic policies related to those who choose to live and work in the United States. As the UN report states, an International Tax Organization would be the perfect institution to undertake the "development, negotiation and operation of international arrangements for the taxation of emigrants."[33]

Full and complete management of the international economy is what the United Nations seeks as evidenced by the Zedillo Report's recommendation to create an "Economic Security Council within the United Nations ... [with] the same standing on international economic matters that the Security Council has with regard to peace and security."[34] Already, Democrats in Congress are more than willing to allow our national defense to be run by the UN Security Council. So there is no doubt that they would be willing to hand the keys to our Treasury Department and Federal Reserve to the secretary-general. And what would a UN Economic Security Council do? The Zedillo Report explains:

> Its tasks would be to monitor the state of the world economy, to supervise interactions among the major policy areas, to provide a strategic framework for policy made in the several international organizations and secure consistency across their policy goals, and to promote intergovernmental dialogue on the evolution of the global economic system.[35]

One of the mistakes the U.S. government makes with respect to the United Nations is to treat it as an ally. It is not. In today's world, and given the offensive the UN has mounted to increase its authority, the organization must be treated as an adversary—one that is persistent, not passive.

As an example, the organization does not rest on the Zedillo Report and hope that the ideas will someday be championed. It ensures they will be discussed until they are implemented. After calling for the creation of an International Tax Organization and a UN Economic Security Council, the report also demanded that the UN "create a global council at the highest political level to provide leadership on issues of global governance."[36]

This is how the United Nations operates—meetings are held; advisory panels are appointed; recommendations for new programs and institutions are made; commissions are formed to endorse the recommendations; summits are organized so world leaders can agree to the formation of more global governing bodies; and working groups are assembled to draft the treaties or documents that will create the organizations.

In other words, the ideas will be rehashed for years—if that is what it takes—until they are successfully implemented. Barry Goldwater's approach that "we begin by not taking [the United Nations] seriously"[37] is no longer applicable. We must take it very seriously.

As former Congressman Bob Barr explained to me, the United Nations "is an organization whose avowed purpose is to supplant national sovereignty with international sovereignty." He says they have been "very good at weaseling their way into to a handful of very, very important, substantive issues," in the United States, in large part because most people in Washington are not paying attention.

But they had better pay attention because the two other major domestic policy areas where the UN intends to stick its nose are in the areas of labor and the environment. Republicans particularly had better pay attention, because these are traditionally two active and effective members of the Democrat coalition. The Zedillo Report recommends that the International Labor Organization be given the authority it needs "to enforce its standards."

International standards for wages and worker safety could easily gain support in Western democracies when viewed through the prism of wanting to help enslaved Chinese laborers or get rid of third-world sweatshops that exploit children. But like so much the UN does, its focus will not be on those who are committing evil. If given a new enforcement mandate, the International Labor Organization is likely to target, among its first priorities, the unionization of Wal-Mart.

The other recommendation of the Zedillo Report is to take the environmental issues that are currently being addressed at the World Trade Organization and spin them off into a new Global Environmental Organization that, like the WTO, would have authority to hold national governments accountable.

World Environmental Organization

When he addressed the UN's Millennium Summit in September 2000, Eduard Shevardnadze, president of Georgia, put his faith fully and completely in the United Nations as the only institution capable of solving the world's emerging problems. As one who formerly served as Mikhail Gorbachev's foreign minister in the communist Soviet Union, Shevardnadze is no stranger to centralized government. His desire to see the UN adopt the policies of the Soviet's good ol' days, is therefore no surprise:

> I therefore believe that global environmental security should be the direct responsibility of the UN and its Security Council. To some degree, world

food security should also become subject to centralized management. The resources and capabilities of the United Nations must dramatically increase.[38]

Five years later, it doesn't look as though the UN Security Council will be issuing resolutions on environmental protection, but Shevardnadze will soon see his dream realized in a slightly different way.

An effort is underway to upgrade the United Nations Environment Program into a full-fledged, stand-alone organization to police the world's environment with the same authority wielded by the World Trade Organization. Wetlands preservation, global warming, and protection of the rain forest will all soon fall under the mandate of a World Environmental Organization.

If you like the Environmental Protection Agency, you'll love the World Environmental Organization. American industries such as oil drilling, commercial fishing, manufacturing, shipping, tourism, land development, and many others are sure to be impacted by an unaccountable international body run by the United Nations. And nobody has done more to advocate the creation of a World Environmental Organization than French president Jacques Chirac. Like Al Gore, who incessantly talked about a "lock box" during the 2000 presidential campaign, Chirac references a global environmental institution in nearly every major speech he makes. A sample:[39]

• Chirac at the UN World Summit on Sustainable Development, Johannesburg, South Africa (September 2, 2002): "To better manage the environment and ensure compliance with the Rio Principles, we need a World Environment Organization."

• Chirac at the Eleventh Ambassador's Conference, Paris, France (August 29, 2003): "We need a world authority able to carry out a global ecological diagnosis, guarantee compliance with environmental protection principles and treaties, and assist the developing countries. This mission should be vested in a United Nations environment agency."

• Chirac at the UN's 58th General Assembly, New York City (September 23, 2003): "Against the chaos of a world shaken by ecological disaster, let us call for a sharing of responsibility, around a United Nations Environment Organization."

• Chirac at a New Year's Greeting for the Diplomatic Corps, Paris, France (January 8, 2004): "In the face of growing ecological hazards an environmental governance should be urgently established on a world scale. Last autumn, France submitted to her partners proposals for creating a United Nations Environment Organization."

• Chirac at Twelfth Ambassador's Conference, Paris, France (August 27, 2004): "We must strengthen global environmental governance organs. The group of States set up at France's instigation to discuss the creation of a United Nations Environment Organization will [soon] submit it proposals."

In 2003, the French sprang into action and proposed a committee be formed to determine how to turn the existing United Nations Environmental Program into what is now being dubbed a United Nations Environmental Organization (UNEO). Twenty-six countries are part of the coalition to create a UN entity that will dictate to other countries what kinds of environmental policies they may or may not have. That coalition includes countries like China, India, Japan, Germany, Indonesia, Brazil, the United Kingdom, and Italy—which are all, by the way, among the top ten water polluters in the world.[40]

A UNEO would be nothing more than a playground for environmental extremists who count among their clan those who want to abolish electricity and flush toilets. The environmental movement has often placed a higher priority on the well-being of rodents and fish than on human beings.

Marc Morano, a reporter for Cybercast News Service who reports extensively on international environmental organizations, told me that the environmental groups that attend UN conferences and summits "want to negate the entire twentieth century, which is a century of technology, prosperity, advancement." They are out to blame the United States for the ills that are suffered in the world and use any resource at their disposal to punish the U.S. Even American environmentalists are willing to sock it to their own country.

As one example, Morano told me that during the United Nations climate conference in Buenos Aires, Argentina, Ken Alex, attorney general for the state of California, showed up to announce his "first-ever climate change litigation against private companies."[41] It is a strategy adopted by organizations such as Greenpeace, Friends of the Earth International, Earthjustice, and others who want to hold private industry responsible for climate change and natural disasters.

Soon, they will have a new enforcement mechanism in a United Nations Environmental Organization and, once again, the United States government and American industry will be wearing the biggest targets. It is a fact to which Morano can attest. "When I was at the UN's climate summit in Argentina," Morano told me, "the United States was getting all these 'awards' from the international groups—like the 'Fossil of the Day Award,' and the U.S. was being bashed continuously."

Kofi Dot Com?

The Internet is simultaneously one of America's great national assets and one of its most generous gifts to the world—and the United Nations wants to control it. In 2003, UN secretary-general Kofi Annan established the Working Group on Internet Governance (WGIG). In the past two years, the group has been meeting in Geneva to build political support and a logistical mechanism for wresting control of the Internet from American hands. "No single Government should have a pre-eminent role in relation to international Internet governance,"[42] the group informed the United States, even though the U.S. created the Internet and generously shared it with the world.

Markus Kummer is the director of the UN's WGIG. He explained that many governments "feel that the United Nations is the natural system of global governance and they hold the view that a UN umbrella would . . . give the necessary political legitimacy to Internet governance."[43] Operating on that belief, the group proposes that a "Global Internet Council" should "take over the functions relating to international Internet governance currently performed by the Department of Commerce of the United States Government."[44]

This Global Internet Council "should be anchored in the United Nations," and should exercise political control over treaties and other agreements related to the Internet; policy issues such as privacy, personal data, and security; and technical control over issues related to the structure of web sites, e-mail addresses, etc.

Such responsibilities currently fall to ICANN—the Internet Corporation for Assigned Names and Numbers—which is a U.S. based organization that manages the Internet under a special agreement with the Department of Commerce. Such a public-private partnership is in keeping with the history of the Internet, which was invented not by Al Gore, but by the Department of Defense in the late 1960s. It started out as a communication system largely for academics, scientists, and researchers. But when the possibilities of the Internet were exposed to entrepreneurs and creative Americans, the Internet exploded.

After America invested its ingenuity and billions of dollars, international ingrates at the UN have knocked on the door of the Department of Commerce demanding to stake their claim in this prize. It is not entirely their fault. They are demanding control of the Internet because the U.S. government has legitimized the United Nations. We have invested in its agencies, tolerated its incompetence, endured its insults, and offered it a home. The United Nations believes, by virtue of the confidence we have shown in it, that it has a right to govern what is ours. Retaining control of the Internet is an unnecessary political struggle in which the United States has, unfortunately, decided to engage. And few people know about it.

One who understands the stakes is Richard Lessner, who represents the Global Internet Governance Alliance, an organization devoted to keeping the Internet in America's hands. Lessner told me that the UN's effort to control the Internet is "rolling downhill and gaining momentum."[45] Unfortunately, he explained, "most Americans are unaware of this major push by the United Nations and the European Union to strip control of the Internet away from the United States and hand it over to some international body under the auspices of the UN."[46]

Although the United States has been generous in sharing the Internet technology and opening it up to the rest of the world, "there's a lot of resentment and envy around the world of the United States' management of the Internet," he explained. Much of that resentment comes from repressive regimes like communist China, Cuba, Venezuela, Iran, North Korea, Syria, Saudi Arabia, and others that see the Internet as a threat to their hold on power. Such nations impose severe restrictions on the content that Internet users in their countries are allowed to see. Web sites that offer political content contrary to the government's view are prohibited; religious content is banned completely in some cases—in others, it is allowed only to the extent that it conforms with national policy.

Personal e-mail communications are also monitored to try to prevent "subversive" activity. The leaders of these countries understand the power of the Internet to open their societies to alternative political viewpoints, which is why one of their biggest complaints is about the amount of "spam" entering their countries via the Internet. "When [these regimes] refer to spam," Lessner explained, "they just mean the free flow of ideas. They don't like the notion that 'subversive' ideas can come into the country and can be accessible to people outside of government control." To allow the UN to exercise authority over the Internet is to give Fidel Castro and Mommar Ghadafi a vote in how it is run.

Cuius regio, eius religio. He who controls the region, controls the religion. The religion of the Internet, under U.S. authority, is freedom, transparency, ingenuity, progress. The web has created new technologies, spawned whole new commercial industries, facilitated the free flow of ideas, brought new efficiencies to government and business, and expanded political dialogue. But the First Church of Kofi is replete with incompetence, bureaucracy, and corruption.

To allow the Internet to fall into the hands of the United Nations would be a mortal sin. Fortunately, there are some in the international community who see the benefit of keeping the Internet in U.S. hands. Carl Bildt, former prime minister of Sweden, wrote in the *International Herald Tribune,*

> It would be profoundly dangerous now to set up an international mechanism, controlled by governments, to take over the running of the Internet. Not only would this play into the hands of regimes bent on limiting the freedom that the Internet can bring, it also risks stifling innovation and ultimately endangering the security of the system.[47]

In the aftermath of the UN's Oil-for-Food scandal, Kofi Annan conceded that he hoped the United Nations would "never have to run that kind programme again," because it was "not a programme that the UN was set up to run."[48] Nor was the United Nations set up to run something like the Internet. It is a medium that has become an integral part of American commerce, communication, and culture. Everyday over the Internet, Americans pay their bills, do their banking, send e-mails to friends and coworkers. Businesses large and small rely on it for purchasing or shipping merchandise. Students use it for research. Libraries store volumes of information on the Internet. Corporations and government agencies have stored private and sensitive information on individuals and programs that cannot be entrusted to an institution with a track record of incompetence.

To give the United Nations control of the Internet would also hand them the power to tax its use. It is an idea that has already been considered by the UN and one they are eager to implement. The potential for mischief is too great.

The United States should prevent the creation of any new institution that would internationalize control over the Internet. But we should also prevent the creation of new global institutions for other purposes as well. They are good for only one thing—undermining the American Republic.

Pistols, Palaces, and Petroleum

The day after Christmas, December 26, 1998, Iraqi vice president Taha Yasin Ramadan threatened the lives of American pilots enforcing the no-fly zones over Iraq. Patrols intended to safeguard repressed minority populations in the north and south of Iraq, Ramadan said, "will be met by Iraqi fire"[1] if believed to enter Iraqi airspace. It was no idle threat. Two days later, Iraqi surface-to-air missiles attacked American pilots patrolling the no-fly zone.

Over the next month, the Iraqis repeatedly fired deadly weapons on American aircraft. It was, in the words of General Anthony Zinni, the commander of U.S. Central Command, "a deliberate onset of repeated attacks against our forces."[2] Saddam Hussein "wants to shoot down an American airplane," Zinni said, and suggested the Iraqi dictator hoped to have "a pilot to parade in Baghdad."[3]

At about the same time young Americans were taking hostile fire by Iraqis, Benon Sevan, a veteran UN bureaucrat and the head of the UN Oil-for-Food program, was taking illegal bribes from Saddam Hussein. By risking their lives enforcing the no-fly zones over Iraq, U.S. pilots were enforcing UN Security Council Resolution 688, which was adopted at the end of the first Gulf War. The U.S. military flew thousands of sorties each year and spent hundreds of millions of dollars to do that which the United Nations wanted done.

Also at about the time that danger was escalating for Americans patrolling the no-fly zones, Kofi Annan's son, Kojo Annan, and a long-time friend of the Annan family, Michael Wilson, were trading on their access to the secretary-general to win a lucrative Oil-for-Food contract for their employer.

This is how the United Nations works. Americans sacrifice their lives and resources for the ideas professed in the UN Charter, while the third-world used car salesmen who run the institution make peace with dictators.

And, as demonstrated by the Oil-for-Food scandal, UN bureaucrats and allies are too often on the receiving end of payoffs from America's enemies.

Those payoffs were exposed on January 25, 2004, when *al Mada*, a newly-liberated newspaper in Baghdad, published a list of 270 people, companies, politicians, and at least one UN official who had accepted bribes from Iraqi dictator Saddam Hussein in the form of valuable oil contracts. Rarely has the power and influence of a free press been displayed as dramatically as it was when *al Mada* unearthed the extent to which the Iraqi dictator was dispensing international "walking around" money.

In exchange for the contracts, these individuals were expected to use their power and influence to advocate the end of international sanctions imposed on Iraq after the first Gulf War. Because it held the currency of the corrupted, Saddam's Ministry of Oil became his diplomatic war room—doling out oil vouchers to those who would gladly serve as a mouthpiece for the Mother of all Madmen. His search began in the UN Security Council. Saddam employed "a savvy public relations campaign and extensive diplomatic effort," explained Charles Duelfer, head of the Iraq Survey Group, "to divide the five permanent members [of the UN Security Council] and foment international public support of Iraq at the UN."[4]

The contracts, or "vouchers," were negotiable instruments that could be exchanged for thousands, sometimes millions of barrels of steeply discounted Iraqi crude oil, which could then be resold on the open market for a handsome profit. The names on the list of voucher recipients were not J.R. Ewing oil tycoons, but rather "non-end users" of oil. As *al Mada* explained, they were names "that have nothing to do with oil, its distribution, storage or sale and that are not known to be interested in oil or to have any affiliation to oil companies."[5]

"A newspaper's duty," Wilbur Storey of the *Chicago Times* once explained, is "to print the news, and raise hell."[6] The editors of *al Mada* did just that. What the newspaper published was a list of prominent but crooked individuals that Iraqi dictator Saddam Hussein used to prop up his brutal regime and undermine international sanctions. Individuals from fifty-two different countries and at least one UN official were named as Friends of Saddam. Many of those participating in the scheme hailed from one of three countries—France, Russia, and China—that are permanent members of the UN Security Council and were instrumental in helping Saddam turn the humanitarian Oil-for-Food program "into a dirty business and a political game to fund his secret purchases of weapons, expensive construction materials for the presidential palaces and mosques, and luxurious items for extravagance."[7] In the process, the editors wrote, Saddam "squandered the homeland's wealth" to buy "loyalty and influence . . . with foreign figures to provide them with crude oil in exchange for helping the regime break free of its international isolation, finance the campaign to lift the economic embargo on it, and brighten its image."[8]

Al Mada was right. Saddam Hussein manipulated a compliant United Nations and pocketed nearly $2 billion from the Oil-for-Food program through kickbacks and illegal surcharges, and another $11 billion by illegally smuggling oil out of the country. It is the biggest scandal in the history of the United Nations, and given the vast sums of money involved, may be, according to Eric Shawn of Fox News, "the biggest financial crime in the history of humankind."[9]

The UN Oil-for-Food program was supposed to provide for the humanitarian needs of 24 million innocent Iraqi citizens—food, clothing, and medicine—while at the same time isolating the regime of Saddam Hussein and preventing him from causing any more trouble in the neighborhood. Like so many projects the UN undertakes, it was a failure. Instead of neutering a brutal dictator, the Oil-for-Food program helped Saddam reinvigorate his economy, stave off a popular revolt, re-arm his military, and enhance his image in the Arab world.

What makes the scandal even more disturbing is the widespread corruption of individuals in many nations throughout the world who were willing to turn a blind eye to the suffering of innocents and enlist themselves as propagandists for one of the most despicable human beings in modern history. This "temporary" program, over the course of seven years, transacted more than $100 billion. More than 2,200 companies from at least 66 nations around the globe paid surcharges on the purchase of oil or gave kickbacks to the Iraqi regime when selling humanitarian goods. Among those who gave themselves to this cause were individuals hailing from Jordan, Egypt, Lebanon, Switzerland, Turkey, Ukraine, Brazil, and forty-five other nations.

As Charles Duelfer of the Iraq Survey Group pointed out, Saddam was trying to win influence in the UN Security Council, which is reflected in the fact that the two countries where most of Iraq's oil was sold were Russia and France—two permanent members of the Security Council. Oil sales to Russia accounted for 30 percent of all oil transactions under the program, while French companies purchased 7 percent of the total Oil-for-Food sales.

In addition to establishing valuable economic ties to countries influential within the UN, Saddam showered individual politicians and prominent activists with oil vouchers that could be traded for handsome sums. Among those individuals in Russia or France were Gennady Zyuganov, head of the Russian Communist Party; Vladimir Zhirinovsky, the ultra-nationalist who founded the Liberal Democratic Party; Alexander Voloshin, chief of staff for Russian president Vladimir Putin; and Charles Pasqua, former French interior minister.

George Galloway, a member of the British Parliament and one of the fiercest critics of the sanctions on Iraq, was identified by the Volcker Commission as having received vouchers—either directly or through an intermediary—for 18 million barrels of oil. Galloway has vehemently denied the charges, even appearing before a U.S. Senate investigative committee in which he gave animated testimony.

One of the names that immediately caught the attention of *al Mada* editors was Benon Sevan, a forty-year veteran bureaucrat of the United Nations. The man entrusted to care for the humanitarian needs of starving Iraqi women and children, the powder blue savior from that oasis of compassion we call the United Nations, was on the take.

Once *al Mada's* story was published and translated for the English-speaking world, hell was indeed raised—at least for Kofi Annan, Benon Sevan, and their cronies at the United Nations. The paper's scoop made headlines around the world and rocked the House of Hammarskjöld. It led to five separate investigations in the U.S. Congress; a vote in the House of Representatives to slash UN funding; the appointment of a special investigator; terminations of key UN employees; an international rift in the Annan family; and calls for the secretary-general's resignation.

The scandal caused a partisan split in Washington with skeptical Republicans commencing investigations into what Congressman Chris Shays said was "probably the biggest rip-off in the history of rip-offs."[10] Senator Norm Coleman said the Oil-for-Food program had turned the United Nations into a "sinkhole of corruption."[11]

But Democrats, sensing that their beloved United Nations was vulnerable to the scandal, circled the wagons and urged caution. Lead by Representative Dennis Kucinich of Ohio, twenty Democrats and one Independent sent a letter to Secretary of State Colin Powell expressing their support for Kofi Annan, hailing his "honesty and integrity." Any attack on their friend the "Nobel Peace laureate," they said, was "disgraceful and premature."[12]

Representative Jose Serrano of New York charged Republicans with starting "another one of their UN-bashing frenzies" and called on them to stop their "preemptive hate campaign against Annan and the UN." After all,

Serrano noted, Kofi Annan is "one of the most distinguished UN Secretaries General the world has ever known."[13] Given that Kofi Annan is in a group that includes a Nazi and the disgraced Boutros Boutros-Ghali, that is high praise indeed.

Richard Holbrooke, U.S. ambassador to the United Nations under Bill Clinton, told the House International Relations Committee that "due to a lack of American engagement, the institution is hijacked by states whose practices are anathema to all that the UN stands for."[14]

Democrats were placing their faith in an institution that had just committed a historic breach of trust. They were taking in stride the fact that UN officials were accepting bribes from a regime that attempted the assassination of a former American president.

Too many Democrats are breaking their bond with Lady Liberty only to cavort and carouse in Kofi Annan's underworld. It is a dark and pessimistic place. And the corruption and mismanagement that have been uncovered in the Oil-for-Food scandal offer only a portion of the evidence as to why the United Nations cannot be trusted with any semblance of responsibility on the world stage.

Laying the Groundwork for Oil-for-Food

Just after midnight on August 2, 1990, three Iraqi divisions of Republican Guard penetrated the border of neighboring Kuwait and effortlessly marched to Kuwait City, causing death and destruction along the way. A few days later, Saddam Hussein claimed Kuwait as Iraq's "19th Province"—a nation to which he laid historical claim. Saddam desperately wanted access to the valuable Kuwaiti oil fields and ports along the Persian Gulf.

President George H.W. Bush immediately decided that Saddam's aggression would not stand. He convened his talented foreign policy team, who began to assemble the troops, build a coalition of foreign nations, and put the issue on the agenda at the UN Security Council.

Four days after Saddam's army invaded Kuwait, the Security Council adopted Resolution 661, imposing trade and economic sanctions on Iraq supported by more than 150 countries.[15] What followed was Operation Desert Storm, commenced on January 17, 1991, by the United States and a broad coalition of international partners to liberate the tiny nation of Kuwait. The war lasted forty-three days, ending on February 28. UN Security Council Resolution 687 served as the formal cease-fire agreement and demanded that Iraq "shall unconditionally accept the destruction, removal, or rendering harmless" of biological, chemical, and nuclear weapons and their components. The resolution also called for on-site inspections of Iraq's weapons facilities and the establishment within the Security Council of a committee—known as the "661 Committee"—to monitor the importation by Iraq of goods for humanitarian purposes and "essential civilian needs."

In the years that followed, the sanctions against Iraq remained in place and could have been lifted had Saddam cooperated by disarming and allowing weapons inspections, but the dictator refused.

The sanctions, along with Saddam's repressive leadership, were taking their toll on innocent Iraqis who were in need of food and medicine. By 1995, the Iraqi economy was in shambles. Former CIA investigator Charles Duelfer reported that from 1989 to 1995, per capita GDP fell from $2,304 to $495 and inflation rose to 387 percent.[16] In an attempt to provide help to the Iraqi population, on April 14, 1995, the UN Security Council adopted Resolution 986 creating the UN's Oil-for-Food program. For thirteen months, Saddam refused to cooperate. Finally, in May 1996, Iraq signed a Memorandum of Understanding that would implement the UN Oil-for Food program. It was intended as a "temporary measure"[17] that lasted for seven years and ended only because Saddam was forcibly removed from power in 2003 by the U.S.-led coalition.

The Oil-for-Food program was supposed "to provide for the humanitarian needs of the Iraqi people"[18]—and by most accounts, it did help reduce the immediate problem of starvation by distributing a monthly ration consisting of sugar, rice, infant formula, and tea, which boosted the average Iraqi's caloric consumption over the course of six years. Unfortunately, however, it did more to enrich Saddam, his military, and the UN bureaucracy than it did to improve the lives of 24 million impoverished Iraqis.

In fact, as Duelfer notes, in the four years following the implementation of the Oil-for-Food program, Iraq's gross domestic product (GDP) increased from $10.6 billion to $33 billion; its oil production more than doubled; and the budget for the Military Industrialization Commission grew from $7.8 million to $500 million by 2003.[19] "In short," Duelfer noted, after the implementation of the Oil-for-Food program, "the state of the Iraqi economy no longer threatened Saddam's hold on power in Iraq."[20] Had the Oil-for-Food program not been implemented, regime change might have come about at the hands of the Iraqis themselves.

Despite the sanctions, Resolution 986 authorized nations to buy up to $1 billion worth of Iraq's surplus oil every 90 days as long as there was appropriate "transparency" for each transaction and the money was paid into an escrow account established and controlled by the UN secretary-general—who at the time was the hapless Boutros Boutros-Ghali. Twice in two years, the Security Council raised the maximum limits on the amount of oil that Iraq could sell—the second time declaring that there would be no limit at all. That action not only increased Saddam's leverage to skim even more money from the program, but lessened the impact of sanctions against Iraq.

The proceeds from the oil sales were to be used to provide the civilian population of Iraq with "medicine, health supplies, foodstuffs, and materials and supplies for essential civilian needs."[21] The secretary-general, working with the Iraqi government, was to ensure that the supplies made it to the Iraqi people who needed them. A portion of the proceeds would also pay compensation to Kuwaiti victims who were so brutally tortured by Saddam's vicious army. But like the oil export aspect of the program, the Security Council liberated many of the restrictions on imports into Iraq, again making it easier for Iraqi officials to manipulate the system.

In the process, the United Nations allotted itself 2.2 percent of the billions of dollars in oil proceeds to administer the program. Over the life of the Oil-for-Food program, the United Nations paid itself a hefty $1.4 billion in administrative fees—an average of $200 million per year. UN officials found no shame in accepting a billion-dollar compensation package for a program that was mismanaged and corrupted.

Setting up the Oil-for-Food Program

In order to set up the Oil-for-Food program, three steps needed to be taken to establish the infrastructure that would run it. A bank was needed to hold the escrow funds and two companies were required to inspect the exports of oil and the importation of humanitarian goods.

These three important but not terribly complicated decisions were all botched from the beginning. The Independent Inquiry Committee (IIC)—the investigative commission headed by former Federal Reserve chairman Paul Volcker—outlined in its first report that the United Nations was playing politics from the start—from Secretary-General Boutros Boutros-Ghali on down. Boutros-Ghali wanted a French bank to administer the escrow account through which billions of dollars would be funneled, and he solicited names of financial institutions from the French ambassador.

Saddam's regime wanted a bank from a country whose government was lenient on Iraqi sanctions. Knowing the French could be counted on in this regard, the Iraqis compiled a list of three French banks and gave it to Boutros-Ghali to choose. Among those on Saddam's wish list was Banque Nationale de Paris (BNP), which eventually won the contract.

But before Saddam's favored bank was chosen, the UN assembled its own list. Over the life of the program, nearly $65 billion of oil would be sold through the program along with $35 billion worth of humanitarian goods. At one point, the UN's file had grown to seventeen major international banks as candidates to manage the Oil-for-Food escrow account. Each of them was ranked according to several criteria such as asset base, potential risk factors, pricing, and credit profile. BNP—Saddam's choice—ranked dead last.

Though BNP did not measure up to the other institutions, it made the cut and remained on the short list that was presented to the secretary-general "because of the preference of the Iraq Government,"[22] according to the Independent Inquiry Committee headed by Volcker. Also on the short list were two American, one German, and two Swiss banks. The U.S. delegation objected to any Swiss bank, believing the country's strict banking laws made it difficult to monitor the transactions. They also feared that funds could be manipulated into Saddam Hussein's personal accounts, which were held in Swiss banks.

From the short list of escrow managers, Saddam vetoed all American banks. Despite the fact that Saddam Hussein invaded Kuwait and forced a war, stockpiled weapons, was shooting at American and British pilots patrolling the no-fly zone, and was starving his own people, it was his approval the United Nations sought. In fact, as Michael Soussan, an Oil-for-Food program coordinator said, "UN leaders approached the implementation of the Oil-for-Food Program with more distrust toward the United Kingdom and the United States than toward the regime of Saddam Hussein."[23]

In a classic case of the inmates running the asylum, when it came time to select the bank, Secretary-General Boutros Boutros-Ghali called the Iraqi government and asked them, "What is your choice?"[24] Saddam Hussein was allowed to choose the business that would help impose sanctions against him. Disneyland justice.

The Iraqis chose the French firm—Banque Nationale de Paris (BNP), though it ranked at the bottom of a list of seventeen banks originally compiled by the UN. Boutros-Ghali was more than happy to accommodate and give the Iraqis what he called "maximum concession"[25] in the choice.

The next step in the process was to employ an inspection firm that would verify the amount and type of oil that was being exported out of Iraq through two pre-selected pipelines. There were two serious competitors for the contract—Societe Generale de Surveillance S.A. (SGS), a Swiss firm, and Saybolt Eastern Hemisphere BV, a Dutch company.

Joseph Stephanides, a twenty-five-year veteran of the United Nations, worked in the UN Department of Political Affairs and played a key role in contracting the company that would oversee the exportation of oil from Iraq. From the start, Stephanides expressed his desire to see the contract go to Saybolt, though its bid was 25 percent more expensive than SGS's proposal.

With Stephanides as an advocate inside the UN, Saybolt was able to manipulate the bidding process, get a second chance to submit a lower bid, and eventually win the contract. The Volcker Commission concluded that the process by which Saybolt won the contract was "neither fair nor transparent in its operation." Stephanides became the first casualty of the Oil-for-Food investigation when he was fired in June 2005 for "serious misconduct."[26]

Less than six months later, Stephanides was reinstated after the UN's Joint Disciplinary Committee found that while he did in fact violate UN staff rules, he was treated unfairly by being fired. The committee gave him back his job and $200,000 to ease his pain and suffering.

It was also revealed in a later report produced by the Volcker Commission that Alexander Yakovlev, a twenty-year veteran of the UN, "purposefully participated in a corrupt scheme to solicit a bribe from SGS."[27] Yakovlev was also involved in the selection process for the oil inspection company. The Volcker Commission was careful to point out that it had no evidence that SGS paid Yakovlev, but the commission did find "persuasive evidence" that Yakovlev had a long history of taking bribes from companies doing business with the United Nations. The Volcker Commission concluded that Yakovlev accepted nearly $1 million into an offshore account from companies that were awarded $79 million in contracts from the United Nations. Clearly, Kofi Annan was not presiding over the most ethical UN administration in history.

The third component in establishing the Oil-for-Food program was hiring a company to inspect the goods that would be permitted into the country. This was an important aspect of the program. The U.S. and Britain were vigilant on this front to ensure that goods entering Iraq met the humanitarian purpose for which they were intended and did not have military value. In the ensuing years, through rigorous oversight, the American delegation to the UN prevented numerous shipments of goods into Iraq that could have been used for military purposes.

The UN procurement department accepted for consideration the bids of five companies for this contract, but ultimately it boiled down to two firms—Bureau Veritas of France and Lloyd's Register Inspection Ltd. of Great Britain. While Veritas had presented a much lower bid, by about 25 percent than did Lloyd's, Joseph Stephanides once again preferred Lloyd's and intervened to Lloyd's benefit. Lloyd's eventually won the contract, in a process that the Volcker Commission said was "tainted" by Stephanides's intervention.

The process was "replete with convincing and uncontested evidence" that the manner in which the three contractors were chosen "did not conform to established financial and competitive bidding rules,"[28] the committee wrote. The Volcker Commission also concluded that the record "clearly and repeatedly demonstrates" that the selection of these three contractors "did not meet reasonable standards of fairness and transparency."[29] The selection of the three contracting firms was old-fashioned City Hall graft on a global scale.

Many criticized the Volcker Commission as a kinder and gentler investigative team—and there is merit to that argument. But the significance of Volcker's findings in this area should not be overlooked. The selection process of these three firms shows how easily career bureaucrats at the UN can manipulate the system, and the lack of accountability or professional management within the UN bureaucracy.

The United Nations comprised more than 350 agencies, departments, commissions, and institutions—and dozens more are planned or are in the process of being created. Most are financed with American tax dollars and staffed with second-rate bureaucrats who cut their teeth in governments where corruption is the norm. They range from the well known like the UN Security Council, to the unnecessary like the World Tourism Organization, to the completely ridiculous like the International Union for the Protection of New Varieties of Plants.

Each of these agencies or programs is susceptible to the same mismanagement and fraud that has plagued the Oil-for-Food program. For example, in just the past few years, there have been reports of embezzlement of millions of dollars at the World Meteorological Association; sexual impropriety in both the peacekeeping and refugee departments; and reports of bribes at the World Intellectual Property Organization, to name a few. The United Nations has not submitted itself to a system-wide audit and only recently created the Office of Oversight Inspection. If it were to submit to a comprehensive audit, American taxpayers would likely find that the 22 percent of UN operations they are funding are being wasted or stolen or worse.

The Case of Benon Sevan

A native of Cyprus, Benon Sevan worked for the United Nations for forty years, holding numerous positions during that time, including two years as deputy head of the Department of Political Affairs and as an assistant secretary-general in the Department of Administration and Management. He was appointed executive director of the Oil-for-Food program in October 1997 and remained in the post through 2004. From the start, Sevan was working hand-in-glove with the Iraqis and helped them by convincing the Security Council to divert $300 million in Oil-for-Food money to upgrade Iraqi oil facilities. The money was supposed to serve humanitarian purposes.

Just days after the Security Council granted the Iraqis their wish, Benon Sevan was on a plane to Iraq where he would meet with Saddam's vice president and oil minister. Both men served on the Command Council, a group of high-ranking officials—to include Saddam Hussein—that decided to whom oil would be sold.

During his meeting with them, Sevan sought an "allocation" of oil—a commodity contract in which the holder has the right to purchase a specific amount of oil at a specified price. This was done in the name of one of Sevan's associates who ran the African Middle East Petroleum Company (AMEP). Iraqi officials, the Volcker Report says, were more than happy to accommodate Sevan as they viewed him as "a man of influence." Though neither Sevan nor AMEP were "end users" of oil, the Command Council approved an allocation of 1.8 million barrels of oil, which AMEP then turned around and sold for a tidy profit of $300,000. Sevan's associates at AMEP were able to get an allocation of oil and resell it despite the fact that AMEP was not registered with or approved by the United Nations, a condition of the Oil-for-Food program.

For three years, this practice continued. Sevan—who graduated from the Hillary Rodham School of Investment—received allocations of 14.3 million barrels of oil. He and his cronies at AMEP actually took possession of 7.3 million barrels from Iraq and turned it around for a $1.5 million profit. At one point, Sevan's associate, AMEP, even paid an illegal surcharge of $160,000 to Iraqi authorities outside the scope of the UN Oil-for-Food program.

117

In return for his ill-gotten retirement fund, Benon Sevan did the Iraqis' bidding. In October 1999, and February 2000, he addressed the Security Council and asked that $300 million—which was intended to feed hungry children—be diverted to rebuild the Iraqi oil infrastructure. It worked. On March 31, 2000, the UN Security Council adopted Resolution 1293, allowing up to $600 million to be used for Iraqi oil infrastructure and spare parts—just what Saddam ordered.

Sevan's UN financial disclosure forms, as detailed by the Volcker Report, indicate that from 1999 to 2003, he received $160,000 in four installments from an elderly aunt living in Cyprus. In fact, it was bribe money (roughly $150,000) that was made possible by the oil vouchers he accepted from Saddam Hussein. He was taking these bribes despite the fact that he and his wife were both earning good salaries from the UN. When Sevan took over the Oil-for-Food program, he was earning $130,000 annually, while his wife was making $70,000—both salaries were tax-free and included allowances and benefits.[30]

The arrogance of life-long UN bureaucrats is evident in Benon Sevan. Their diplomatic immunity and tax-free salaries give them a sense of entitlement they don't deserve. Most of them are nothing more than international paper pushers who instruct the rest of us on how we should live.

Median household income in the United States in 2003 was $43,318, yet Sevan was earning five times that amount. The United Nations paid Benon Sevan and his wife in just three months what it took the average American all year to earn. And the average American had to pay taxes on his income, where Sevan did not. In spite of all those advantages, Sevan was still living well beyond his means. The Volcker Report explained:

> With a combined take-home pay of about $14,000 per month, the Sevans' finances were frequently stretched thin from the monthly burden of funding two residences, debt obligations, credit card charges, and related living expenses. During much of the period, the monthly balances in their checking accounts hovered at or near zero, as their monthly expenditures more than kept pace with their monthly incomes. This caused frequent overdrafts . . . and an inability to accumulate further savings.[31]

Cry me a river. When the Iraq war began in March 2003, the one-time death gratuity paid to the spouse of a U.S. soldier killed liberating Iraqis from Saddam's oppression was less than what Benon Sevan was taking home every month—living the high life in New York City. He had no problem accepting—perhaps he even thought he was entitled to—Saddam's blood money.

Benon Sevan was in charge of a $100 billion project. As director of the Oil-for-Food program, he had to oversee sales and purchases of billions of dollars of Iraq oil; sales and purchases of billions of dollars worth of humanitarian goods; hundreds of millions of dollars in monthly cash flows; banking records; escrow agents; exchange rates; and numerous other financial details. Yet in a period of 22 months, the Sevans' personal bank accounts were overdrawn 198 times![32] The man was not only corrupt; he was wholly unqualified.

During the course of the investigation, while still working for the UN, Sevan tried to impede journalistic and independent inquiries into the matter by sending letters to companies who did work for the Oil-for-Food program telling them that all documents related to OFF "shall be the property of the United Nations, shall be treated as confidential and shall be delivered only to United Nations authorized officials."[33] The Volcker Commission found that Benon Sevan breached the UN Charter and UN staff regulations in at least four different ways. His actions constituted a "grave and continuing conflict of interest, were ethically improper, and seriously undermined the integrity of the United Nations."[34]

Despite that, the UN found it only appropriate to take $300,000 out of the Oil-for-Food account to pay Benon Sevan's legal bills. They were forced to reverse that decision only after Iraqi officials, with the support of the Americans and British, objected.

Kofi, Kojo, and Cotecna

Throughout the Oil-for-Food investigation, Kofi Annan faced intense criticism. First, as the man in charge of the United Nations and having the final authority on the Oil-for-Food program, Annan was seen by some as an oblivious dunce—a man who could spend a week in hell and not find sin. Columnist Dale McFeatters wrote that Kofi Annan was "willfully inattentive to the point of negligence" and "stunningly incurious" when trouble surfaced.[35]

By others, he was pegged as the devil's accomplice—a CEO who preferred to look the other way while corruption surrounded him. In addition, Kofi Annan, along with his son Kojo, were the targets of intense scrutiny to determine if the secretary-general was personally involved in steering a valuable $10 million per year contract to Cotecna, the inspection services firm that employed Kojo Annan.

Cotecna is a Swiss firm run by Elie Massey and his son Robert that replaced Lloyd's Register as the inspector of the humanitarian imports into Iraq. Cotecna carried its own baggage, having been under investigation for allegedly paying kickbacks to the family of Prime Minister Benazir Bhutto as the price to win business with the government of Pakistan.

From 1995 through 1998, Cotecna employed Kojo Annan, and it was during this time that the company was awarded the UN contract for the Oil-for-Food program to inspect humanitarian goods entering Iraq. While Cotecna won the contract on the basis that it was the lowest bidder, it was only days later that the company raised its price—a move that should have sparked a new bidding process.

After Kofi Annan was sworn in as secretary-general on January 1, 1997, Kojo's career blossomed; he received two promotions within two months of his father being sworn in as the head of the United Nations. After 1998, Kojo continued to receive payments from Cotecna through February 2004 while he worked for them as a consultant. It was a sweet deal for Kojo. He was paid $2,500 per month and only had to work seven days each month— the equivalent of $96,000 per year for a young man who had only recently graduated from college. Kojo originally got the job with the help of Michael Wilson, a family friend of the Annans and a vice president for Cotecna.

The media learned of Kojo Annan's employment with Cotecna as early as January 1999, which presented a political problem for both Kofi and Kojo. So, "at the beginning of 1999, following the award of the contract, Cotecna and Kojo Annan took steps to conceal the fact of their continuing relationship."[36] Though Kojo was still on Cotecna's payroll, the company made it more difficult to "follow the money." They made payments to Kojo through two different companies affiliated with Cotecna and deposited the monies into a Swiss bank account controlled by a friend of Kojo Annan. Based on records Kojo Annan surrendered to the Independent Inquiry Committee, Cotecna paid him as much as $582,000 during the course of his relationship with the company.

Kofi Annan knew his son worked for Cotecna, a company with which he was also familiar, as Cotecna sought UN contracts when Kofi served as the controller of the United Nations. Annan twice met with Elie Massey before Cotecna was awarded the contract for inspection of humanitarian goods into Iraq in December 1998, a fact he misrepresented to the IIC before being forced to admit to the encounters. The first meeting was one month after Kofi was sworn in as secretary-general during the World Economic Forum in Davos, Switzerland.

The meeting is interesting for this reason: Kofi Annan did not know Elie Massey, though he knew his son worked for him at Cotecna. Yet Kofi Annan took time out of what was a very busy schedule, within weeks of becoming secretary-general, to meet with an unknown businessman. In other words, Kofi Annan's schedule that day in Switzerland included meetings with President Hosni Mubarak of Egypt, Prime Minister Benjamin Netanyahu of Israel, the minister of defense for Portugal, the crown prince and princess of Luxembourg, the president of Hungary, and his son's boss.

Kofi Annan met a second time with Elie Massey before the Cotecna contract was awarded, this time in a private setting at UN headquarters in New York. The meeting was facilitated by Kojo Annan, and because it was private, there is no record of what was discussed. Both Massey and Annan say they talked about a lottery scheme for the United Nations, an idea that was never acted upon. Annan also met with Massey once after the awarding of the Oil-for-Food contract to Cotecna. The meetings were described by Annan's chief of staff, Mark Malloch Brown, as "innocent encounters"[37] when he took a page out of the Clinton playbook and leaked the information ahead of the Volcker Report's release.

Despite the circumstances that clearly show a relationship between Kofi Annan and the CEO of Cotecna—and evidence that Kojo Annan facilitated at least one meeting between his father and his employer—the Volcker Commission let Kofi Annan off the hook. On March 29, 2005, the Independent Inquiry Committee issued the second installment of its findings on the Oil-for-Food program. "There is no evidence," the report stated, "that the selection of Cotecna in 1998 was subject to any affirmative or improper influence of the Secretary-General in the bidding or selection process." It went on to conclude that "the evidence is not reasonably sufficient to show that the Secretary-General knew that Cotecna had submitted a bid on the humanitarian inspection contract in 1998." This is where Volcker ran into trouble.

Many believed that short of Kofi Annan prostrating himself before the world and pleading guilty, Volcker would not travel where the evidence was leading him. In writing his conclusions, Volcker took the Mark Twain approach. When he started his career as reporter, Twain was cautioned by his editor never to write anything to which he could not personally attest. Heeding the advice, Twain covered his next assignment—a local social event—and upon returning to his office, he submitted the following for publication in the paper:

> A woman giving the name of Mrs. James Jones, who is reported to be one of the society leaders of the city, is said to have given what purported to be a party yesterday to a number of alleged ladies. The hostess claims to be the wife of a reputed attorney.

Without a signed affidavit from God Almighty, Volcker was not willing to suggest impropriety on Kofi Annan's part. The secretary-general took that lead and ran with it. Kofi Annan immediately took to the podium in the UN briefing room and declared that "the inquiry has cleared me of any wrong-doing."[38] "After so many distressing and untrue allegations have been made against me, this exoneration by the independent inquiry obviously comes as a great relief,"[39] Annan said.

The media, as they usually do, echoed Kofi's assessment. "Kofi Annan Cleared in Corruption Probe," blared the headline in the *Washington Post*.[40] But not everybody on Volcker's team was as certain. An IIC investigator, Mark Peith, responded to Annan's claims, saying "we did not exonerate Kofi Annan. We should not brush this off. A certain mea culpa would have been appropriate."[41]

But there was no way Kofi Annan would give a mea culpa. When asked during a press conference if the scandal had taken its toll on his leadership and if he would resign, the soft-spoken diplomat replied "hell, no." After the Volcker Report was issued, Annan was emboldened. Two weeks later before a group of former UN spokesmen, Annan laid the blame for the Oil-for-Food fiasco at the feet of the Americans and the British. "The bulk of the money that Saddam made came out of smuggling outside the Oil-for-Food programme, and it was on the American and British watch," he charged.[42]

It's the kind of tactic we've seen again and again from Kofi Annan. When his back is against the wall he attacks fiercely and unfairly. But it was not long before more questions were raised about Annan himself.

Two months after the Volcker Report was issued, new evidence surfaced that cast doubt on Volcker's findings and once again put the secretary-general in the spotlight. On June 14, 2005, the *New York Times* reported the details of two newly discovered e-mails written in 1998 by Michael Wilson, Annan family friend and a Cotecna executive, that suggest Kofi Annan not only knew about Cotecna's bid for the lucrative inspection contract, but supported it. "We had a brief discussion with the SG [Secretary-General] and his entourage," the first e-mail stated, and "[were told] that we could count on their support."[43]

The Volcker Commission did find that Kofi Annan failed to act properly when he learned that a UN contract was awarded to a company for which his son worked. The commission wrote in its report:

> In light of [media reports] and the complaint of a conflict of interest because of Kojo Annan's employment, as well as the published information concerning the alleged illicit payments to the Bhutto family, the inquiry initiated by the Secretary-General was inadequate, and the Secretary-General should have referred the matter to an appropriate United Nations department for a thorough and independent investigation. Had there been such an investigation of these allegations, it is unlikely that Cotecna would have been awarded renewals of its contract with the United Nations.[44]

It was a diplomatic slap on the wrist for Kofi Annan.

The IIC reserved harsher judgment for the secretary-general's son and his employer. "Kojo Annan," Volcker concluded, "actively participated in efforts by Cotecna to conceal the true nature of its continuing relationship with him." They found that Kojo Annan "was not forthcoming" and "failed to cooperate fully" with the Independent Inquiry Committee. The IIC also found that "Cotecna has made false statements to the public, the United Nations, and the Committee."[45]

It may never be known conclusively if Kofi Annan steered a lucrative contract to his son's employer or if Kofi Annan or other UN employees committed crimes, because as the Oil-for-Food investigation commenced, so did the document destruction in Kofi Annan's office.

Beginning in April 2004 and continuing for nine months, three years of files were destroyed at the order of Iqbal Riza, Kofi Annan's chief of staff at the time. The document destruction began the day after the UN Security Council authorized the Independent Inquiry Committee to commence an investigation into the Oil-for-Food program. The files that were destroyed were from the years 1997 through 1999—prime years of the Oil-for-Food program.

There were no copies kept. Undoubtedly, those files contained information that would have shed light on what happened and who should be held accountable. Just ten days before Riza began destroying documents, he had written to UN agency chiefs to "take all necessary steps to collect, preserve and secure files, records and documents . . . relating to the Oil-for-Food programme."[46] Mr. Riza conveniently retired from the UN the same day he informed the Volcker Committee that the documents had been destroyed.

The Volcker Committee found that Iqbal Riza "acted imprudently" when he "permitted documents of potential relevance to the Committee's investigation to be shredded by his secretarial staff during the pendency of the Committee's investigation."[47]

The Right Man for the Job?

On April 21, 2004, under increasing pressure, Kofi Annan appointed Paul Volcker to lead the Independent Inquiry Committee (IIC) into the United Nations Oil-for-Food Programme. Having served nearly thirty years in government—at the Treasury Department and the Federal Reserve Bank of New York, before he served two terms as the chairman of the Federal Reserve System—Volcker was respected in Washington. "I hold Volcker in very high regard,"[48] said Representative Howard Coble of North Carolina.

But in this instance, Volcker was a neutered tiger, and the respect he earned over his career was overshadowed by widespread skepticism about whether or not he had the tools or the stomach to get to the bottom of this scandal. Coble tempered his faith in Volcker with an indictment of the UN. "Unfortunately, I do not have the same sterling endorsement for the United Nations,"[49] he commented, and went on to say that Kofi Annan should have picked somebody else to run the investigation—somebody more independent.

Kofi Annan handcuffed Volcker from the start. The IIC was a UN-created investigation. Volcker was appointed by Annan himself—whose actions were under investigation—and the operation was funded with $30 million from the Oil-for-Food fund—money entrusted to the United Nations but belonging to the Iraqi people. In Volcker's first installment of the Oil-for-Food report, he admitted that he and Kofi made up the rules. "The Committee's investigation proceeds on the authority of the terms of reference agreed upon between its Chairman and the Secretary-General of the United Nations."[50]

Volcker's ability to conduct a credible investigation was further called into question when it was discovered that he was associated with the United Nations Association of the United States (UNA-USA)—a highly influential non-governmental organization (NGO). From 2000 to 2004, Volcker was listed by the group as a member of its board of directors. The group describes itself as an "organization that supports the work of the United Nations."[51]

But UNA-USA does more than just support the UN. It is one of the leading agitators for yielding American sovereignty to a stronger United Nations. Through its Model United Nations program, the group targets high school students and plants the belief that the United Nations is more important than the United States in world affairs. UNA-USA is a driving force behind the creation of the International Criminal Court (ICC) and vigorously advocates U.S. ratification of the Law of the Sea Treaty, which would give the United Nations control over the world's oceans and their natural resources.

It was not only Volcker's independence that was questioned, but that of at least one of his staff. Anna Di Lellio was the director of communications for the IIC before being forced to step down due to incendiary remarks she made to the *Guardian* in 2002 that were highlighted by the Heritage Foundation's Nile Gardiner in a column he penned for *National Review*. In her comments, Di Lellio suggested that George W. Bush and the United States were greater threats than Osama bin Laden.

> I see the major threats coming from ourselves, rather than the east. I find deeply unsettling both the ascendance of George Bush and his puppeteers to the U.S. government, and the mix of self-serving hypocrisy and incompetence prevailing in European governments. I don't like it that the two nations whose citizenship I hold, Italy and the U.S., have leased their institutions to a couple of families. With defenders like W. and Berlusconi, largely unchecked by a sycophantic media, who needs bin Laden to destroy culture, personal freedom, respect for other human beings, integrity, and the rule of law—all the things that make our life worthwhile?[52]

And in the end, it was Volcker who saved Kofi Annan's job. Annan was most vulnerable where his son was concerned—on the issue of the Cotecna contract. Did Kofi Annan influence it as a way to help his son? Did he allow himself to be used by Kojo while maintaining plausible deniability? Or was Kofi Annan completely oblivious to how he was being used by his son? Those questions were hotly debated in the Independent Inquiry Committee, and in an interview with Maggie Farley of the *Los Angeles Times*, Volcker conceded that "I felt uncomfortably" that the fate of the secretary-general was in his hands. Farley reported,

> Hours before the publication of Volcker's report in September assessing Annan's culpability, the U.N. chief and his lawyer asked Volcker to change

language about business dealings by Kojo Annan that they thought could force his father's resignation. Volcker agreed.[53]

But Robert Parton, one of Volcker's investigators, resigned from the committee in protest believing that the final report was too lenient on Annan. When a committee member told the press that Parton resigned because his work was finished, Parton issued a statement saying, "contrary to recent published reports, I resigned my position as senior investigative counsel for the IIC not because my work was complete, but on principle."[54]

Throughout the Oil-for-Food investigation, many Republicans expressed concern that Mr. Volcker did not have "subpoena power"—the authority to compel testimony from reluctant witnesses and force individuals or businesses to hand over documents. Critics of the United Nations are rightly eager to see those responsible for corrupting the Oil-for-Food program brought to justice. But in their desire for justice, they are calling for a dangerous precedent to be set. "The fact that [Volcker] doesn't have subpoena power, he doesn't have a grand jury, he can't compel testimony, he can't compel production of documents and witnesses and documents that are located in other countries might be beyond his reach—those are tremendous handicaps," complained Jack Danforth, former U.S. ambassador to the United Nations.[55]

But do we Americans really want to entrust the secretary-general of the United Nations or his self-appointed designee with the authority to breach the Fourth Amendment rights of our citizens against unreasonable searches and seizures? Though Paul Volcker is a U.S. citizen, in his capacity as chairman of the Independent Inquiry Committee, he was acting as an agent of the United Nations. To give Volcker the kinds of tools some requested would be to give the United Nations the authority to subpoena U.S. citizens and haul them before a UN tribunal—among the very concerns cited when President Bush refused to agree to the International Criminal Court.

In practical terms, subpoena power for the Volcker Commission was unnecessary other than to satisfy curiosities. To suggest that Paul Volcker needed additional legal authority to make a proper assessment of the United Nations is like saying a vice cop who walks into a house of ill repute needs a search warrant to figure out what's going on behind closed bedroom doors. It should be obvious.

The Oil-for-Food program was corrupted and mismanaged. UN bureaucrats are unaccountable and open to political payoffs. The French can't be trusted. The Russians were in bed with Saddam. We knew all that before Volcker even began his investigation.

The real question is what are U.S. policymakers going to do with the information contained in Volcker's conclusions? He found that "far too much initiative was left to the Iraqi regime in the Programme's design and subsequent implementation." Will this finding be heeded the next time the Security Council imposes sanctions? The Independent Inquiry Committee concluded that there was "a grievous absence of effective auditing and management controls" and "serious instances of illicit, unethical, and corrupt behavior within the United Nations."[56]

As comprehensive as Volcker's examination was, it only examined the Oil-for-Food program—a tiny piece of the overall United Nations puzzle. The case of Alexander Yakovlev is instructive. Though Volcker found no evidence that Yakovlev accepted a bribe for an Oil-for-Food contract, he did solicit one, and he accepted bribes for many years in other programs. If competent and trustworthy auditors were set loose in Turtle Bay, there is no telling the extent of the corruption they would uncover.

Trick or Treaty

In *The Prince*, Niccolo Machiavelli advised that "a wise prince cannot, nor ought he to, keep faith [with a treaty or agreement] when such observance may be turned against him, and when the reasons that caused him to pledge it exist no longer."[1] It is advice President George W. Bush wisely followed when he withdrew the United States from the 1972 Anti-Ballistic Missile Defense Treaty. Speaking in the Rose Garden on December 13, 2001, the president reasoned that the agreement was made "at a much different time, in a vastly different world," and explained that "the ABM treaty hinders our government's ability to develop ways to protect our people from future terrorist or rogue state missile attacks."[2]

It was a welcome move. The ABM treaty was outdated and enacted with the Soviet Union—a country that no longer existed. The U.S. and Russia had put the Cold War behind them and the administration needed flexibility to fight a new kind of war against an unpredictable enemy. Blindly adhering to an outdated piece of paper to avoid his critics' juvenile claims of "isolationism" would have been foolish.

The president's withdrawal from the ABM treaty, along with his reluctance to join the flawed Kyoto Protocol, showed that he held a healthy skepticism for the bilateral and multilateral commitments of which the international pols are so fond. Treaties are the arsenal of the internationalists, for each new agreement adds another page to the bible of global government and creates new bureaucracies. Treaties are also favored by homegrown globalists like Bill Clinton who, in a 1997 speech to the UN General Assembly, praised the "forces of global integration" that are "inexorably wearing away the established order of things."[3]

According to the Treaty Database Online—a study conducted by the Institute for Agriculture and Trade Policy—President Clinton signed thirty-two treaties and ushered thirty more to ratification during his presidency, more than any other president. In contrast, the study was critical of President

George W. Bush for being "particularly reluctant to participate in the multilateral treaty system."[4] As of April 2005, Mr. Bush signed six treaties, fewer than any other president according to the study.

The United States is party to hundreds of treaties that deal with a wide variety of topics—everything from arms control; to the treatment of prisoners; to aviation, trade, and intellectual property rights. Many of these agreements have served American interests well. But international agreements proposed in more recent years are so fundamentally flawed that they are injurious to our Constitution.

Unfortunately, that means little to some senators in Washington who view treaties as a vehicle for appeasing America's global critics. Presidents and senators need to view UN treaties with much more skepticism before committing U.S. prestige to them. Under Article VI of the Constitution, treaties are "the supreme Law of the Land" and today, the United States is being asked by the UN to enter into numerous multilateral treaties that are contrary to U.S. interests.

Many treaties contain provisions to create new international governing bodies that exercise authority over public policy and the American people. California congressman Tom Lantos says he is "sick and tired of the world's dictatorships making key decisions at the United Nations"[5] and points out that for too many years, these global institutions have been "polluted by the machinations of rogue regimes."[6] But if we were not creating international institutions through the treaty process, the rogue regimes of which Lantos speaks wouldn't have the influence that they do.

Historically, treaties have been a way for countries to make peace and improve relations. But unfortunately, the UN and its allies in the United States are using international agreements as a way to advance their controversial agenda. Treaties are a perfect vehicle for internationalists to manipulate American jurisprudence and legislate from the global bench. Phyllis Schlafly, president of Eagle Forum, explains why legislators should be reluctant to enter into new global agreements:

> The first lesson we should learn . . . is the folly of signing UN treaties that are called voluntary. Any treaty called voluntary will surely morph into Other Countries' Great Expectations, which in turn will morph into demands by foreigners abroad and globalists at home that we meet our alleged "obligations."[7]

The Kyoto Protocol is one example. This accord is aggressively pushed upon the United States by wild-eyed environmentalists who demand that greenhouse gas emissions be reduced to levels that existed in 1990. Such reductions would throw the American economy into a tailspin. For this reason, along with the fact that the treaty exempts two-thirds of the world's countries from similar sacrifices, the Senate denounced the treaty embraced by Al Gore with a 95-0 vote in 1997. It was a shot across the Clinton administration's bow that it ought not ask for ratification of an agreement so manifestly unfair to American citizens.

But it hasn't stopped a whole coalition of Bush-haters from using it as a public relations punji stick against the administration. Criticisms that the United Nations is "ineffective" or that "it doesn't do anything" are misguided. In fact, the organization is tremendously effective and does a great deal. But what it does do well are those things that are unfamiliar to American interests. The UN creates chaos for the United States. Much of that mischief is caused through treaties and their accompanying regulatory bodies. So it is no longer enough for the United States to protest from the sidelines—we must stop the game.

Though the United States has not ratified the Kyoto Protocol, which entered into force in February 2005, "American businesses operating in countries that have ratified the treaty will have to comply with requirements imposed by those nations,"[8] reports the U.S. Chamber of Commerce. Billions of dollars in compliance costs is a steep price for adhering to a treaty that will do nothing to solve global warming.

The Rome Statute of the International Criminal Court (ICC) is another example of a treaty the U.S. found to be objectionable but could not prevent from being enacted. And though the U.S. has declined to ratify the accord, the ICC is causing headaches at both the Pentagon and State Department. Continued U.S. participation in the United Nations only encourages more of this kind of renegade diplomacy targeted at American interests.

The creation of international enforcement mechanisms through the adoption of treaties is what globalists like Bill Clinton want to see. "Through this web of institutions and arrangements," Clinton told the General Assembly, "nations are now setting the international ground rules for the twenty-first century . . . and shaping the emerging international system."[9]

At present those broadsides at American policy are in various stages. Some sit in Senate committees awaiting a full Senate audience; others are being drafted by UN bureaucrats. Let us review a few of those agreements that are likely, if ratified, to rewrite significant portions of Mr. Jefferson's finest composition.

Law of the Sea Treaty

When John Kerry declared during the 2004 presidential campaign that U.S. foreign policy needed to pass a "global test" before it could be implemented, the Bush administration correctly denounced him. America's national security is too important to be put in the hands of the United Nations. But the administration seems perfectly willing, through the UN's Law of the Sea Treaty (LOST), to allow the United Nations to control the seas and oceans—venues from which the U.S. military defends our national interests and where U.S. businessmen conduct commercial operations. The president "would certainly like to see it pass as soon as possible . . . and we very much want to see it go into force," Condoleezza Rice told the Senate Foreign Relations Committee in January 2005 during her confirmation hearings to be the next secretary of state.

The Law of the Sea Treaty entered into force in November 1994 without the consent of the United States. The agreement dates to the early 1960s when, once again, internationalists demonstrated their persistence for building international government; negotiating for two decades an agreement that gives the UN "sovereignty over the territorial sea [which] is exercised subject to this Convention,"[10] the document states. As such, the same United Nations, which corrupted the Oil-for-Food program, would have control of the seas, oceans, and their natural resources. When it was presented to President Ronald Reagan in 1982, he refused to sign it because of the damage it would do to American sovereignty. Caring little about such things, President Bill Clinton dusted off the LOST and renegotiated portions of it.

Fortunately, those were the days when there were individuals in the Senate like Jesse Helms who took threats to American sovereignty seriously. Now that Helms is retired, the chairmanship of the Senate Foreign Relations Committee is in the hands of Indiana's Dick Lugar—the most vocal cheerleader for the Law of the Sea Treaty. But conservative leaders in Washington have been trying to prevent the treaty from getting a ratification vote before the full Senate. The reasons are numerous—to protect national security, defend sovereignty, prevent global taxation, and safeguard the rights of exploration on the high seas.

Frank Gaffney, president of the Center for Security Policy, has marshaled conservative forces to keep the LOST in a lock box. Among the numerous reasons he cites in opposition to the LOST are these:

It was drafted more than 20 years ago at the behest of the Soviet Bloc and "non-aligned" nations as the centerpiece of their so-called "New International Economic Order," a scheme to transfer wealth from the industrialized to the developing world . . . . LOST also would infringe in significant ways on the movement and activities of U.S. military and intelligence operations at sea. It would oblige the U.S. to transfer sensitive data and technology to potentially hostile nations.[11]

Under the theory that the oceans are part of the "global commons," the General Assembly in 1970 declared that the seabed and ocean floor are the "common heritage of mankind," and any "exploration and exploitation" of the seas "shall be carried out for the benefit of mankind as a whole."[12] It is that socialist reasoning that has Gaffney concerned, for there are several provisions of the LOST, including Article 144, which requires "State Parties [to] cooperate in promoting the transfer of technology and scientific knowledge . . . so that . . . all State Parties may benefit therefrom."[13]

Throughout history, American explorers have climbed to the highest peaks and swum to the lowest valleys in the world. They have tested the limits of human endurance and spent billions of dollars to fly within and beyond earth's boundaries. Yet, the United Nations demands that the research they risked their lives to collect must be shared with others around the world who risk nothing.

Not only would the U.S. have to share whatever we find as a result of ocean exploration, but as Phyllis Schlafly points out, the Law of the Sea Treaty gives the United Nations "the power to impose production quotas for deep-sea mining and oil production so the United States could never become self-sufficient in strategic materials."[14] Such quotas would be administered through a powerful and unaccountable International Seabed Authority (ISA), yet another global institution created by the Law of the Sea Treaty. The ISA would rule more than 70 percent of the world's surface area, "a territory greater than the Soviet Union ruled at its zenith,"[15] as Schlafly points out.

LtCol Oliver North, founder of Freedom Alliance and a staff member of the National Security Council under President Ronald Reagan, is not only concerned about the national security implications of ratifying the LOST, but also the power to levy taxes and fees on private companies that is given to the International Seabed Authority in the Treaty. North writes,

Under LOST, [the International Seabed Authority] is empowered to levy fees and other taxes on private companies to which mining contracts are awarded and can compel industrialized nations to share technologies with others unable to obtain sophisticated seabed mining equipment. The billions of dollars this would put under the control of UN bureaucracy makes the Oil-for-Food program look like pocket change. To an "entrepreneur" in Nepal, Central African Republic, Paraguay, the PLO, or any other land-locked entity, LOST is better than a globalized Small Business Administration.[16]

In fact, the International Seabed Authority, which in 2003 was led by Jozef Franzen of Slovakia—a land-locked country—adjudicates disputes among parties, has taxing power on member states and contractors, forces private mining and fishing companies to acquire permits at hefty price tags, and collects royalty fees from their successful acquisitions. It is an international license to steal.

Doug Bandow, while a senior fellow at the CATO Institute, has studied and wrote extensively about the Law of the Sea Treaty—an instrument he worked on directly when he was a special assistant to President Reagan. Bandow believes that while parts of the treaty are "unobjectionable," the seabed provisions are so flawed that they alone require it to be defeated. Bandow writes,

> The LOST remains captive to its collectivist and redistributionist origins. It is a bad agreement, one that cannot be fixed without abandoning its philosophical presupposition that the seabed is the common heritage of the world's politicians and their agents.[17]

Also under the LOST, U.S. national security would take a back seat to the naïveté of UN officials who can't define terrorism and are unwilling to confront evil in the world. U.S. naval vessels would be prevented from interdicting ships on the high seas that are under the control of terrorists or carrying weapons of mass destruction, or both.

The treaty, in Article 29, also fails to account for new terrorist threats by narrowly defining a warship as only "belonging to the armed forces of a State . . . under the command of an officer duly commissioned by the government of the State . . . and manned by a crew which is under regular armed forces discipline." This provision is a gold-plated invitation to terrorists to hijack civilian ships in international waters.

The LOST would violate American sovereignty, hurt national security, stifle America's economy and exploration for natural resources in the sea, and allow taxes and fees to be imposed on American industry by a UN agency.

Multilateral treaties have long been the sticks with which the United Nations whacks at the protective piñata of American sovereignty. If the Senate ratifies the Law of the Sea Treaty, Kofi Annan and his pals will have just what they need to crack open the fragile vessel of U.S. independence.

Arms Trade Treaty

Liberals love to accuse the National Rifle Association (NRA) of being "the most powerful lobby in Washington," as if there was something inherently wrong with such a distinction. By most accounts, the NRA is the biggest, most effective grassroots advocacy organization working in our nation's capital. It is also one of the oldest. But the NRA is only as effective as its membership, and the principle reason the organization is such a force is because it represents millions of American hunters and sportsmen who cherish their right, as guaranteed in the Constitution, to keep and bear arms.

For well over a century, the National Rifle Association has defended the rights of gun owners from well-connected lobbies who want to eliminate the ability of individuals to own firearms. Many activists on the Left won't be satisfied until the Second Amendment is repealed and our citizenry disarmed. To date, they haven't been able to achieve that objective in the United States, but in countries like Great Britain and Australia, citizens who want personal protection and sportsmen who want to hunt have had their firearms confiscated by government authorities.

Those same abolitionists are now working through the United Nations to impose global restrictions on the private ownership of firearms. Their liberal counterparts in the United States are joining them. For the past three decades, liberals have followed the policy that when their candidates are rejected by the electorate, when their ideas fall short in the political free market, or when their policies are voted down by duly elected governing bodies, they turn to the courts and find legislator-judges who are more than willing to enshrine their opinions into law. Today, they are adopting a similar strategy wherein they are asking the United Nations to forbid that which our Constitution guarantees—the right to keep and bear arms.

The chief agitator of this effort is Rebecca Peters, an aggressive anti-American lobbyist who heads the International Action Network of Small Arms (IANSA), a conglomerate of 600 gun-grabbing non-governmental organizations (NGOs). Peters believes that the United States "contributes disproportionately to many of the world's problems, and it should cooperate with other UN member states to solve those problems."[18]

That is exactly where Peters's full faith and allegiance is invested—the United Nations. "The way to get freedom," she explains, "is to have stronger institutions," like the UN. Peters's anti-gun mindset is perfectly consistent with her idea of liberty. While conservatives believe freedom is a gift from God that no government may take from us, Rebecca Peters and her friends at IANSA believe freedom is something that belongs to governments, and government institutions should dole out to the people only the kind, and amount, of liberty the institution wants them to have. Rebecca Peters explains, "It's not up to each individual person to be like a hero in a movie defending against this threat to freedom."[19]

IANSA's goal is simple—they want to outlaw the private ownership of firearms in every country in the world. Like many NGOs that work through the United Nations, IANSA is skilled at adopting rhetoric that will advance their agenda. In the spirit of creating "world peace" and building "international harmony"—ideas that find no opposition anywhere—IANSA professes to want to disarm rogue militias in third-world countries and keep dangerous military weapons out of the hands of those who would commit genocide.

"That's nonsense. That's the veneer they use," Bob Barr told me. Barr is a board member for the National Rifle Association and attended several UN conferences, including the UN Small Arms Conference in 2001 as a member of the official U.S. delegation. But, he explained, "the ultimate agenda of the UN is to outlaw the civilian possession of firearms and, of course, they would do it in such a way that would put them in charge of making sure that there are proper legally binding regulations in all member nations for registration, tracking and so forth."

IANSA doesn't like to explain exactly what is meant by "small arms" to which they are opposed. But the United Nations has defined the term. The UN says small arms are "weapons designed for personal use," and examples of small arms include "revolvers and self-loading pistols" as well as "rifles."[20] Millions of Americans own and use these kinds of firearms for hunting, sport shooting, and defending their person or property. But to Kofi Annan, they are "weapons of mass destruction."[21]

Because Kofi Annan and IANSA fail to see any benefit in shooting as sport or the right of individuals to protect themselves, they are working hand in glove to create an Arms Trade Treaty that will undermine, if not eradicate, the Second Amendment of the Constitution. In fact, Rebecca Peters cares nothing about the rights of sport shooters. In an October 2004 debate with the NRA's Wayne LaPierre in London, Peters celebrated the destruction of a sport with a rich tradition. She explained, "Pistol shooting used to be a sport that was allowed in the U.K. and it no longer is. I'm sad for you. I suppose if you miss your sport, take up another sport."[22]

Similar losses of liberty could easily occur in the United States with the adoption of an Arms Trade Treaty that is the "legally binding international instrument,"[23] for which IANSA is lobbying. The danger of an Arms Trade Treaty (ATT), like a Law of the Sea Treaty or an International Criminal Court, is that over time, case by case, the anti-American values enshrined in these documents seep into American case law, legislation, and culture and become precedent to which judges and politicians give fealty. Through existing and proposed international treaties, our Constitution is dying the death of a thousand edits.

Already, IANSA and its allies at the UN have held two working meetings to lay the groundwork for the ATT. The real discussions and negotiations for the Arms Trade Treaty will begin in 2006. There is no doubt that global gun grabbers will closely monitor the presidential race in 2008 and try to implement their agenda in a way that is most beneficial to the Democrat candidate for the White House. Any one of the leading Democrats would likely be favorable to such a proposal.

IANSA won't let a little thing like the U.S. Constitution get in their way of confiscating guns on a global level. Rebecca Peters openly laments that there is yet "no international regulation"[24] of firearms and admits that her idea should be universal. "I'm for global standards, applying across the world,"[25] she says.

That is why they are aggressively lobbying at the United Nations to implement "global Codes of Conduct"[26] that would govern the sale and purchase of firearms, so that "American citizens [are not] exempt from the rules that apply to the rest of the world."[27] But they don't want other nations to conform their laws to those of the United States; they want the U.S. to adopt the policies of Great Britain, where guns are prohibited.

IANSA states clearly that their goal is to "reduce the availability of weapons to civilians in all societies," and as such, they ask citizens to "surrender" their firearms.[28] On this and other measures, IANSA is getting a lot of support. During the UN's Small Arms Conference in March 2001, four countries—Great Britain, Brazil, the Netherlands, and Mali—sponsored a resolution recommending the creation of a "Small Arms Destruction Day" and called upon all countries to organize "public events of destruction of small arms and light weapons."[29] IANSA believes that only "an international arrangement or mechanism" can appropriately "monitor adherence to international norms and rules" regarding firearms that will be established once an Arms Trade Treaty is adopted.[30]

But it is not only the private ownership of firearms that IANSA wants the UN to control. Arsenals held by police or military forces should be open to inspection by international busybodies. In order to "increase transparency and accountability," IANSA says, governments like the United States should "establish and maintain complete national and regional inventories of arms and ammunition and related equipment held by security forces and other state bodies."[31]

In addition, the U.S. and other countries should be required to "exchange information" on certain police and military equipment "to promote a common understanding of appropriate levels of armaments required for national self-defense."[32] What Rebecca Peters and her crowd are asking Donald Rumsfeld to do is open the doors to the Pentagon, invite in al Qaeda operatives, the communist Chinese, and leaders of international drug cartels and host a year-round show-and-tell. An Arms Trade Treaty like the one IANSA proposes will turn U.S. national security on its head.

Just Say No to Tobacco Treaties

According to Article 1 of its charter, the United Nations was formed "to maintain international peace and security" and to "develop friendly relations among nations." So why is the United Nations in the business of banning cigarettes? While corruption runs rampant at the UN, and problems abound across the globe, the powers that be in Turtle Bay concern themselves with the global regulation of legal consumer products.

On February 27, 2005, after being ratified by only 20 percent of the world's countries, a new United Nations treaty became international law—the Framework Convention on Tobacco Control. The United States joined the treaty when the May 10, 2004, signature of Tommy Thompson, the secretary of Health and Human Services, added the U.S. as a party. Fortunately, the administration hasn't yet sent the treaty to the Senate for ratification, but it may only be a matter of time.

The treaty demands curbs on tobacco advertisements and hefty taxes on tobacco products. It seeks to expand New York City's "Bloomberg Doctrine," which states that tobacco may not be used anywhere at any time. A Democrat president who rails against the evils of the "powerful tobacco lobby" would be sure to push for its ratification.

The treaty received little attention in the press, and there are few who are willing to defend smoking. It has been banned in small businesses and on airline flights, and insurance companies charge smokers hefty premiums. Cigarettes stink. Smoking is disgusting. It's unhealthy and even deadly, some would say. So three cheers for Kofi Annan and the World Health Organization, right? Wrong.

The United States had no business signing this treaty. Ratifying it would legitimize the role of the UN as the Global Nanny and give Rebecca Peters the precedent she wants in order to go after firearms. The Framework Convention on Tobacco Control is an end run around the Constitution and the democratic process. It is an effort to have the so-called global community achieve that which anti-smoking activists in the United States have failed to do—ban cigarettes and tobacco products.

The objective of the convention, we are told, is to "protect present and future generations"[33] from this evil product. The document demands that governments inform "every person . . . of the health consequences, addictive nature and mortal threat posed by tobacco consumption."[34] This is not the role of the United Nations. If it were, Richard Simmons would be secretary-general.

But even that is not as far-fetched as it sounds. Now that the precedent has been set for the UN to regulate that which can harm us, global do-good-ers will use their new authority to attack the whole politically-incorrect product line. Ronald McDonald, meet Kofi Annan.

Sports utility vehicles have been attacked as environmentally unfriendly by both Arianna Huffington and Hugo Chavez. Clearly, they have to go. Advertising slogans like "Built Ford Tough" will have to be replaced by "Built UN Friendly." Red meat and alcohol—you're next.

Once these products find themselves on the UN hit list, they are subject to international pressures to put them out of business. Each country that is party to the anti-tobacco treaty, for example, will "implement tax policies and . . . price policies, on tobacco products so as to contribute to the health objectives aimed at reducing tobacco consumption."[35]

If global taxation doesn't remove the harmful product from the shelves, then it must be regulated. In Article 11 of the treaty, the United Nations insists that each party "implement . . . effective measures to ensure that . . . each unit packet and package of tobacco products and any outside packaging and labeling of such products also carry health warnings describing the harmful effects of tobacco use."[36] But the UN doesn't stop there. It also mandates that these warnings and messages:

- "shall be large, clear, visible, and legible";
- "should be 50% or more of the principal display areas but shall be no less than 30% of the principal display areas";
- "may be in the form of or include pictures or pictograms."[37]

What does any of this have to do with "maintaining international peace and security"? Was Secretary Tommy Thompson at all concerned that an international institution was imposing such detailed, parochial mandates on U.S. legislators and regulatory bodies before he signed us up for this global Smokers Anonymous meeting?

And just for good measure, the United Nations also included in the treaty a provision requiring state parties to "undertake a comprehensive ban of all tobacco advertising, promotion, and sponsorship."[38]

Say what? Your Founding Fathers attached a First Amendment to your Constitution to guarantee your right of free speech? Fair enough, the UN says. In those cases, the treaty states, "A Party that is not in a position to undertake a comprehensive ban due to its constitution or constitutional principles shall apply restrictions on all tobacco advertising, promotion and sponsorship."[39]

The fate of tobacco products in America lies with the American people and their elected representatives at the local, state, and federal levels. The use of any consumer product in the United States may not be regulated by Kofi Annan. It may not be restricted by the World Health Organization. It may not be regulated by some international ambassador for alcohol, tobacco, and firearms.

Who in our government will stand up to this global group of self-help gurus? When liberal activists killed the concept of personal responsibility, they dug the grave of self-government.

Reliance on International Law

"Our Constitution," John Quincy Adams once wrote, "professedly rests upon the good sense and attachment of the people. This basis, weak as it may appear, has not yet been found to fail."

But it is failing now. During one of the many low points of his presidency, at a time when Republicans in Congress were dominating the public policy debate, Bill Clinton was asked if he were still relevant. Today, the same could be asked of our Constitution.

Liberals have long used the Constitution as a judicial inkblot test—seeing in it only those words that fit their needs. But today they are taking their end run around the Constitution to a new level—the global level—using the work of the United Nations and the opinions of foreign tribunals to justify that which the American public does not support.

In a 2003 speech to the Southern Center for International Studies, Justice Sandra Day O'Connor admitted that she and her colleagues were buying into this strategy. Referring to her colleagues on the Supreme Court, O'Connor told the audience, "I suspect that over time we will rely increasingly . . . on international and foreign courts in examining domestic issues." To do so, she said, will help America "create that all important good impression."[40]

Members of the court, like John Kerry, crave the affection of foreigners. But it is not the job of the Supreme Court to "create a good impression." That responsibility falls to Karen Hughes at the State Department. But that is one of the many problems in Washington today. Nobody wants to do the job for which they are responsible. Members of Congress outsource their responsibilities to UN institutions. Senators want to be president. Supreme Court justices want to be secretary of state. And presidents want to do the jobs of governors and mayors.

Justice Anthony Kennedy agrees with O'Connor's theory of judicial appeasement of foreign courts. He explained it to author Jeffrey Toobin, who wrote a lengthy profile of Kennedy for *The New Yorker*. Kennedy explained to Toobin,

> The European courts, in particular the transnational courts, have been somewhat concerned, and some feel demeaned, that we did not cite their decisions with more regularity. They cite ours all the time. And, basically, they were saying, "Why should we cite yours if you don't cite ours?" If we are asking the rest of the world to adopt our idea of freedom, it does seem to me that there may be some mutuality there, that other nations and other peoples can define and interpret freedom in a way that's at least instructive to us.[41]

Good God. Kennedy has enlisted the United States in a perverted judicial game of "I'll show you mine if you show me yours." This is no different than John Kerry's "global test." It is no different from those who are willing to let American soldiers be paraded before international tribunals just so we don't offend other countries. It is no different from those who invited United

Nations officials into our country to inspect our prisons or judge our elections. It is an irresponsible mindset infesting every facet of government, believing we must turn our backs on the Constitution and American culture lest we offend foreigners.

One of the problems with federal judges looking beyond America's shores for precedent to make their case in U.S. courtrooms is that there is so much more ammunition out there with which they can get creative. They may look to any one of the court systems in 190 other countries for an argument that might help them. They can pull "evidence" from international treaties. Or they may read through the reports or advisory opinions of hundreds of UN international governing bodies to help them make their case. This is how liberal activists are using international bodies—to give ideas rejected by the American public "credibility" by virtue of the fact that it was mentioned favorably by an international institution.

In a case like *Roper v. Simmons*, we see how willing Supreme Court justices are to invoke international law and European opinion to find in the Constitution a right of immunity from the death penalty for minors. "Our determination that the death penalty is disproportionate punishment for offenders under 18," Justice Kennedy wrote, "finds confirmation in the stark reality that the United States is the only country in the world that continues to give official sanction to the juvenile death penalty."

Kennedy cited the International Covenant on Civil and Political Rights, the United Nations Convention on the Rights of the Child, and a 1930 report from the Select Committee on Capital Punishment from the British House of Commons to support his thesis. Kennedy then argued, "it does not lessen our fidelity to the Constitution or our pride in its origins" to take into account the opinions of foreigners. But in fact, it does. To rely on foreign law when adjudicating cases in U.S. courtrooms is worthy of impeachment from the bench. There is no place for it. To do so is to perpetrate a fraud on the American public who comport themselves within the boundaries of American law.

But once American citizens are dragged into a modern-day courtroom, they have no idea to what standard they might be held. Having adopted the role of imperial legislators, judges and justices are looking abroad for no other reason but to appease their own selfish motives.

The abolition of the death penalty is a perfect example. It has been a mainstay of liberal ideology for many years. The issue garnered a great deal of attention during the 2000 campaign for president, as activists and the media demanded that Texas governor George W. Bush explain the prevalent role capital punishment played in the state's penal system. Over the years, anti-death penalty advocates have used Hollywood and the media—and more recently DNA evidence—to try to eliminate the practice. They even tried unsuccessfully to use the French to convince Americans to change our ways.

In 2000, a group of French legislators sent a letter to members of Congress hoping to influence them to abolish the death penalty. Such a grave concern is the matter to the French that the friendship of the two nations could be at stake if the cold-blooded Americans can't find it in their hearts to make nice-nice with vicious killers. "It is in all candor," the French pols wrote, "that we say to you that maintaining the death penalty in your country profoundly affects the friendship which we feel for you."[42]

Members of Congress were heartbroken. Historians may yet conclude that it was this letter, and not France's betrayal of her American ally over the issue of Iraq, which ultimately sealed the fate of the French fry in the House Dining Room.

The American public appreciates law and order candidates who support the use of the death penalty as a way to punish those who commit the most horrific crimes. Those who are openly disdainful of it tend to have a harder time. Just ask Michael Dukakis.

If, when, how, and under what circumstances the death penalty may be used in the United States are legitimate questions. They should be raised and debated and fought over. Americans are more than capable of having that debate amongst ourselves. We don't need the unsolicited advice of the French or Kofi Annan.

But while our elected representatives were ignoring the opinions of foreign busybodies, the Supreme Court was writing their opinions into law. In *Atkins v. Virginia*, the court held that executions of mentally retarded criminals are "cruel and unusual punishments" prohibited by the Eighth Amendment. They arrived at that decision with the help of foreign law.

In this case, Daryl Atkins was convicted of abduction, armed robbery, and murder. He was sentenced to death because on August 16, 1996, Atkins, along with a friend, kidnapped Eric Nesbitt and robbed him. They then drove him to a nearby ATM machine, where he was forced to make a withdrawal of funds for his abductors. Once the transaction was finished, they took Mr. Nesbitt to another location and shot him eight times, killing him. Atkins was found by a psychologist to have a mild case of mental retardation.

In writing the majority opinion for the court, Justice John Paul Stevens said that the practice of executing mentally retarded criminals "has become truly unusual, and it is fair to say that a national consensus has developed against it."[43] In coming to that conclusion, he relied on a brief by the European Union filed in another case, *McCarver v. North Carolina*, and stated that "within the world community, the imposition of the death penalty for crimes committed by mentally retarded offenders is overwhelmingly disapproved."[44] To which any constitutional jurist should answer, "Who cares what the 'world community' thinks?"

Stevens's opinion is judicial activism at its worst. The mind of this justice was made up before he ever set foot in the courtroom or typed a word of his opinion. He wants to abolish the death penalty, and so he looked for any reason to support his belief. In this case, Stevens committed the sin of constitutional adultery—cheating on the one to whom he took an oath. It is a sin that is becoming more commonplace with the activist justices on our nation's highest court.

The practice has also caused concern among the more conservative justices. In *Atkins v. Virginia*, Chief Justice William Rehnquist chastised Stevens's decision to rely on foreign opinion. In a dissenting opinion Rehnquist wrote,

> I write separately, however, to call attention to the defects in the Court's decision to place weight on foreign laws . . . . The Court's suggestion that these sources are relevant to the constitutional question finds little support in our precedents and, in my view, is antithetical to considerations of federalism, which instruct that any "permanent prohibitions upon all units of democratic government must [be apparent] in the operative acts that the people have approved."[45]

The trend in all federal courts over the past thirty-plus years has been one in which judges impose their personal will on the people. The federal court system is now little more than an outpost of liberal activism. What makes this more dangerous is their new strategy of using a body of socialist opinion written by the United Nations, the European Union, multilateral institutions, international treaties, and global gadflies. In *Atkins*, Rehnquist went on to say,

> I fail to see, however, how the views of other countries regarding the punishment of their citizens provide any support for the Court's ultimate determination . . . . For if it is evidence of a national consensus for which we are looking, then the viewpoints of other countries simply are not relevant.[46]

Justice Antonin Scalia was even more direct in making the point. In a dissenting opinion in *Atkins*, Scalia wrote, "Equally irrelevant are the practices of the 'world community,' whose notions of justice are (thankfully) not always those of our people."[47] Then Scalia quotes from an opinion he himself wrote in *Thompson v. Oklahoma*:

> We must never forget that it is a Constitution for the United States of America that we are expounding . . . . [W]here there is not first a settled consensus among our own people, the views of other nations, however enlightened the Justices of this Court many think them to be, cannot be imposed upon Americans through the Constitution.[48]

Both Scalia and Rehnquist write that foreign opinion or precedent is irrelevant in shaping the body of U.S. law. It is a point that one would think is self-evident to those scholarly enough to sit on the nation's highest court. American citizens never elected those who wrote the laws, but somehow our federal judges believe U.S. citizens should nonetheless be governed by them.

Unfortunately, there have been many other cases in which the Supreme Court is issuing edicts by which the American people must live—edicts rooted in illegitimacy. A few examples:

• *Stanford v. Kentucky*, decided June 26, 1989. In another death penalty case decided more than a decade before *Atkins*, Justice William Brennan wrote in a dissenting opinion,

> Many countries, of course—over 50, including nearly all in Western Europe—have formally abolished the death penalty, or have limited its use to exceptional crimes such as treason . . . . In addition to national laws, three leading human rights treaties ratified or signed by the United States explicitly prohibit juvenile death penalties. Within the world community, the imposition of the death penalty for juvenile crimes appears to be overwhelmingly disapproved.[49]

• *Lawrence v. Texas*, decided June 26, 2003. When Justice Anthony Kennedy's majority opinion in *Lawrence v. Texas* landed on the desks of constitutional scholars, they must have known they were in for an interesting ride when Kennedy began his opinion by writing, "The instant case involves liberty of the person both in its spatial and more transcendent dimensions."[50] Upon reading these words, one can almost hear Scalia mocking from his chambers, "right on, dude."

In this case, the court threw out decades of precedent and, Arlen Specter not withstanding, said to hell with *stare decisis*. Then they ruled that a Texas statute forbidding two people of the same sex to engage in certain intimate sexual conduct violates the Constitution's Due Process Clause. Kennedy arrived at his decision with the help of the European Court of Human Rights and international precedent. He blathered,

> A committee advising the British Parliament recommended in 1957 repeal of laws punishing homosexual conduct . . . . Parliament enacted the substance of those recommendations 10 years later . . . . Of even more importance, almost five years before [*Bowers v. Hardwick*] was decided the European Court of Human Rights considered a case with parallels to Bowers and to today's case. An adult male resident in Northern Ireland alleged he was a practicing homosexual who desired to engage in consensual homosexual conduct. The laws of Northern Ireland forbade him that right. He alleged that he had been questioned, his home had been searched, and he feared criminal prosecution. The court held that the laws proscribing the conduct were invalid under the European Convention on Human Rights.[51]

What in God's name does an alleged practicing homosexual in Northern Ireland have to do with the proper interpretation of the Constitution of the United States of America? Absolutely nothing. Kennedy's arrogance got the better of him. His opinion makes clear that he was determined to overturn a precedent of U.S. law for which he could not find much support in American law or customs. So he set off on an international adventure, cherry picking from liberal screeds written in inferior courts. Kennedy even adopts his own illogic to try to make his point, arguing that *Bowers*—an American legal precedent—didn't hold up in foreign courts. Why should it? Argued Kennedy, "[I]t should be noted that the reasoning and holding in *Bowers* have been rejected elsewhere. The European Court of Human Rights has followed not *Bowers* but its own decision in *Dudgeon v. United Kingdom*."[52]

Yes, Mr. Justice, that is the way it is supposed to work. Courts in foreign lands rely on the laws and precedents of their own governments. Kennedy continued, searching for a reason to edit the Constitution by creating a protected right for homosexual behavior:

> Other nations, too, have taken action consistent with an affirmation of the protected right of homosexual adults to engage in intimate, consensual conduct . . . . The right the petitioners seek in this case has been accepted as an integral part of human freedom in many other countries.[53]

Once again, Justice Scalia, in a dissenting opinion did his best to remind his colleagues that their job is to interpret the U.S. Constitution, not cite global galimatias:

> Much less do [constitutional entitlements] spring into existence, as the Court seems to believe, because *foreign nations* decriminalize conduct. The *Bowers* majority opinion *never* relied on "values we share with a wider civilization" . . . but rather rejected the claimed right to sodomy on the ground that such a right was not "deeply rooted in *this Nation's* history and tradition." . . . The Court's discussion of these foreign views (ignoring, of course, the many countries that have retained criminal prohibitions on sodomy) is therefore meaningless dicta. Dangerous dicta, however, since [as Justice Thomas said] "this Court . . . should not impose foreign moods, fads, or fashions on Americans."[54] [emphasis his]

• *Grutter v. Bollinger,* decided June 23, 2003. In one of the more controversial Supreme Court decisions of 2003, the justices handed down a 5-4 decision in *Grutter v. Bollinger,* which allowed the University of Michigan Law School to discriminate on the basis of race, saying the school's "narrowly tailored use of race in admissions decisions to further a compelling interest" does not violate the Constitution's Equal Protection Clause.

In a concurring opinion, Justice Ruth Bader Ginsburg invoked the International Convention on the Elimination of All Forms of Racial Discrimination, which was ratified by the Senate during Bill Clinton's presidency, to bolster her argument for legalized discrimination. The logic of Ginsburg and her friends in the "international community" goes as follows:

> The Court's observation that race-conscience programs "must have a logical end point" accords with the international understanding of the office of affirmative action. The International Convention on the Elimination of All Forms of Racial Discrimination, ratified by the United States in 1994 . . . endorses "*special and concrete measures* to ensure the adequate development and protection of certain racial groups or individuals belonging to them, for the purpose of guaranteeing them the full and equal enjoyment of human rights and fundamental freedoms."[55] [emphasis added]

Wendy Wright of Concerned Women for America is troubled by this trend of judges citing international documents to make their case in U.S. courts. "What is happening at the UN can and does affect us here in the United States," Wright explained to me. "In fact," she said, "Supreme Court justices have cited UN documents and treaties that the United States is not party to, but they cited them in their decisions."

Wright was referring to *Grutter v. Bollinger*, wherein Justice Ginsburg cited the Convention on the Elimination of All Forms of Discrimination Against Women, a controversial treaty that the United States has not ratified. "Our revolution," Wright added, "was based on the concept that 'we the people' should be able to decide our own laws and our culture for ourselves. It should not be determined by somebody in a foreign land." If only we could get the Supreme Court to agree.

The problem with turning to international law and foreign courts is basically twofold. First, the American people never consented to be accountable to these institutions and legislatures. Second, there is no standard. This should be obvious to learned scholars of law, but their lifetime tenures have led too many of them to adopt the snotty standards of elitism, which makes them quasi dictators ruling over the American public.

When a Supreme Court justice refers to a law in France, why not China? When they adopt a policy of Great Britain, why not Libya? What makes one better than the other? Because Anthony Kennedy says so?

In a dissenting opinion in the 1999 case of *Knight v. Florida*, Justice Breyer cited Jamaican law, the Supreme Court of Zimbabwe, the European Court of Human Rights, the Supreme Court of Canada, the United Nations Human Rights Committee, and the Universal Declaration of Human Rights.

The practice of judges relying on foreign opinion has become such a problem that it is not enough simply to take the Supreme Court to task. Congress should set aside opinions of the court that rely on international law. After that, they should impeach judges who place more faith in the Charter of the United Nations than in their own Constitution.

How shall we be governed? By the genius of our Founding Fathers, whose Constitution has served us well for more than 200 years and helped make America the greatest nation in the world? Or shall we be governed by jurists who put America's fate in the mysterious whims of an international judicial Ouija Board?

It's Party Time, UN Style

The United Nations is a playground for international delinquents, and the international conferences it sponsors are little more than anti-American rallies. That fact was displayed during its most recent World Summit held at UN headquarters in September 2005 when many of the world's despots and dictators rolled into town under the protective cover of the Secret Service and New York City Police Department.

During the summit, one of those delinquents was on prominent display in Room 226 of UN headquarters, where roughly 150 members of the international press corps gathered. The tiny briefing room where UN spokesmen regularly make their press announcements was packed so reporters could witness one of America's most vocal critics.

The individual the political paparazzi were stalking was the new star on the international stage—Hugo Chavez, dictator of Venezuela. But the press would have to wait while Chavez's large entourage conducted a security sweep, tested his chair for height and comfort, adorned the speaker's table with their country's flag, distributed communist propaganda, and laid out el presidente's writing utensils.

Finally, when the preparations were completed, Chavez took his seat—and he did not disappoint his fans. Within minutes, he had labeled the United States a "state sponsor of terrorism," accused America of "using napalm and chemical substances" in Iraq, and called George W. Bush "the father of all terrorists on this continent." Chavez denounced the liberation of Iraq, calling it an "illegal and immoral war," and said he had pity for the American people who are "victims" who are kept under the dictatorial thumb of President Bush.

Armed with considerable financial assets derived from Venezuela's vast oil resources, and with mentoring from Fidel Castro, Chavez is building a power base for himself throughout Latin America. He has a growing propaganda machine and is buying weapons for his army from various countries around the world. It has even been reported that Chavez is cozying up to Iran's mullahs in the hope that they might share their nuclear know-how with him.[1]

When he spoke to the General Assembly, he was given, as were other world leaders, five minutes to speak. After ten minutes, the presiding officer of the assembly approached the podium and handed Chavez a note requesting him to abide by the time limit. Chavez ignored it and informed the delegates that since President Bush spoke for twenty minutes, so would he. Indeed, Chavez spoke for more than twenty minutes, attacking the U.S., and received a standing ovation. The United Nations—funded by U.S. tax dollars—provided Chavez a world stage on American soil wherein he planted seeds of hatred against the United States.

In June 2005, President Bush nominated his long-time advisor Karen Hughes to serve as ambassador for public diplomacy and public affairs. Her job is to improve America's battered image in the world. It is a necessary mission, but one that will ultimately fail unless we first end our subsidies for the "Hate America Club" that meets regularly at the United Nations.

Another member of the club who entered the United States with the help of a State Department-issued visa is Mahmoud Ahmadinejad, the new president of Iran. Many of the 52 Americans who were held for 444 days after the 1979 seizure of the U.S. embassy in Tehran believe Ahmadinejad to have played a leading role in their capture.

Like Chavez, Ahmadinejad came to attack the United States. Despite the fact that he leads a country that is a state sponsor of terrorism, and he was allowed into the U.S. to visit the United Nations, Ahmadinejad lectured the United States that as the host country it must allow "all governments, civil society organizations and NGOs from all over the world to freely travel to [UN] headquarters without the selective hindrances of the host country."[2] In fact, the United States has never denied a head of state from entering the country to visit the UN.

America's tolerance of her adversaries is well documented. By contrast, Mr. Ahmadinejad's anti-Semitism was displayed at the UN's World Summit when he twice refused to answer questions from Israeli reporters, citing the fact that Iran does not recognize the state of Israel. Then he demanded a permanent seat on the Security Council for an Islamic state.

But he was not finished. The new president of Iran used this, his first major address on the world stage, to accuse the United States of supporting terrorism. He vowed that his pursuit of nuclear technology was entirely peaceful because, after all, his country's religious principles prohibit nuclear weapons. But if the United States tries "to impose [its] will on the Iranian people . . . we will reconsider our entire approach to the nuclear issue," he warned.[3]

Once again, in a desire to appease the United Nations, America helped to put her enemies on display for the world. Global thugs from countries like Venezuela, Cuba, Syria, and Iran are given more deference than some of the administration's political foes at home.

The Bush administration, like other administrations before it, sanitizes public events to ensure protestor-free meetings and constructs protest zones that are so far removed from the president's public appearances as to be meaningless. But avowed enemies of the United States are welcomed into the country and driven by chauffeur to the UN, where they decry all that is American.

Why do we allow the United Nations to force us into this position by which we treat dictators with more courtesy than we show to some of our own citizens? It is not only heads of state who use the international forum provided by a UN-sponsored conference to advance their agenda against the United States. A United Nations conference is to UN delegates and liberal activists what spring break is to college fraternities. It's a time to run wild, blow off steam, and live the high life. Some UN events draw tens of thousands of people. More than 60,000 activists and bureaucrats met in Johannesburg, South Africa, for the UN World Summit on Sustainable Development; 50,000 were on hand in Beijing for the UN's women's conference; and 47,000 took planes, cars, and buses to Rio de Janeiro for the 1992 Earth Summit.

The gatherings get wide media attention from a fawning press. Reporters rely heavily on the propaganda they are fed by the UN's public affairs office and the powerful NGOs that dominate the UN. The average U.S. daily newspaper runs headlines and stories praising the work of the United Nations but avoids any critical interpretation or alternate viewpoints.

Like pigs to a trough, UN conferences are an appetizing attraction for globalists because their goal of building a global governing structure is advanced through these fora. A UN fact sheet on global conferences admits as much. Global conferences, the document states, are essential for "establishing international standards . . . for national policy."[4]

While NGOs affiliated with the United Nations are notorious for never being satisfied with the pace at which global governance is built, they know they are effective. One conference builds on the next. The 1992 Earth Summit, for example, spawned four new international treaties governing the environment and one new agency—the UN Commission on Sustainable Development.[5]

United Nations world conferences are held not to solve problems to create global bureaucracy, because every new institution or agreement that is created is yet one more check on the influence of the United States. This is their goal—keep the money flowing from the United States, but cut the strings that are attached to it.

One leader who wants to reduce U.S. influence in the world is Jacques Chirac of France. Chirac is a votary of world government run by the United Nations and explains that we are living in a world in which "borders are slowly disappearing . . . [and] the world taking shape before our eyes needs common rules, principles and ambitions."[6]

But Chirac is not alone. Many world leaders use the occasion of a UN conference to endorse more supranational bureaucracy. During the 2000 Millennium Summit, many leaders rose to the podium to endorse world government. Some, like the Netherlands' Wim Kok, are straightforward: "global governance needs to be strengthened,"[7] he said. Others, like the Sultan of Oman, embrace it with a little more flair: "The United Nations shall always remain the blooming tree for the nations to rest under its shade and for their peoples to benefit from its fruits."[8]

America must never rest under the shade of the United Nations. In fact, that would be impossible, for it is Americans who provide the money and resources to the UN from which other countries benefit. For decades, poor countries have treated the UN as a welfare office of the international nanny state.

Being a forum for the advancement of global government is only one part of the UN's international gatherings. There is a circus aspect carried out by the UN-accredited NGOs that take the form of angry protests, marches, or demonstrations and often require heavy security by the local police.

Participating in them are environmental extremists like Jessica Coven of Greenpeace International who, during the United Nations climate conference in Buenos Aires, called President George W. Bush "immoral" and said his decision to withhold America's signature from the flawed Kyoto Protocol "condemns millions of people around the world to suffer the devastating consequences of global warming."[9]

A United Nations world conference attracts socialists, anti-gun advocates, and opponents of private property. Special-interest organizations demanding gay rights, abortion rights, and animal rights turn out in force. Many of them are devotees of Marxism; others advocate a return to primitive lifestyles. Third-world despots like Fidel Castro and Robert Mugabe find a special place in the hearts of UN loyalists, who burn American flags and hang the U.S. president in effigy.

But not everybody is angry at a UN conference. Some, like Mechai Viravaiday, head of Thailand's Population and Community Development Association, take a little too much pleasure in their work. Viravaiday is known in his country as "Mr. Condom." He was on hand during the 2002 Earth Summit in Johannesburg, South Africa, to argue that only politicians who have sex and enjoy it should be able to sit on their national AIDS councils. When it comes to preventing the spread of AIDS, he believes "the only lifesaver we have is the condom." Viravaiday said that in his country, every agency is urged to promote use of the condom—even the police—who attach condoms to parking tickets in what is known as a "cops and rubbers" program.[10]

Another example of the crazy ideas that are given credence at UN summits are those of the anti-toilet activists. During the Earth Summit, Sunita Narain, an environmentalist from India, crusaded for the abolition of the flush toilet. In an interview with PBS's Bill Moyers, she denounced the creation and use of the flush toilet as an "ecologically mindless technology."[11] A year later, hundreds of anti-sanitation aficionados got together in Tampere, Finland, for the First International Dry Toilet Conference.

Whether their interest is in international finance or bathroom fixtures, most of these NGOs advocate a one-size-fits-all policy for international governance of their issues by the United Nations. Central management of the economy, environment, education, international relations, and other issues would all be better off, they believe, if only run by Kofi Annan's troops. Their beliefs were expressed at the organization's Millennium Summit in New York by British prime minister Tony Blair when he said, "Our desire is that the [United Nations] does more, not less. If it did not exist, we would need to invent it."[12]

The NGOs and internationalists are committed to the United Nations—and believe in the people who run it—in large part because UN bureaucrats take them and their ideas seriously. But while these activists and their ideas are outside the mainstream, they should not be taken lightly as political adversaries. They are aggressive and determined to have their views heard. They have effective communications operations. And what starts as a crazy idea today is UN policy tomorrow and U.S. policy the day after that. UN activists inspired the Kyoto Protocol. They made the International Criminal Court a reality. They are the lifeblood of a UN that feasts off the

American taxpayer. The no-flush toilet that was introduced at the Earth Summit was given a $2 million earmark in a Defense Appropriations bill in the House of Representatives in 2005. If left unchecked, there is no telling the damage UN activists can cause.

A Backstage Pass

"The thing about the UN," Marc Morano of *Cybercast News Service* told me, "they know how to throw a party." He was speaking, of course, about the UN's treatment of the news media that cover these lavish world summits. Keeping the media happy greatly increases the likelihood of a positive story being written about the UN and its activities. That, in turn, advances Kofi Annan's goal of winning more support from individual citizens around the world—especially Americans.

Morano has covered three major UN summits in Mexico, South Africa, and Argentina. "They really do serve reporters well," he said. "You get fed, you get taken care of." The United Nations provides the media with hundreds of computer stations with high-speed Internet access, phone lines, and technical assistance to help them cover these events. Audio and video of the conference proceedings are piped into the media room so reporters don't have to leave their comfortable confines.

The exception is for reporters the UN doesn't like. "They don't tolerate anything that is skeptical of what the UN agenda is—they really don't," Morano told me. Morano compares these conferences to a major political convention or the campaign of a political candidate. "It is image control," he said. "UN summits are very tightly controlled."

But that is part of the UN's strategy. When covering UN summits, many reporters lose the healthy sense of skepticism they should have when reporting on the activities of any large government or bureaucracy. Many of them write only what is being said from the main podium of the convention, and they copy the self-congratulatory pronouncements of UN press releases. They fail to ask tough questions. They refuse to play devil's advocate.

Morano believes that in their stories, some reporters downplay criticism delegates make of the United States so that it doesn't reflect poorly on the United Nations. They do this because they are sympathetic to the UN and its goals. "They are supportive of the UN," Morano explained. "They think anyone who's opposed to it, anyone who promotes national sovereignty is a crackpot or extremist."

But it is not enough for the United Nations to look good at these conferences—it is also important for the United States to look bad. Speakers and events are organized in such a way as to make the United States look like a cheap nation that does not live up to its so-called "international obligations." America is portrayed as an aggressor—an imperialist bully on the one hand and a disinterested, uncaring superpower on the other if we fail to intervene in every hot spot around the world. Although the U.S. has some of the highest environmental standards of any country in the world, activists routinely accuse the United States of destroying the environment.

To listen to the critics, the United States is responsible for war, famine, poverty, disease, malnourishment, and natural disasters. It is the kind of commentary the media love to report—especially *Al Jazeera* and other terrorist-friendly outlets.

Thomas Jacobson is the representative to the United Nations for Focus on the Family. He has participated in dozens of UN conferences and meetings, primarily those focusing on family and social policy such as human cloning, same-sex marriage, and gender and sexual rights issues.

These can be some of the most divisive kinds of meetings at the UN, as pro-family advocates have to tussle with those who have little use for God or organized religion. During the meetings leading up to the UN's Child Summit in May 2002, three issues dominated the discussions—"sexual rights," "reproductive health services," and "the definition of family."

These controversial topics "captivated the attention of the delegates and dominated the deliberations," Jacobson told me. So instead of focusing "on the true needs of children like nutrition, clean water, or helping mothers deliver their babies safely and reducing the maternal mortality rate," Jacobson explained, the UN's Child Summit was hijacked by social activists bent on advancing a radical social ideology.

Abortion rights advocates used the Child Summit to try to insert language about "reproductive health services" into the document which member governments would approve because the term has been interpreted by many to mean a universal right to abortion. Once the term was included in an approved UN document, courts in many nations could point to it as a rationale for the national government to provide state-funded abortions.

In a similar way, homosexual rights activists lobby to include the phrase "various forms of the family" into UN documents to pave the way for acceptance of same-sex marriage and homosexual adoption. It is this kind of subtle manipulation of public policy at the international level that is beginning to influence American public policy through the U.S. court system.

Wendy Wright, executive vice president with Concerned Women for America explained that "those that are in favor of destroying the concept of the family . . . have joined in a strategy to push the envelope on the legal concept of customary international law." Liberal social activists use UN conferences to manipulate customary international law by inserting phrases or principles with loaded definitions into what Wright calls "softball documents." These are agreements adopted by consensus at the UN but are rarely given much attention by official delegations.

When these documents are negotiated, Wright explained, "your country's delegate may not have been in the room the entire time . . . [because] none of them expect that the document will be binding upon their countries." But liberal NGOs take these documents that now contain pro-abortion or pro-homosexual language and shop them to courts all over the world and convince judges that nations are bound by the agreement and forced to provide government-funded abortions or homosexual adoption or some such thing.

This is the importance of the "outcome document" that is produced every time the United Nations holds a world conference. The negotiated agreement is adopted by countries and may address environmental policy, international trade, development, family and social matters, legal issues, or any public policy initiative the conference purports to address. Often many of these issues are wrapped into the outcome document.

Each conference treatise contains political principles or financial goals that must be met by all parties signing the agreement. But in most cases, it is only the United States that is criticized in the international press if it does not sign the document—as is the Bush administration policy on the Kyoto Protocol—or honor its commitments.

The agreements are given noble and authoritative-sounding names and generally include the city in which the conference was held: the "Monterrey Consensus," the "Kyoto Protocol," the "Rome Statute," the "Rio Principles," and the "Beijing Declaration." The documents and the agreements that are drawn up are then used to try to influence U.S. policy. With increasing frequency, they are being cited by courts in the United States in support of liberal policies that cannot be won by popular referendum.

International Conference on Financing for Development

A case in point is the UN's long-running attempt to institute a historic transfer of wealth from self-sufficient countries like the United States to poor nations in the developing world. Trying to emulate Franklin Roosevelt's expansion of the U.S. federal government in the 1930s, Kofi Annan has referred to the program as the Global New Deal, but more recently it has been wrapped in a neat package called the Millennium Development Goals. The program is a UN-imposed tax on America's national income—or Gross Domestic Product (GDP)—ostensibly to reduce international indigence.

The global levy on GDP has long been a goal of the United Nations. It was born in 1969 when the Pearson Commission—named after former Canadian prime minister Lester Pearson—issued its report "Partners in Development." The report, written at the behest of the World Bank, demanded governments contribute the arbitrary amount of 0.7 percent of gross national product to international development.

The United Nations embraced the finding and declared the UN's "Second Development Decade" in 1970. To mark the occasion, and the UN's twenty-fifth anniversary, President Richard Nixon announced in his address to the General Assembly a "major transformation of the American foreign aid program." There was considerable debate in the administration on whether or not the United States ought to embrace the 0.7 percent target. And while they decided not to accept specific targets, President Nixon nonetheless announced to the UN that the United States would "place larger shares of American assistance under international agencies."[13]

That the United Nations would now be able to administer vast amounts of American largess for developing countries was not enough for the greedy globocrats at the UN. The next day, October 24, 1970, the General Assembly adopted Resolution 2626 demanding that countries like the United States fork over at least 0.7 percent of national income to the United Nations:

> In recognition of the special importance of the role which can be fulfilled only by official development assistance, a major part of financial resource transfers to the developing countries should be provided in the form of official development assistance. Each economically advanced country will progressively increase its official development assistance to the developing countries and will exert its best efforts to reach a minimum net amount of 0.7 per cent of its gross national product at market prices by the middle of the Decade.[14]

Since then, the United Nations has never given up on this demand. The idea was resuscitated twenty years later in the Agenda 21 document produced by the United Nations Conference on Environment and Development held in Rio de Janeiro in June 1992.

While the United States is criticized by the media and Democrat politicians in our own country, few realize the magnitude of the levy. A 0.7 percent assessment on America's gross national product would require American taxpayers to fork over $80 billion each year. In 2004, the U.S. paid 25 percent of this tax—$19 billion.

But America's generosity is never enough for Kofi Annan. On May 21, 2000, while delivering the commencement address at Notre Dame University in South Bend, Indiana, Annan condemned the American government for not giving more. In his address he said,

> It is particularly shameful that the United States, the most prosperous and successful country in the history of the world, should be one of the least generous in terms of the share of its gross national product it devotes to helping the world's poor. I am sure many of you share my feeling that this is unworthy of the traditions of this great country.[15]

There was virtually no media coverage of this incredible insult. Annan was speaking about the U.S. contribution to Official Development Assistance—the UN's global welfare plan. But even there, the United States provides more funding than any other country. The next highest contributor is Japan at $8.8 billion. The United States provides twice as much as our Japanese friends. In fact, if you add up the total amount given to the UN's ODA fund by the fourteen countries of Canada, Italy, Norway, Denmark, Australia, Belgium, Switzerland, Portugal, Austria, Finland, Ireland, Greece, Luxembourg, and New Zealand, it still does not exceed the amount given by the United States.

Yet the UN keeps trying. Ten years after the Rio conference, the UN's global tax was once again included in the "Monterrey Consensus" and was a major point of negotiation at the International Conference for Financing and Development. The Monterrey Consensus stated in part, "We urge developed countries that have not done so to make concrete efforts toward the target of 0.7 percent of gross national product as Official Development Assistance to developing countries."

In Monterrey, UN delegates played on the fears of Americans who, only six months earlier, had experienced the terrorist attacks of September 11 in order to gain momentum for their global tax. Though the UN sat on its collective hands after September 11, they saw an opportunity to exploit the memory of 3,000 dead Americans.

To understand how shameful some UN delegates can be, one need look no further than Monterrey and their behavior at the financing and development conference. Global panhandlers showed up with their tin cups to guilt Uncle Sam into a generous contribution. To do so, they suggested that Americans would see more days like September 11 if we didn't pay up.

The unofficial theme of the conference was "Poverty Equals Terrorism," and it was displayed everywhere—on posters, lapel buttons, fliers, and in meeting rooms. The theme was recited in speeches made by representatives of NGOs, finance ministers, and heads of state. Kofi Annan warned that "no one in this world can feel comfortable, or safe, while so many are suffering and deprived."[16] James Wolfensohn, president of the World Bank, declared that aid is an "insurance policy against terrorism." Romano Prodi, president of the European Commission, instructed the conference that the world faces two choices: "poverty and . . . war" or "peace and prosperity." Russia's deputy minister of finance said Kofi Annan's goal of 0.7 percent of GDP will be a "determining factor" for a world "free from terrorist threat."

But poverty itself does not breed terrorism. Osama bin Laden is a wealthy man who self-financed a global terrorist network. None of the September 11 hijackers was living in poverty in the United States. Hatred breeds terrorism, and wealthy Islamists finance much of it.

But even a strong president committed to fighting terrorism like George W. Bush can be negatively influenced by the constant drumbeat of UN platitudes. When President Bush addressed the delegates in Monterrey, he gave credence to their mantra that "poverty equals terrorism" by declaring that "we fight against poverty because hope is an answer to terror."[17] Yet only a week before, in a speech to the Inter-American Development Bank in Washington, Mr. Bush was more accurate in his diagnosis. "Poverty doesn't cause terrorism," the president said. "Being poor doesn't make you a murderer. Most of the plotters of September 11th were raised in comfort."[18]

Helping the impoverished people of the world to lift themselves out of destitution is a noble and worthy goal. But it should not be undertaken as the result of political blackmail—and paying blood money to the United Nations or any country to "prevent terrorism" is financing one kind of terrorism to prevent another.

World Summit on Sustainable Development

I was not surprised to see yet another anti-American rally when I traveled to the UN's World Summit on Sustainable Development in Johannesburg, South Africa, in fall 2002. Although the United States had only a year before suffered a devastating terrorist attack on our homeland, delegates and activists were not about to let that stop them from making their hostile point of view known.

These professional complainers should not be confused with the local citizens of Johannesburg and surrounding areas of South Africa who welcomed visitors at the airport with warm smiles. Though language was sometimes a barrier, the locals were eager to accommodate.

Having the opportunity to leave the conference proceedings for a few days, I traveled to the Northern Province—the site of the famed Kruger National Park. Seeing African wildlife in its natural habitat was breathtaking. I also had the opportunity to visit with local villagers who, despite their incredible poverty, welcomed our group into their village with warmth and hospitality.

But back in Johannesburg, it was a circus. As the delegates arrived in their limousines, organizers of the conference predicted an end to poverty would be found in the days ahead. The conference was held in the Sandton City section of Johannesburg, and the shops and malls were as glitzy as the most upscale stores in New York City or Beverly Hills.

The hotels accommodating the delegates were on par with the finest hotels in Paris or London. Exotic game and fine wine were served in the restaurants. Other than police cars, stretch limousines and Mercedes Benz automobiles were the only vehicles in sight. Male delegates wore expensive suits, and females were studded with glitzy jewelry. Lavish cocktail parties featuring champagne and caviar were all the rage.

But this is also where U.S. secretary of state Colin Powell was booed and jeered when he arrived with tens of millions of dollars in U.S. aid. At the conference, and in the months that preceded it, the Bush administration announced numerous initiatives in support of the UN's Millennium Development Goals. These goals include reducing child mortality, alleviating poverty and hunger, preventing the spread of HIV/AIDS and the deadly impact of malaria, and increasing aid to impoverished nations.

Among the new spending the Bush administration announced was $200 million for teachers and education projects in Africa; $100 million for a global school lunch program; $15 million for housing construction in South

Africa; $144 million worth of food and nutritional items to southern Africa to combat starvation as a result of the famine caused by policies of the Zimbabwe government and its dictatorial leader, Robert Mugabe. At the time of the World Summit, the Bush administration had either committed or requested more than $2 billion for the Global Fund to fight HIV/AIDS. They also committed hundreds of millions more for hunger programs, clean water initiatives, health care, and environmental and educational initiatives.

The only caveat the administration attached to new funding was that nations now had to show that they were going to use the money responsibly, and the United States would make every effort to ensure that aid was given only to nations committed to serious reform. But when Powell tried to speak, he was shouted down. Protestors yelled, "Shame on Bush," until they had to be dragged out of the room by police. Powell said, "Thank you, I have now heard you. I ask that you hear me."[19] Marc Morano told me that when he goes to a UN conference, "as bad as the European journalists are . . . and as bad as it is to get attacked by the international NGOs," he said, "the worst attacks come from Americans."

That was the case when Secretary of State Colin Powell spoke to the delegates. "I was ashamed for my country because the people representing us were acting like selfish children," said Michael Green, the executive director of the Center for Environmental Health. Green stormed the pressroom at the summit and said, "as an American, I was so embarrassed . . . that the U.S. delegation is obstructing very important environmental issues like global warming and the World Trade Organization." He said, "I am embarrassed by the government that is currently representing me."[20]

Outside the conference center, protestors marched in the streets carrying signs reading "Forward to Socialism" and "Israel USA UK—The Toxic Axis of Evil."[21] Pins and placards with anti-American slogans were seen throughout the conference facilities.

It was not only the NGOs and activists who condemned the United States. Leaders like French president Jacques Chirac took a direct swipe at the U.S., saying "the American economy [has an] often-ravenous appetite for natural resources."[22]

Unfortunately, these kinds of remarks go unreported by the major media outlets. Jacques Chirac, the leader of a country that shares a permanent seat on the Security Council, attacks the American people as gluttons, and not a word about it is printed. If the media did a better job of reporting the way in which the United States is treated at the UN, there would be much more skepticism of the institution. "What these conferences are all about," Marc

Morano told me, is trying to "drain Uncle Sam of his resources and his reputation."

World Summit on Racism—Durban, South Africa

Many Americans' perception of the United Nations is that it is an institution of peace and tolerance, hope and optimism. It's not. It is an institution dominated by emissaries of anti-Americanism and anti-Semitism. Like the United States, the state of Israel is routinely denounced in the General Assembly. Such behavior is not only tolerated, but facilitated.

Here in the U.S., if a restaurant chain or a country club or an individual of public stature is accused of bigotry or discriminatory practice, it is front-page news—often for weeks. Talk shows feast on such subjects. Investigations are launched and press conferences held and apologies demanded. Boycotts are organized, managers are fired, lawsuits are filed, and sensitivity training is ordered.

But at the United Nations, hatred is rampant, bigotry is condoned, and racism is institutionalized. Contrary to its reputation in some quarters as an oasis of compassion, the United Nations is a cesspool of ill will largely directed at the United States and Israel.

A well-crafted insult at the United States will win a dictator a photo-op with Kofi Annan and draw more international media to watch his every move. There is no better example of this fact than the failed World Conference on Racism that was held in Durban, South Africa, in 2001.

When the General Assembly adopted Resolution 52/111 in 1997, it agreed to hold a "World Conference against Racism, Racial Discrimination, Xenophobia and Related Intolerance." The conference was chaired by Mary Robinson, former president of Ireland, who said it had "the potential to be among the most significant gatherings at the start of this century."[23]

But the conference was a political farce. Every two-bit political interest group around the globe tried to get under the conference's umbrella as victims of racism and discrimination. Those who had legitimate historical grievances tried to leverage the event for a narrower political goal. Led by the likes of Jesse Jackson, black activists used the conference as a vehicle for advancing the cause of reparations. Even a hotly debated, controversial topic such as that would be overshadowed by the hate of one people for another.

Twice previously—in 1978 and 1983—the United Nations held world conferences on the subject. On both occasions, the United States was forced to boycott the events precisely because racism infested the conferences that were supposed to combat it.

The 2001 World Conference Against Racism (WCAR) was supposed to be a constructive international dialogue to address the historical wounds of slavery and end the trafficking of women and children—the modern-day slave trade. Conference documents called for respect for human rights and the dignity of all people. But these noble goals were overshadowed by hatred and racism of a different kind.

Major world conferences such as the WCAR are generally preceded by "prepcoms," which is UN-speak for preparatory conferences. These are the sessions wherein the working delegations and NGOs craft the documents that will be officially adopted at the main conference. Prepcoms are where the real debates occur.

Four prepcoms preceded the WCAR—one of them in Tehran, Iran. The moral relevancy of the United Nations once again reared its ugly, two-faced head. To debate the issue of human rights and racism in a nation that has no respect for human rights is a self-defeating premise. Why reward the country of Iran with the so-called honor of hosting a major United Nations conference when such a country shows no respect for human rights?

While one of the main themes of the WCAR was to denounce and try to prevent trafficking in persons, they held their deliberation in a country whose law "does not prohibit specifically trafficking in persons."[24] In 2000, the year before the Tehran Prepcom, the State Department cited reports "that women were trafficked to the United Arab Emirates (UAE) for the purpose of forced prostitution [and] . . . young boys were trafficked through the country to be camel jockeys in the UAE."[25]

In selecting Tehran for one of the prepcoms of the WCAR, the United Nations ignored its own pleadings to respect the rights and the dignity of women. While delegates crafted strongly worded platitudes about such topics, they did so in a country where discrimination against women is not only commonplace, but is written into its repressive Islamic-based law that allows, in some cases, stoning as a form of capital punishment.

In addition to the negative signals sent on the women's front, holding the prepcom in Tehran set a decidedly anti-Jewish tone. Representative Tom Lantos served as a delegate for the United States to the WCAR. In a detailed report he wrote for the Fletcher Forum of World Affairs about the conference, he explained that citizens holding Israeli passports and Jewish NGOs were being barred from the conference by Iranian officials. Credentials were also denied to countries like Australia and New Zealand, which were sympathetic to Israel.

In many cases, prepcoms consist of hours or days of excruciatingly boring debate. But for many of the skilled activists and diplomats, that is exactly their goal—to lull other participants to sleep or force them out of the room and then slip in language to which they would otherwise object.

"The communist Chinese are masters at this," former congressman Bob Barr told me. Barr has sat through numerous negotiating sessions at the UN. They wait patiently and look for an opportunity to attach an amendment to a document that either changes the meaning of what has just been debated for hours or exempts the Chinese from what was just agreed upon.

At the other end of the spectrum, there are conferences like the WCAR where delegates have no use for subtle jibes and veiled biases. They prefer instead, as was the case with Islamic delegates at the Tehran Prepcom, to openly spit venom at Israel, turning it into an international infomercial of anti-Semitism.

With a compliant United Nations, and opposition from Jewish supporters quelled, delegates in Tehran were able to craft a document that accused Israel of "ethnic cleansing," "apartheid," and "racist practices."[26] This is what would be sent to Durban for consideration of governments and their high-level delegations. It was a replay of the debate in 1975 in which the General Assembly adopted, by a vote of 72-35, Resolution 3379 declaring that "Zionism is a form of racism and racial discrimination." The resolution stood until its repeal in December 1991—sixteen years.

The United States takes great pride in the fact that our delegation overturned such an odious statement by the world body. The individuals who worked to accomplish this task—among them the late senator Daniel Patrick Moynihan and the current ambassador to the UN John Bolton—have reason to be proud.

But as a nation we should be ashamed—not because it was repealed, but because we allowed it to stand for so long. During those sixteen years, the United States continued to send ambassadors to the institution and remained the most generous financial contributor to the United Nations. And today, while the official resolution has been repealed on paper, its sentiment still resides in the heart of the UN. It is a stain on our national reputation that we continue to prop up this international collection of Hitler Youth just because they drive cars with diplomatic license plates.

Before the WCAR opened in Durban, South Africa, the Bush administration found itself in an unfortunate situation. Lead by Secretary of State

Colin Powell, many in the administration wanted to participate in a conference that might be helpful in addressing some of the disturbing human rights problems like trafficking in women and children and the modern slave trade. It might also help, they had hoped, to heal some of the historical wounds of racism. But having been hijacked by radical Islamic forces, the administration could not in good conscience attend.

"We have made it very clear," President George W. Bush stated from his ranch in Crawford, "that we will have no representative there, so long as they pick on Israel, as long as they continue to say Zionism is racism. If they use the forum as a way to isolate our friend and strong ally, we will not participate."[27]

The administration had little choice. As Congressman Tom Lantos pointed out, Israel was the only country singled out for criticism in the official document of the conference—a document Lantos described as an "absurdity."

> It does not criticize Sudan, which currently practices slavery. It does not criticize the Taliban in Afghanistan, which is running a medieval dictatorship. It doesn't criticize China for its treatment of Tibet, but it criticizes one country on the face of this planet, the country of Israel.[28]

Lantos was referring to the written text of the document the delegates were asked to adopt. The speeches at the conference only reinforced the hatred on paper.

Yasser Arafat, who before his death in 2004 was the media's favorite terrorist, delivered a viciously anti-Semitic speech in which he accused the Israelis of "savage aggression" whose goal was to force the Palestinian people "to their knees" in order to "liquidate" them. He got help from Cuba's Fidel Castro, who demanded an end to the "ongoing genocide" against Palestinians.

Outside the conference hall, rallies were held and literature distributed of an anti-Israeli nature. Congressman Lantos, the only Holocaust survivor to serve in Congress, said it "was the most sickening and unabashed display of hate for Jews I had seen since the Nazi period."[29] Lantos lays much of the blame for the conference debacle at the feet of Mary Robinson, the UN's conference chairman. He cites too the failure of NGOs and human rights advocates strongly to denounce the actions of the Islamists.

In the end, the Bush administration, along with Israel, walked out of the conference—a move Fidel Castro declared "no one has the right to [do]."

The final declaration adopted by the UN serves as evidence that in spite of the UN's claims of wanting to eradicate racism, it serves to facilitate it.

The Durban conference, it turned out, was just a preview of the hate that would be unleashed against the United States. Two days after it concluded, the terrorists stopped talking and started acting by flying planes into buildings in Washington, D.C., and New York City.

With Friends Like These . . .

"There is a law in America: nobody can take your life. That's what makes me believe in peace."[1] The promise of America is that simple for Hassan Lamungu, a refugee from Somalia's Bantu tribe who, along with his wife and children, settled in the United States in 2003. Writing for the *Smithsonian* magazine, Gregory Jaynes chronicled the travails of the Lamungu family, who for twelve years wandered like nomads from one refugee camp to another, crossing African borders to escape war, poverty, famine, and persecution. The Somali Bantus are perhaps the world's poorest and most persecuted people. Unable to speak English and possessing no money, Hassan Lamungu jumped at the chance to come to America. "I cannot describe my happiness,"[2] he said when informed he would be relocated to the U.S.

The inherent greatness of the United States attracts immigrants, refugees, and asylum seekers from the far corners of the earth. For generations, God's children have aspired to the peaceful and promising pastures that only America provides. For it is here, more so than in any other country, where human dignity is respected, religious tolerance is practiced, opportunity is afforded, and hard work is rewarded. America is home to the most enterprising, creative, and generous people in the world. It is also, unfortunately, home to some of the most ungrateful citizens any country could know.

During the 2000 presidential election—while people around the world were literally dying to get to America—film director Robert Altman threatened that "if George W. Bush is elected president, I'm leaving for France."[3] Altman's mindset is troubling—not because he believes George Bush would make a lousy president—but because he grossly misunderstands the presidency and his country. Moreover, he is not alone. There is a significant and growing class of Virtual Americans—those who are happy to exploit American wealth and freedom but who openly commit patriotic adultery.

This belief—that political foes of an American president must seek asylum abroad—equates our constitutional Republic with despotism and mocks the rule of law by which we are governed. It gives rise to international paranoia that the American president is all powerful.

Contrary to what Altman believes, the election of one man does not make or break the United States. What makes America great are three things—the blessings of God, the heart and ability of her people, and the genius of her Constitution.

But those attributes are increasingly under attack by antagonists who challenge the greatness of America from within, cast doubt on her motives, and tear down her leaders. And as they try to tarnish the reputation of the greatest country in the world, they pledge their allegiance to another institution—the United Nations.

The Celebrity Set

From Jane Fonda's VIP tour of North Vietnam to Sean Penn's 2002 weekend getaway to Baghdad on the eve of war with Iraq, many celebrities in the United States have had a tortured relationship with national fidelity. While Fonda "apologized" many years later, most Vietnam Vets never forgave "Hanoi Jane's" betrayal of her country. After his visit with representatives of a government with which America was about to go to war, Penn conceded that he was used as a propaganda tool by Saddam's regime. He could not bring himself to apologize. But then, why would he, given his feelings for his country.

"I was brought up in a country," Penn told reporters at the Cannes Film Festival in 1991, "that relished fear-based religion, corrupt government, and an entire white population living on stolen property that they murdered for and that is passed on from generation to generation."[4] Such sentiments were undoubtedly well received in Baghdad.

These Virtual Americans—at least those of the Hollywood variety—are a valuable asset to Kofi Annan and the United Nations. The UN is aggressively recruiting and embracing Americans who are willing to publicly denounce the United States and espouse the goals and ideals of the United Nations. In spite of his mismanagement and moral cowardice, Kofi Annan is not a fool. He understands the power of celebrity and the need for the UN to capture the American culture. With that in mind, Annan is trying to win the imagination and allegiance of the next generation of Americans.

It began in April 1998, when Kofi Annan visited California to speak to the Los Angeles World Affairs Council and court Tinseltown's trendsetters. In the heart of Hollywood, he was feted by Jack Valenti, the influential president of the Motion Picture Association, and a host of celebrities that included James Woods, Tony Curtis, Jacqueline Bisset, Merv Griffin, and Los Angeles Lakers star Earvin "Magic" Johnson, whom Annan named as a United Nations "Messenger of Peace."[5]

During his visit, Annan lectured the stars of the entertainment industry about America's "obligation to pay its debt to the UN"[6] and asked for their help to win support for the global body. "But if the public . . . realizes how the UN impacts on their daily lives, what the UN and its agencies are doing to make this world a better place, I think they will support us,"[7] he said.

To help build that support, Annan courts celebrities and recruits them as "UN Goodwill Ambassadors" or "Messengers of Peace." These cultural emissaries, Annan explains, are prominent personalities who "give life to the role of the United Nations."[8] But it is not enough for these people to praise the global institution. In many cases, the UN selects as its spokesmen what Sun Tzu referred to as "native agents"—Americans who have a record of, and a penchant for, protest against their own country.

Their complaints are myriad, harsh, and often contradictory. The United States doesn't spend enough money to feed the world's hungry, help the poor, or find a cure for AIDS, they claim. War and upheaval are blamed on Uncle Sam. Terrorism is spawned by U.S. policy; the United States spends too much on our military; our military doesn't do enough to stop genocide; and so forth. They can't be satisfied. Virtual Americans harbor resentment for their country, and the United Nations is quick to exploit it by giving them a platform and a microphone.

One of the UN's most outspoken critics of the United States is entertainer Harry Belafonte, who in 1987 was named a Goodwill Ambassador to the United Nations Children's Fund (UNICEF). "I work for the United Nations," Belafonte explained to CNN's Larry King in October 2002. "I go to places where enormous upheaval and pain and anguish exist. And a lot of it exists based upon American policy."[9] Belafonte's twisted beliefs and animosity to his country only serve to feed the world's resentment toward the United States.

A few months later, in December 2002, Belafonte traveled to Cuba with fellow actor and America basher Danny Glover for an international film festival. Belafonte told the Cuban newspaper, *Granma*, that the terrorist attacks of September 11, 2001, allowed the Bush administration "to extend its imperialist, economic and political domination all over the planet."[10]

He accused the Bush administration of censorship, ignoring the fact that hundreds of journalists were embedded in military units for front-line reports of the Iraq war. "Many of my friends are journalists and they tell me that there has never been as much censorship as now,"[11] Belafonte ironically explained to a Cuban state-controlled newspaper.

It wasn't true, of course, because other than not being able to reveal the location of American troops for security reasons, journalists covering the Iraq war were under few restrictions. In fact, the embedment process allowed Americans to watch much of the war in real time on their televisions. That didn't stop Belafonte, however, from spreading false information about his own country while on hostile soil.

But Belafonte is perfectly willing to trash his country whether at home or abroad. In an address to the 2004 Global Exchange Human Rights Awards Ceremony in San Francisco, Belafonte took pity on those who "choose not to see or to hear or to taste or to believe that we can perpetuate and involve ourselves as a nation in the kind of villainy that is so dramatically identified in so many parts of the world."[12]

Advocating a kinder and gentler policy toward both communists and terrorists, Belafonte criticized former attorney general John Ashcroft, saying, "McCarthyism is very much Ashcroftism."[13]

UN Goodwill Ambassadors, explains Gillian Sorensen, assistant secretary-general for external relations, "can reach audiences that we cannot . . . they have voices and outreach that we don't have."[14] The United Nations is building support for itself while trying to weaken the United States. And therein lies the value to the United Nations of somebody like Harry Belafonte who demands that America "find a new code of honor in which to deal with the world."[15] Such a code, Belafonte insists, would begin with the United States stopping "your military interventions and your military impositions."[16]

The United States is by far the largest financial contributor to the United Nations and the host country of the institution, and the UN shows its gratitude by encouraging anti-American propaganda from its so-called Goodwill Ambassadors. Far from spreading "goodwill," Belafonte is the Mike Tyson of UN spokesmen—a pit bull who aggressively promotes animosity toward, and resentment of, the United States.

In 2005, the U.S. government contributed $125 million to UNICEF. Businesses and individuals in the United States donated hundreds of millions more. In turn, UNICEF employed Belafonte—one of America's fiercest critics—and unleashed him to the global media. "As I go around the world," Belafonte explained, "when I go to Somalia and to Rwanda and Kenya . . . when I go to the oppressive places in Eastern Europe and in Latin America and Central America, I'm aware how vast America's villainy extends itself because I see in the faces of the wretched millions who make up poverty globally, who are languishing from HIV-AIDS, hunger, and malnutrition."[17]

That kind of anti-Americanism wins Kofi Annan's approval. "You have good reasons to be proud of yourselves," Annan told Belafonte and a group of other Goodwill Ambassadors when they visited the UN in 2002 for a seminar to help them "act as advocates and spokespersons for the United Nations family."[18]

The UN family is clearly where Belafonte feels at home. I am "a servant of the United Nations,"[19] he explains, and says it is his duty to inform people in the countries he visits "to let them know that we, in America, are made up of different people other than the ones they have come to know who carry guns and bombs and lies and deceit."[20] As a representative of the United Nations, Belafonte ignores Article I of the UN Charter, which states that the UN exists to "develop friendly relations among nations." To the contrary, Belafonte, who says, "I speak for Kofi Annan and the United Nations,"[21] is bellicose and antagonistic.

"I not only think that [America's leaders] are misguided," Belafonte said just before the start of the war in Iraq in 2003, "I think that they are men who are possessed of evil."[22] Kofi Annan has never repudiated Harry Belafonte's insults to America and her leaders. Nor have members of Congress who fret about America's image at the United Nations.

When considering the nomination of John Bolton to be the next U.S. ambassador to the UN, many senators expressed concern that Bolton was too blunt in his criticism of the world body. "I do have concerns" about the Bolton nomination, worried Nebraska senator Chuck Hagel, "because the United Nations is a very important institution,"[23] and we don't want to send Bolton "up there [to] kick the UN around."[24] Delaware senator Joe Biden said Bolton's "stated attitude toward the United Nations gives me great pause."[25]

But members of Congress show no such concern about the UN's ministers of anti-Americanism. One of them is actor Danny Glover who, for eight years, the UN has proudly placed before the international media and who has praised the UN while denouncing President George W. Bush as a "racist."[26] Appointed as a Goodwill Ambassador to the UN Development Programme in 1998, Glover now works under the UNICEF umbrella and pulls no punches when criticizing the United States. Three months after the terrorist attack that brought down the World Trade Center and claimed the lives of thousands of Americans, Glover—a self-described member "of the

UN family"—charged the U.S. with being "one of the main purveyors of violence in this world."[27]

Glover's observation was made at Princeton University just two months after the September 11 attacks, in a community located less than 100 miles from Ground Zero. To further insult residents still grieving from the attacks, the actor offered his sympathy to Osama bin Laden. "When I say the death penalty is inhumane, I mean [it's inhumane] whether that person is in a bird cage or it's bin Laden,"[28] Glover noted.

Joining Belafonte and Glover in Kofi Annan's kennel of UN attack dogs is actress Susan Sarandon. Sarandon was named a UN Goodwill Ambassador for UNICEF in 1999—just in time to use the United Nations microphone to attack Republican presidential candidate George Bush. "We stand a chance," she told Britain's *Sunday Express*, "of getting a president who has probably killed more people before he gets into office than any president in the history of the United States."[29]

What qualifies Miss Sarandon to speak on behalf of the United Nations is her ability to attract attention and her belief that "the United States is a land that has raped every area of the world."[30] To Sarandon, the United States is no better than al Qaeda. Speaking at a 2002 rally in the nation's capital, the actress equated our American government with terrorists. "Let us find a way," she pleaded, "to resist fundamentalism that leads to violence. Fundamentalism of all kinds, in al-Qaeda and within our government."[31] She pleaded with protestors to "resist this war"[32] because of what it might do to "our relationship with the UN."[33] Sarandon also found a silver lining in the horror of September 11, suggesting the attacks may cause "American arrogance [to] be diminished,"[34] a sentiment that finds favor in the halls of Turtle Bay.

Sarandon, Glover, and Belafonte are spokespeople for the UN. They generate support for the United Nations by denigrating their own country. They are just three of numerous Hollywood celebrities who use their fame to proselytize on behalf of Kofi Annan and the United Nations.

It has been that way since 1954 when Danny Kaye signed on as the first UN Goodwill Ambassador. Kaye has been followed by celebrities such as Mia Farrow, Audrey Hepburn, Vanessa Redgrave, and Angelina Jolie. But in recent years, it has become much worse. In Hollywood today, the United Nations is the "cause de jour."

Celebrities show their support for the UN by wearing a "Dove of Peace" pin, which many of them did when the stars met at Hollywood's Kodak Theatre for the 2004 Academy Awards. It was a year after the start of the

Iraq war, and an anti-American protest took place as several dozen award recipients and presenters—lead by actress Drew Barrymore—sported UN Dove of Peace pins on their lapels. These "Artists for the UN" professed their belief that the United Nations is "the best organization to promote peace across the globe."[35]

At a UN news conference announcing Artists for Peace, Ms. Barrymore displayed the intellectual heft of the group by saying, "We wake up every morning thinking, like, what more can we do in this world to make it a better, happier, more peaceful and beautiful place."[36] A Nobel Prize no doubt awaits her.

Hollywood's support for the UN was showcased in the movie *The Interpreter*, which was shot at United Nations headquarters in New York. It was the first time the UN opened its doors to a Hollywood movie crew, but Secretary-General Kofi Annan, seeing the public relations value, was enthusiastic about the project. Director Sydney Pollack also assured him that "there would be nothing in the film that would in any way embarrass the UN or be hurtful or harmful to the UN."[37] In fact, Pollack explained, he made the lead character a figure who was "passionately sympathetic with the values of the UN."[38]

That lead character is played by Nicole Kidman—also a UN Goodwill Ambassador. In the film, Kidman is a UN translator who becomes involved in an assassination plot against a genocidal African leader, President Zawani. Sean Penn plays a U.S. Secret Service agent who must prevent Zawani's assassination so that Zawani can be handed over to the International Criminal Court (ICC).

Through the movie, Hollywood shows its bias, as the ICC is portrayed as the only legitimate arbiter of justice and the American delegation is portrayed as the bad guys for opposing the global court. In the end, the ICC gets to put the genocidal Zawani on trial; the United Nations comes out on top; and the Americans are forced to see the error of their ways.

Actress Catherine Keener said the idea of shooting *The Interpreter* at the United Nations was "mind-blowing," and the opportunity to see the General Assembly and stand at the podium was "breathtaking." Just the idea of being at the UN, Keener said, was "thrilling" and an "amazing experience."[39]

As ridiculous as *The Interpreter* is, it is Oscar material compared to how some movies inflate the importance of the UN. In *The Day After Tomorrow*, Dennis Quaid plays a scientist who has long cautioned politicians of changing climate patterns. In one of the opening scenes, his character is the featured speaker at a UN-sponsored climate conference and warns of imminent catastrophes if the U.S. administration doesn't immediately change its environmental policies. At the UN conference, Quaid's character Professor Hall is challenged by the U.S. delegate, the vice-president, who invokes his opposition to the Kyoto Protocol. When he does, Hall, to the delight of the other assembled delegates, dresses him down and explains that the UN-sponsored climate treaty is the only hope for mankind to prevent an environmental disaster.

Intelligentsia

While the Hollywood crowd is condemning the United States, another group of elitists is openly advocating the transfer of American sovereignty to the United Nations. Hailing from academia, journalism, government, and think tanks, these people have the ability to shape public opinion.

One of the leaders of this pack is former *CBS Evening News* anchor Walter Cronkite. In October 1999, Cronkite was presented with the Norman Cousins Global Governance Award during a gala dinner held at the UN Delegates Dining Room. He began his presentation by declaring that "the first priority of humankind . . . is to establish an effective system of world law."[40] Cronkite fully understands that to create such a system would mean radical changes to our government. But no matter. He advocates a process in which authority over issues of war and peace, the economy and finance, law and justice would be stripped from elected members of the United States Congress and given on a platter to the United Nations.

Cronkite explained,

> We must strengthen the United Nations as a first step toward a world government patterned after our own government with a legislature, executive, and judiciary, and police to enforce its international laws and keep the peace. To do that, of course, we Americans will have to yield up some of our sovereignty. That would be a bitter pill. It would take a lot of courage, a lot of faith in the new order . . . . Within the next few years we must change the basic structure of our global community from the present anarchic system of war and ever more destructive weaponry to a new system governed by a democratic UN federation.[41]

He did not stop there. Cronkite went on to demand that the United States pay its dues to the United Nations because it would do wonders for our "national self-esteem."[42] He called for the ratification of a host of international treaties to include the Law of the Sea Treaty, the Convention to

Eliminate All Forms of Discrimination Against Women, the Convention on the Rights of the Child, and the Rome Statute of the International Criminal Court, which had not yet been signed by Bill Clinton. To do otherwise, Cronkite explained, would be a "failure to live up to our obligations to the United Nations."[43]

Walter Cronkite occupied the anchor's chair at CBS for twenty years— at a time when CNN and FOX News did not exist and when CBS still had its reputation intact. Millions of Americans tuned in to hear "Uncle Walter" report some of the most significant news stories of his day, including the assassination of President John F. Kennedy, the Cuban missile crisis, and Neil Armstrong's first steps on the moon.

In 2003, the former CBS anchor began writing a weekly syndicated newspaper column. In it, Cronkite—once known as "the most trusted man in America," called the United Nations "the world's best hope for a lasting peace."[44] He has also used his influence to raise money for the World Federalist Association—one of the leading advocates of the United Nations and world government. Unfortunately, people still listen to him.

They also listen to people like Strobe Talbott. A journalist with *Time* magazine for twenty-one years, Talbott handed in his press pass in 1993 to join the administration of his former classmate at Oxford, Bill Clinton. Talbott began his government service at the State Department as ambassador-at-large and went on to serve for seven years as deputy secretary of state.

In 1992, just before he joined the Clinton administration, Talbott penned a widely quoted article in *Time* magazine titled "The Birth of a Global Nation," in which he argued that throughout history "the best minds" advocated some form of international government, wondering if "perhaps national sovereignty wasn't such a great idea after all."[45] Talbott argued that sovereignty, national identity, and economic freedom must give way to international government. He wrote,

> Within the next hundred years . . . nationhood as we know it will be obsolete; all states will recognize a single, global authority. A phrase briefly fashionable in the mid 20th century—"citizen of the world"—will have assumed real meaning by the end of the 21st century.[46]

Talbott believes that "the best mechanism for democracy" is to create on a global level the same relationship between nation-states and the UN that exists between states and the federal government in the United States. For countries such as the United States to "allocate certain powers" to the United

Nations, Talbott wrote, "would be the logical extension of the Founding Fathers' wisdom, therefore a special source of pride for a world government's American constituents."[47]

Today, Talbott constructs the new world order from his platforms as the president of the Brookings Institution, one of the oldest and best-funded think tanks in the country. Talbott also heads the Yale Center for the Study of Globalization, which advocates the establishment of a "global governance for peace and security" and a system for "global economic governance." Today, intellectuals with influence have wholeheartedly embraced Talbott's outlook for the future of the world with the United Nations at the center of political, military, and economic influence.

Another leading agitator for UN dominance is Professor Jeffrey Sachs. Long affiliated with Harvard University, Sachs is now a professor at Columbia University in New York City and director of the school's Earth Institute. He is also the director of the UN Millennium Project and a special advisor to UN secretary-general Kofi Annan. In Sachs, Kofi Annan has recruited a pit-bull who will stand by his side and attack the United States at the drop of a hat.

While there is hardly a UN institution that Sachs would not defend, he is most animated in promoting the Millennium Development Goals—a tax on gross domestic product (GDP) that would force the United States to give the UN $80 billion each year. The last time the United Nations was in charge of that kind of money, it resulted in massive amounts of corruption in the form of the Oil-for-Food scandal.

Not only does Professor Sachs want to slap an international levy on Uncle Sam's GDP, but he told *Esquire* magazine in May 2004 that there should be a "save the world" tax on the richest Americans. He estimates such a tax would generate $35 billion annually that could be given to the poor. That kind of thinking lead *Time* magazine in 2004 to include Sachs on its list of the "100 Most Influential People in the World."

For the United States to give anything short of the UN-imposed 0.7 percent tax on GDP causes Sachs to condemn his country. In South Africa at the World Summit on Sustainable Development in August 2002, Sachs attacked the United States for what he considered paltry contributions to the world's poor. During a press briefing I attended, Sachs was asked if the United States was contributing enough to the UN for development assistance. He responded,

When the U.S. was rich and booming, it was giving little money. When the U.S. was in recession, it was giving little money. When the stock market had raised wealth by more than $10 trillion, it gave little money. When the stock market had come down, it had given little money. When there was a $4 trillion cumulative projected budget surplus over the next ten years, it gave little money. Now that the budget surplus is vanquished, it gives little money. When there was ample resources in the budget [the Bush administration] decided to give huge amounts of that in tax cuts for the American people. It did not choose to address even a small amount in a meaningful way to the issues that are at this summit.[48]

It's all America's fault. That is what Jeffrey Sachs believes, and he proclaims it incessantly to every domestic and international news outlet that will listen to him—and most of them do. Three years after Johannesburg, Sachs was still singing from the same sheet of music as President Bush prepared to meet with leaders of the G-8 in Scotland—a meeting in which aid to Africa played a major role. A few weeks prior to that meeting, Sachs penned a column in the *Los Angeles Times* titled "Africa's Suffering is Bush's Shame" and declared that "the millions of Africans who die young and the hundreds of millions going hungry are not victims of fate. They are the consequences of U.S. policy."[49]

Because he is willing to attack the United States in such stark terms, Jeffrey Sachs is valuable to Kofi Annan, and it doesn't hurt that Sachs commands significant media attention at home and abroad. Sachs is not just another dubiously opinionated economist. He can influence the bureaucracies of government to spend more money on Kofi Annan's pet projects.

In his most recent work, *The End of Poverty*, Sachs argues for a modern-day Marshall Plan for the continent of Africa. As part of that strategy, he wrote, "it is time for the debts of the highly indebted poor countries to be cancelled outright as part of the financing package for the Millennium Goals-based poverty reduction strategies."[50]

Sachs got his wish. On June 13, 2005, President Bush announced in the Eisenhower Executive Office Building, with the presidents of Botswana, Ghana, Mozambique, Namibia, and Niger at his side, that the United States, along with other G-8 countries, were canceling more than $40 billion in debt for mostly African countries.

Kofi Annan views Jeffrey Sachs as an asset for another reason. Sachs believes—and has accused the United States—of being "as capable of barbarism as anyone else."[51] Whether the topic is economics or national security, Sachs is ready to blame America first, last, and always. "Much of the time the barbarism in Iraq goes unrecorded, as when American tanks sweep into Iraqi neighborhoods and kill dozens of innocents in the name of fighting 'insurgents,'"[52] he wrote. He called the United States a "supposedly civilized country"[53] and expressed more disdain for the "torture"[54] by Americans on Iraqi prisoners at the Abu Ghraib prison than for the savage beheading of American Nicholas Berg.

But lest you think too little of Jeffrey Sachs, he did go out of his way to clarify his thoughts. "I am not saying," Sachs explained, "that the U.S. is more depraved than other countries," only that Americans are capable of "barbaric thinking."[55]

When he's not attacking his country, Jeffrey Sachs is advocating global government. Like Strobe Talbott, Sachs acknowledges that globalization "requires international governance and rules . . . it cannot function without international law and international institutions," and strongly believes that "globalization is a powerful and generally positive force."[56]

Bill Clinton: President of the World

The presidency of the United States is the most powerful office on earth. But there are those who would like to see the post of UN secretary-general be just as powerful and influential. The ambitions of one former American president—William Jefferson Clinton—are at the forefront of this effort.

Within weeks of leaving the Oval Office, the self-described "Comeback Kid" was plotting his redemption strategy that would have him become the first U.S. secretary-general. By virtue of his previous position, Clinton would be considered "President of the World."[57]

For Clinton, the attraction of being secretary-general is more than just a way to keep himself busy. He and his partner Hillary Rodham are all about making history. From their earliest days in the White House, the Clintons plowed new ground. The First Lady led the effort to socialize the health care system. Mr. Clinton manipulated the Middle East peace process in an attempt to get his hands on the Holy Grail of the international intelligentsia—the Nobel Peace Prize. Hillary Clinton has become the only First Lady to go on to serve in Congress, and she is determined to become the first female president.

Clinton has an insatiable appetite for power and the limelight. The secretary-general's post would satisfy that thirst, and, given Clinton's experience in presiding over an administration that was part street gang, part fraternity house, he is perfectly suited to lead the asylum that is the United Nations. After writing his memoirs and opening his library in Little Rock, Clinton believes he must finish out his post-presidential career in a way no other former president has.

It was once rumored that Clinton would serve as chancellor of his alma mater, Oxford University. But two of his predecessors have already worked in higher education—Thomas Jefferson founded the University of Virginia, and John Tyler served as chancellor at the College of William and Mary.

Running for Congress or mayor of New York City was also believed a possibility for Clinton. But that would only add Clinton's name to a list that already includes John Quincy Adams and Andrew Johnson. Donning the black robe of a Supreme Court justice would bore Bill Clinton; besides, it's already been done by William Howard Taft. It was also believed that Clinton might move to the West Coast and lead a major Hollywood studio. But comparisons to the ever-popular Ronald Reagan would get under his skin. But as secretary-general, Clinton would hold a post no other U.S. president has ever held.

But what is good for Bill Clinton would be a disaster for the country. It would be seen as a pedestal for challenging and undermining the U.S. presidency, which is more than just another political office. Strength, justice, and generosity are among the many characteristics embodied by the occupant of the Oval Office. Our president is not only the head of state and the commander-in-chief; he is our First Citizen—America's representative to the world through whom our benevolence is offered.

The Bully Pulpit of which Teddy Roosevelt spoke is not confined to America's shores. Ronald Reagan used it to great affect when, standing at the Brandenburg Gate in 1987, he demanded that Mikhail Gorbachev "tear down this wall" that separated the people of Germany into two states—oppressed and free. When the need arose for the president to confront a hostile regime, would Secretary-General Bill Clinton stand with America, or would he undermine his country by claiming a responsibility to serve the world community?

For Bill Clinton to hold the greatest political office in the world and later try to "improve" on that by presiding over a bunch of third-world thugs is to place his personal ambition over national interest. "Our country is that spot to which our heart is bound," Voltaire once remarked. Not so for Bill Clinton. He, like Diogenes, sees himself as a "citizen of the world."

Even considering such a move shows that Bill Clinton still doesn't understand our national character. On overseas trips while president, he constantly apologized for what he perceived to be America's mistakes. Unlike most Americans, he loathes, not loves, the young people who put their lives on the line in our nation's military. He never understood the anger and disappointment citizens had in him when he disgraced the Oval Office through his personal failings.

Americans place our national pride on a pedestal that is forever guarded by citizen-sentries. That pride would be undermined by a former president treating the Oval Office as a stepping stone to a "higher calling." Simply put, the United Nations is not worthy of a former American president—even one like Bill Clinton.

With Clinton as secretary-general, the United Nations would consolidate power at the international level. Throughout his two terms, Bill Clinton tried to strengthen the United Nations—an effort he kicked off in his first address to the General Assembly when he implored delegates to "think anew about whether our institutions of international cooperation are adequate to the moment."[58]

With Clinton at the helm, the United States would be under greater pressure to "lead by example" and sign on to the Kyoto Protocol and the International Criminal Court. American taxpayers would be expected to fund fully the Millennium Development Goals, provide troops for endless UN peacekeeping missions, assent to the creation of a World Environmental Organization, and sign on to an Arms Trade Treaty.

In addition to his post-presidential perks, Secretary-General Clinton would receive a hefty salary and a mansion on New York's posh Sutton Place replete with servants, drivers, and entertainment expenses. More importantly, as a former president, Mr. Clinton is entitled to national security briefings and has access to classified materials. Would it really be a good idea to allow Mr. Clinton—as secretary-general—to broker deals between the United States and other nations? But as secretary-general, Clinton could easily undermine U.S. goals in any part of the world with a statement, a visit, or by sending his own special envoy to counter an American dignitary.

It has long been believed that the membership of the General Assembly would not tolerate an American in the post of secretary-general. While that is true of most Americans, Bill Clinton is the exception the General Assembly and the professional UN staff would not only tolerate, but would wholeheartedly embrace. He would be seen as their advocate. To allow a former American president to lead the United Nations would be to create a "super-presidency" that would only compete for the attention and affections of the American public and our allies abroad. It would be a mistake of grand proportions.

United Nations Election Monitors

One of the most disgraceful displays of propping up the United Nations occurred during the 2004 presidential election. Throughout our history, the United States has been a beacon for freedom and democracy to the rest of the world. Ours is the example oppressed peoples across the globe pray they can replicate in their own countries. But many liberals in the U.S. no longer believe in our democracy. They see our system as corrupted; our Constitution as outdated. They see the electoral process in the United States badly in need of repair. The savior to whom they have turned is the United Nations.

During the 2004 election season, thirteen members of the House of Representatives sent a letter to UN secretary-general Kofi Annan requesting the United Nations to monitor our national elections—elections in which we chose 535 members of the House, one-third of the Senate, and, of course, the next president of the United States. The cast of globalists was led by Congresswoman Eddie Bernice Johnson, a Democrat from Texas, and included Representatives Corrine Brown (FL), Julia Carson (IN), William Lacy Clay (MO), Joseph Crowley (NY), Elijah Cummings (MD), Danny Davis (IL), Raul Grijalva (AZ), Mike Honda (CA), Barbara Lee (CA), Carolyn Maloney (NY), Jerry Nadler (NY), and Edolphus Towns (NY).

On July 1, 2004, just days before the nation's 228th birthday, this group pleaded with Kofi Annan to dispatch election observers from the scandal-ridden United Nations, saying they were "deeply concerned that the right of U.S. citizens to vote in free and fair elections is again in jeopardy."[59] "International oversight is critical," Johnson and her colleagues wrote, because of "issues related to the methodology of elections inside the United States."[60]

The group claimed that the 2000 Florida recount violated the Universal Declaration of Human Rights, the International Covenant on Civil and Political Rights, and the Convention on the Elimination of All Forms of Racial Discrimination.

Representative Shelia Jackson Lee demanded on the floor of the Congress, "we need international observers to affirm the fact that we have lived up to our own obligations, duties and values."[61] Indiana congressman

Steve Buyer called their request to the UN "foolish, nonsense and silly."[62] But it was worse than that.

The thirteen individuals who made the request of the UN are all elected members of the United States House of Representatives—the greatest democratic body on earth—and each swore an oath to protect and defend the Constitution. Yet they were willing to entrust the most sacred act of American democracy—our presidential election—to an international institution that is unaccountable to the American people and mired by scandal and corruption.

Johnson reached out to the UN's Electoral Assistance Division (EAD), which was created in 1991 by General Assembly Resolution 46/137 "to assist Member States in their efforts to hold credible and legitimate democratic elections in accordance with internationally recognized criteria." In so doing, she and her colleagues asked for help from an institution comprising of state sponsors of terrorism, human rights abusers, dictatorships, and repressive monarchies.

The Group of 13 was unfazed. Only UN election monitors can prevent "questionable practices and voter disenfranchisement on Election Day," they wrote. Their actions show they have no faith in their own people and their own institutions of government.

Democrats no longer have faith in a process that is filled with checks and balances. To them it is not enough that voters are protected by the Voting Rights Act of 1965, the Help America Vote Act, the Justice Department, the U.S. Commission on Civil Rights, the courts, the Election Assistance Commission, appeals to interest groups, state or national political party organizations, independent media investigations, and myriad other local, state, or federal agencies. The only institution with the moral authority and integrity to process voter complaints, Democrats believe, is the United Nations. By asking the UN for help, these Democrats put the United States on par with third-world embarrassments like Angola, Cambodia, Ethiopia, Haiti, Mozambique, Nicaragua, and Namibia to which the UN has dispatched observers or otherwise provided assistance in national elections.

Their goal was to embarrass the United States and the Bush administration. Elitist global bureaucrats were elated at the opportunity to kick Uncle Sam. Once the Group of 13 sent their letter to the UN, the terrorist mouthpiece, *Al Jazeera*, wasted no time in posting a headline on their web site: "U.S. lawmakers ask for poll observers."[63]

Democrats showed no sense of embarrassment or concern for national pride. Representative Corrine Brown of Florida charged that Republicans "stole the election" in the 2000 Florida recount in what she described as a "coup d'etat." "We are not going to get over it," she declared, and in the next election, she demanded, "we want verification from the world."[64]

As a final arbiter, the Supreme Court was not good enough for them. In their petition to Kofi Annan, the Group of 13 complained that "the [2000] election was finally determined by the U.S. Supreme Court."[65] But if the United States Supreme Court does not qualify as the final word in American jurisprudence, who does? The International Court of Justice? The International Criminal Court? The UN Security Council? The International Olympic Committee?

Some Democrats have no problem appealing the Supreme Court's decision to an international body. "What in the world are we worried about?" asked Representative Carolyn Maloney. Congressman Steny Hoyer of Maryland wondered aloud on the House floor why it is okay for the United States to send election monitors to other nations but refuse them here. "Are we too proud, too arrogant," Hoyer inquired, to ask for help from third-world election monitors?

Why should we? The United States is the greatest country in the world. We practice democracy better than any other nation on earth. The great sin of liberalism is the belief that the United States really is no better than other countries. We are.

That's not to say that Americans have all the answers. Russia has contributed greatly to the arts and Germany to engineering and Cubans to cigar making. The French dominate the pastry industry.

But let's not pretend that Libya or Cuba or Iran or any other Kofi Annan-approved dictatorial UN member state can teach us more about representative government than could Jefferson and Madison. By requesting UN election monitors, Democrats turned their backs on their neighbors and placed their trust in a corrupt institution. By insisting that only foreigners can adjudicate the outcome of our elections, Democrats believe that we Americans can no longer govern ourselves.

Unfortunately for Eddie Bernice Johnson and the Group of 13, Kofi Annan turned their request down on a technicality. But that didn't stop them. They simply changed the salutation on their letter and fired it off to Secretary of State Colin Powell.

When the request for international election monitors reached Foggy Bottom, it clearly fell into the hands of somebody who misread the Constitution. Believing that the "State Department," not the "States," run our federal elections, an invitation was immediately issued to the

Organization for Security and Cooperation in Europe (OSCE). That was the only way to ensure "that citizens have the ability to exercise their vote in a free, fair, and transparent election," wrote Paul Kelly, assistant secretary for legislative affairs, in his correspondence to Johnson. The Europeans, upset with Mr. Bush for a host of reasons, were more than happy to assemble a crack team of French, German, and Bulgarian poll watchers and dispatch them to the United States.

It was the first time this Republic's presidential election was monitored by representatives from foreign nations. Representative Eddie Bernice Johnson glibly applauded the State Department's decision, stating that "the presence of monitors will assure Americans that America cares about their votes."[66]

But the OSCE, Congressman Ron Paul pointed out, has a "terrible record," noting that in 2004, the organization approved the election of Georgia's Mikheil Saakashvili "with a Saddam Hussein-like 97 percent of the vote."

The Group of 13 was joined by the San Francisco-based Global Exchange, which organized international monitors from Ghana, Nicaragua, and Zambia to proctor the elections in five battleground states. Global Exchange reasoned that "honest scrutiny, serious reporting, and thoughtful recommendations from outside observers can help rebuild public trust in our democracy."[67]

But who, exactly, has lost trust in our democracy? If we can't come together as Americans and trust one another as fellow countrymen, how exactly are powerbrokers from third-world countries supposed to help?

It was not far back in our nation's history that Democrats and Republicans viewed the transfer of power as evidence that our system worked. In 1995, when Dick Gephardt had to concede Democrat control of the House of Representatives for the first time in forty years, he handed the gavel to newly elected Speaker Newt Gingrich, saying, "This is a day to celebrate a power that belongs not to any political party, but to the people, no matter the margin, no matter the majority."[68]

Such comments stand in stark contrast to the "Electoral SOS" the Group of 13 blared around the globe, inviting the world community to poke America in the eye. After the OSCE decided to deploy election observers to the United States, foreign journalists immediately ordered more ink to run their splashy headlines. "Russian Observers to Monitor U.S. Presidential Poll," crowed *ITAR-TASS*, the official Russian news agency. A Canadian newspaper headline read, "Third World Monitors U.S. Elections."

Such logic leads one to believe that the nation that won the Cold War, rebuilt Europe after World War II, put a man on the moon, implanted the first artificial heart, and has led by example on human rights, women's rights, civil rights, and voter's rights is incapable of fixing problems with our electoral system without the help of outsiders.

Beyond the issue of national pride are the practical implications of allowing foreigners a voice in our electoral process. When OSCE monitors arrived in the United States, they met predominantly with liberal organizations that do the bidding of the Democratic Party. They held meetings with organizations such as the Lawyers Committee for Civil Rights Under Law, NAACP, People for the American Way, and the Leadership Conference on Civil Rights, among others. The OSCE also met with eight representatives from Congress—all but one of them were Democrats.

In its preliminary report, the OSCE complained that without a national election guru in Washington, secretaries of state "were left without needed guidelines, and found it impossible to avail themselves of the funding for new voting technology."[69] They carped that voter identification is made more difficult because Americans are not required to carry a "national identification document."[70] This group of outsiders ginned up anxiety prior to Election Day by predicting (wrongly) "greater controversy" in the 2004 election than there was in 2000 because voting machines do not "produce the necessary paper trail."[71]

The group also charged that states that allow overseas voters voluntarily to waive their right to a secret vote by faxing a marked ballot are "not consistent with . . . the Universal Declaration of Human Rights and OSCE commitments."[72] What the OSCE sees as a violation of a United Nations declaration is what we in America call freedom of choice. If the OSCE demanded we apply Kofi Annan's standards, thousands of U.S. military personnel living and fighting abroad could be deprived of their right to vote.

The OSCE report bemoaned the fact that the U.S. has no "central election body" like the IRS that would efficiently administer the presidential election. Our Founders called that federalism, and they purposely decentralized the voting process. We believe citizens can better administer elections at the local level than can bureaucrats in Washington, much less third-world novices.

After Election Day, the OSCE lived up to expectations. One day after Senator Kerry conceded defeat, election monitors from the OSCE called a press conference to critique U.S. elections and lobby for fundamental changes in the American system. The international observers proposed an

IRS-like federal election agency and attacked the Help America Vote Act (HAVA), which Congress passed after the 2000 Florida recount, alleging its sweeping reforms were inadequate. "In order to meet all its OSCE commitments, the U.S. election reforms will have to go beyond HAVA, particularly regarding access for international observers," said Rita Suessmuth, head of the OSCE long-term election observation mission. Apparently it's not enough to have free and fair elections—the United States also needs to satisfy OSCE demands.

The OSCE also blamed state legislatures for creating congressional districts that produce insufficiently competitive voting districts, implying that the system in inherently illegitimate and unfair. They failed to note that redistricting is both a constitutional and democratic process in which citizens vote for their state representatives who later draw congressional districts based on the constitutionally mandated census.

In the elections of 2004, Democrats got their wish—international inspections of elections and global pressure to adhere to international standards. They are helping the UN achieve its long-term goal of building itself into an international superpower that can challenge the United States on all fronts.

Epilogue: Connecting the Dots

The alternate title for this book might have been *Connecting the Dots*. It is a phrase that has been used frequently in our nation's capital after September 11, 2001, by lawmakers and analysts both, who blame each other for the failure to recognize and pinpoint the al Qaeda attacks, which not only killed thousands, but forced dramatic changes in U.S. foreign policy and in the way Americans live.

The months prior to that fateful day offered plenty of evidence. The hijackers were in the United States and were taking flight lessons, but they eschewed those classes dealing with landings. The previous terrorist hits on U.S. targets were leading to something bigger. Even Osama bin Laden's explicit warnings that more was to come should have triggered an alarm for the nation's caretakers.

But few in Washington wanted to "connect the dots" and risk their reputations to issue such a dramatic warning. It may be hard to believe in the aftermath, but alerting the country—in 1999 or 2000—to the possibility of the carnage we saw on 9/11 would have gotten a member of Congress laughed out of town. Terrorism was not a problem according to Washington. The mainstream media would have never considered pulling cameras from celebrity courtroom trials to discuss the topic, and Democrats were obsessed with what they believed was a "stolen" election.

There were many reasons the dots were never connected and the issue never reached the public's attention. There was a failure to communicate among the various national security agencies. There were shortcomings in capturing intelligence. There was wholesale indifference to the subject in the media. But above all was the simple fact that officials in Washington were too arrogant to believe such a thing could happen in the United States.

Unfortunately, we find ourselves in a similar situation with an adversary that is dangerous for different reasons. Just as we failed to heed the "pre-9/11" evidence that forced us to change our lives, our laws, and our foreign policy, we are now ignoring the overwhelming evidence that our sovereignty is under attack by the United Nations. The UN's offensive is not of a military nature; there will be no homicide bombers in blue helmets. It is an attack of a much more insidious nature.

At the same time, the United Nations is using American tax dollars to promote its own reputation across the world while undermining the reputation and legitimacy of the United States. The United Nations is outlining a system of global government to which all nations would be subordinate. They are challenging our national sovereignty every chance they get. They are building, with U.S. resources, the institutions that make up the global bureaucracy. They have forged alliances with the guardians of America's popular culture to shift the allegiance of America's next generation from the Republic to the UN.

These are but a few of the signs—and more are evident. But will members of Congress "connect the dots" and take action? Or will Americans wake up one morning to find one of their own answering to a foreign judge at the International Criminal Court? Will caskets with the remains of American servicemen one day return to Dover Air Force Base draped with the powder blue UN flag? Will we realize after it's too late that a "user fee" has been slapped on selected consumer services in the United States to fund the operations of the United Nations? Perhaps lost sovereignty will come in the form of American businesses and National Park authorities having to abide by global regulations written by a World Environmental Organization. After all, such is already the case in matters of international trade.

Congressman Ron Paul of Texas has alerted his colleagues to these warnings for many years. Some—but not nearly enough—are beginning to listen. His legislation, the American Sovereignty Restoration Act, would terminate America's membership in the United Nations and its specialized agencies, a goal that is supported by the American public.

But Congress is ruled by the lobbyists and the media, and the K Street crowd does not champion the cause of Middle America. Their attention is caught by the sight of powerful international interests with extensive financial resources. And unfortunately, no media outlet is willing to slap a warning label on the slick packaging of the United Nations' utopian ideals that promise peace, stability, and global happiness—but deliver instead corruption, greed, incompetence, and chaos.

One need only look to February 2006 to understand the split between the American people and the government. It was then that the public learned that a shipping company from the United Arab Emirates would be allowed to conduct operations at six of America's busiest ports. When the public outcry reached the tin ears of the Bush administration, the response was that critics are nothing more than a bunch of racist rubes who don't understand the complexities of globalization and national security. But public opposition to the port deal is no different from Mr. Bush's expressed opposition to putting America's national defense in the hands of the UN Security Council or leaving America's fate to the United Nations.

The warning signs of lost sovereignty abound, and the course of action that must be taken is clear. The United States must reclaim its destiny and sever its relationship with the United Nations.

A National Doubt No More

"Isolationist!" "Protectionist!" "Nativist!"

That is what the critics will shout after reading the advice in *Diplomatic Divorce* if, in fact, the detractors read the book. They may simply glance at the cover, determine that the author dared to question the authority of the United Nations—the golden calf of utopians—and charge him with wanting to "withdraw from the world."

Let detractors call names and hurl epithets, for that is all they have left in their arsenal of excuses. With six decades passed, the test phase of the UN is over. In its stated mission—to maintain international peace and security and advance the cause of human rights—the grades are in and the results are disastrous. Billions of dollars have been transferred from over-worked Americans to UN peacekeeping missions in Haiti, Bosnia, Somalia, Congo, Rwanda, and others, only to see those missions fail. And to add insult to injury, the "good guys" in the blue helmets have terrorized and exploited children for sport. While teenage girls struggle through labor, bringing to life the child who was conceived against their will by a UN peacekeeper, bureaucrats in Turtle Bay organize their social calendars.

At its founding, there actually was a requirement for membership in the United Nations. Countries wishing to join the new institution at the close of World War II had to have declared war on one of the Axis powers—proof that they were willing to choose good over evil. The United Nations of today is incapable of such distinctions. It does not choose sides. It refuses to be a voice of moral authority. At the UN, the dais on which the terrorist sits is the same height as that of the statesman. The institution has no standards and imposes no punishments. Evil cannot be defeated when the UN refuses to recognize it. The rules under which the United Nations purports to maintain international peace and security are inherently flawed and inimical to American goals and values.

The United Nations is influencing our foreign policy. After the 1993 UN debacle in Mogadishu, Somalia, and the court-martial of Michael New—a decorated Army medic who refused orders to wear the UN insignia—conservatives stepped up their efforts to keep U.S. troops out of UN peacekeeping missions. But Americans are still placed in those operations. The creation of the International Criminal Court (ICC) forces the president to limit where and how American forces can be deployed throughout the world and makes it imperative to keep American troops from serving under the UN banner.

The UN threatens American citizens. In two consecutive years, the UN Security Council was asked to exempt U.S. citizens from ICC proceedings, a request the Security Council was unwilling to grant. To Kofi Annan, American soldiers, sailors, airmen, and Marines are fair game for prosecution in The Hague. By creating an international court that is hostile to the United States, the UN has made it more difficult for American presidents to carry out their foreign policy.

Participation in the United Nations injures our national pride. In other countries, children are sold into slavery; young women are traded into prostitution; genocide is taking place in Sudan, and men and women of all ages are forced to work long hours under extreme conditions on the factory floor. But the leaders of governments that condone and encourage that kind of behavior are invited to join the UN Human Rights Commission. Yet, the United States was booted off the Commission in 2001.

The American investment of time and money in the United Nations must now come to an end. The sixty-year international orgy at the UN has left Uncle Sam with a diplomatically transmitted disease. It is called "national doubt."

The Democratic party no longer believes that the United States is capable of carrying out our own foreign policy. The approval of the French, the Germans, and the Secretariat of the United Nations is needed before members of Congress are willing to endorse a policy to protect the American homeland. It is the "global test" to which John Kerry would have us submit. After U.S. soldiers, sailors, airmen, and Marines liberated the Iraqi people, leading Democrats demanded the keys to the country be turned over to the United Nations because they did not trust their own government to carry out the mission.

Democrats and Republicans both have doubts in America's ability to trade with other countries. Unlike our Founding Fathers, they don't believe Congress is capable of regulating U.S. commerce among nations. They simply don't believe Americans can manage the intricacies of foreign trade, so they subcontract that constitutional responsibility to the World Trade Organization (WTO).

Democrats believe the American public to be incapable of conducting and policing our own elections. Instead of trusting our friends and neighbors, instead of believing that an electoral cheat will be found out by the numerous checks and balances built into our system, Democrats insist on having Kofi Annan's stamp of approval before the manner in which we choose our leaders is considered valid.

The liberal establishment no longer trusts their government and their elected leaders. Friendly challenges to what was believed to be misguided policy is no longer part of their game plan. There is no such thing as legitimate debate on points of political nuance. What was once a "Loyal Opposition" is now a kennel of rabid attack dogs that no longer trust the President or believe in their institutions of government. To them, George W. Bush is a terrorist, inherently evil and unworthy of trust, and the United States is a purveyor of violence, disease, famine, and sorrow throughout the world. To liberal extremists, our military men and women are not heroic characters who choose national service, but wild-eyed, would-be postal workers who carry out their violent ambitions on the less fortunate in the world, and under the protective legitimacy of the uniform. The only alternative to this chaos is Kofi Annan and the United Nations, liberals believe.

When the suggestion is made that the United States should leave the UN, the question I am most often asked is, "What would we do then?" This mindset into which many Americans have fallen is a dangerous one. Only the United Nations is keeping us from falling into an economic and diplomatic abyss from which we will never emerge, they believe. They feel as though our government cannot conduct diplomacy of its own accord. They actually believe that countries like Iraq, Iran, and Sudan fear referrals to the Security Council. They don't. In fact, they welcome it. Given the Council's record of incompetence and impotence, leaders of dictatorial regimes know they have years to build power and alliances before the United Nations would ever take meaningful action to challenge their authority.

Though they live in a country that has the strongest economy in the world, the greatest military the planet has ever known, the most effective bully pulpit, and the most creative and generous people to be found, the Left gives higher approval ratings to the United Nations than to their own country.

Faith in the Republic must be restored. One prescription for curing the Left's patriotic illness is to remove the cancer from American policy that is the United Nations. This does not mean, as the critics charge, that the United States will withdraw from the world—not at all.

The United States should be engaged with other nations; we should have dialogue and carry out diplomatic efforts in as many countries as possible. Our State Department maintains more than 250 embassies, consulates, and missions around the world. That is how it should be. Secretary of State Condoleezza Rice will likely go down as the most-traveled cabinet secretary in our history. A strong diplomatic effort pays off, as in the case of Libya, which volunteered to give up its nuclear program rather than challenge the United States.

American citizens value their ability to travel abroad—whether for business or personal reasons—and meet people from other cultures. Withdrawal from the United Nations does not mean that they should stay home. Cultural and student exchanges with foreign nations are a welcome component of an engaged diplomacy, but a certain degree of security and discretion is required. America's nuclear labs, for example, should not be open to foreign tours as they were during the Clinton administration.

The U.S. economy is reliant upon international trade for much of its strength, and the United States should continue to trade with as many foreign nations as will fairly trade with us. But it should not be at any cost, and it should not be regulated by the World Trade Organization, for international commerce that is regulated by the WTO is anything but free. Congress must reclaim its role in foreign trade and begin once again to represent the interests of its constituents against foreign competitors. What is objectionable is not the fact that the United States is engaged around the world, but that politicians of both political parties allow America's foreign and economic policies to be chaperoned by Kofi Annan and the United Nations.

Alternatives to Failure

Some analysts agree with the prescription for American withdrawal from the United Nations, but they defend the concept of multilateral security arrangements, and on that basis, argue that a different international organization should be created to take the place of the United Nations. A working title for such an institution is a "League of Democracies." But recent events show the problem with trying to address the unique and ever-changing challenges to U.S. foreign policy through an "entangling alliance" such as a permanent international institution.

The "League of Democracies" theory gained favor as President Bush advanced his dream to spread democracy throughout the world. But the electoral process in places like Venezuela, Iran, Egypt, and other areas of the Middle East have lately produced governments with which the American public is not necessarily enamored. These are among the most anti-American regimes on earth. But they may very well qualify to be included in a League of Democracies. France and Germany are democracies, but they were among America's most vociferous critics on the question of the 2003 Iraq war.

This "League of Democracies" or "Alliance of Free Nations" as others have called it, in a sense already exists—it's called NATO—the North Atlantic Treaty Organization. The expansion of NATO since the collapse of the Soviet empire includes many of the significant members who would otherwise be included in a world league.

The real problem with creating an alternative to the United Nations is one of the main issues with the UN itself—its effect on national sovereignty. Most analysts interpret this from the American perspective. Is U.S. sovereignty being undermined by the United Nations? That is a fair, and obviously, significant component of this book.

But policy makers should also be concerned that U.S. participation in the United Nations undermines that sovereignty of foreign nations and makes them dependent on American generosity. National sovereignty is to the country what personal responsibility is to the individual. We need only to look at certain events and cultural trends in America to see the diminished value our society has placed on personal responsibility.

In the U.S., it has become widely (but wrongly) accepted that obesity is not the fault of the individual but of the fast food restaurants. Lung cancer is never caused by the habits of the smoker, but by tobacco companies. The alcoholic blames the bartender. More and more in the United States, we rely on the federal government to raise our children, fund our charities, buy us prescription drugs, and upgrade our televisions when new technologies come along. For as much as we question the policies of socialist Europeans, the United States is well on its way to nanny-state status.

Those socialist and maternal instincts are not only taking place on the home front, but on the international stage as well. The May 2005 edition of *Frontlines*, the official publication of the U.S. Agency for International

Development, boasted that the United States led a coalition of nations in transferring $78.6 billion worth of welfare to third world nations. The report stated:

> The United States led other nations in ODA [Official Development Assistance] in 2004, handing out $19 billion.... The U.S. ODA was 14 percent above its assistance in 2003 and marked a doubling in the government's development aid since 2000. Under the Bush administration, U.S. assistance rose from $10 billion in 2000 to $19 billion in 2004. At a State Department briefing April 11 [2005], spokesman Richard Boucher said: "Official development assistance from the United States constitutes 24 percent of the world total, the highest share of such support in nearly 20 years. Our current assistance levels are more than twice the commitment made by President Bush at the Monterrey Financing for Development Conference in 2002."

Official Development Assistance is a diplomatic name for global welfare, and it is not an achievement the Bush administration ought to tout. Instead, like Republicans did when they reformed welfare in the 1990s, we ought to ask how many nations are self-sufficient enough to no longer require financial assistance from the United States. That, however, is not what the United Nations wants. Like Democrats who thrive on keeping people on welfare so they can campaign for more federal assistance, the United Nations would lose much of its mandate if third-world nations were able to take care of themselves. And what is the incentive for less-than-reputable leaders of governments to reform their corrupt systems if they know the United States—through the United Nations—will take care of their problems?

All nations must do more to provide for their own economic and security needs. But a League of Democracies, like a United Nations Security Council, only provides an outlet for countries to dump their problems. It can also provide false hope to citizens who need to do more themselves to resist or turn back the forces of tyranny within their own nations.

The United Nations was created in part to provide a forum for world leaders to discuss issues of international importance and to ease the process of communication. Again, this is a worthy goal—presidents and prime ministers should have the opportunity to speak on a regular basis. But a formal institution costing hundreds of millions of dollars and requiring thousands of staff is not necessary. Advancements in communications technology and access to rapid global travel make a permanent substitute to the United Nations less important.

Many others argue that the United Nations needs to be reformed, and they bicker only over the kind and amount of necessary changes. Former House speaker Newt Gingrich and former senator George Mitchell chaired a bipartisan commission in 2005 that examined UN problems and possible reforms. The commission looked at five areas: human rights, proliferation of weapons of mass destruction, ending conflicts, poverty, and the UN's institutional integrity and accountability. From the outset, the commission was flawed in that it did not examine the impact the UN has on American sovereignty. In its report, *American Interests and UN Reform*, the commission wrote,

> As important stakeholders in the institution, Americans are vested in a United Nations that embodies values of honesty, decency, and fair play. An honest, decent, and just headquarters for effective multilateralism will serve the American people well...because it can serve as a valuable instrument for promoting democratic political development, human rights, economic self-sufficiency and the peaceful settlement of differences.

But the United Nations has failed on each of these fronts and will continue to fail. It has been unsuccessful, in part, because America's priorities are not shared by the permanent UN bureaucracy. And to believe that honesty and decency will soon bloom in Turtle Bay is to chase a dream.

Efforts to reform the UN Human Rights Commission are, at this writing, failing because the thugs who dominate the UN's General Assembly are resisting change and are unwilling to give up their seats that allow them to pass judgments on responsible governments like the United States. The news that garnered the most attention during the reform debate was a report issued by the Human Rights Commission demanding that the United States close its terrorist detention facility at Guantanamo Bay, Cuba. The UN accused the U.S. prison personnel of torture and mistreatment of prisoners, though the authors of the report never visited the facility. The report made news around the world and incited more anger from domestic liberals. The report was not only an effort to embarrass the United States but makes it more difficult for the U.S. to keep terrorists behind bars. It also was issued to distract the public's attention from the failure of the United Nations to reform its own human rights commission.

One area where the United Nations is giving its full effort is the issue of reforming the UN Security Council. It is only because the Security Council is dominated by the permanent five members—the United States among them—that the UN wants to reform the body in order to dilute the influence of the U.S. Just as Franklin Roosevelt tried to pack the Supreme Court to neutralize his political enemies, so too is Kofi Annan trying to pack the UN Security Council. The only "reforms" that are offered by the United Nations are those that would make the UN more powerful and influential.

And it is this consolidation of power and influence that is most disturbing about the United Nations. The idea that the United States holds a veto over UN actions, or is able to influence UN policy may have had some truth to it at one time in the institution's history, but that is no longer the case. We saw this born out in the creation of the International Criminal Court, and we are finding that because of the growing influence of the UN, America is being dragged into agreements that are not in our interests.

A case in point is the UN Law of the Sea Treaty which would give the United Nations control over the seas and oceans, including the exploration and commerce which is conducted on the high seas. U.S. Senator Richard Lugar is a firm supporter of the treaty, as is the Bush administration.

Writing to a constituent on the Law of the Sea Treaty, Lugar revealed a dangerous mindset which shows why the United States should not only withdraw from the UN, but encourage other nations to do the same.

Regarding the Law of the Sea Treaty, Lugar wrote,

> It is important to note that failure to ratify the Convention will not insulate the U.S. Navy or American industry from its provisions. Already, 145 countries have ratified the treaty. Our Navy, our fishermen, our oil and natural gas explorers and our shipping fleet tell us that they have to deal with the Convention whenever they interact on ocean issues with foreign governments or companies.... We should not let the rest of the world make ocean policy that will affect U.S. interests.

What Lugar describes above is a component of international government to which the United States is accountable. He obviously doesn't realize it because earlier in his letter, he incorrectly states that "the Law of the Sea provides *no decision-making role* for the United Nations." Yet the United Nations is making the decisions about the earth's oceans and waterways by which Lugar himself says the American Navy and commercial fishermen must abide. The solution he proposes is that the United States join the other

145 countries in signing and ratifying the Law of the Sea Treaty so we can try to influence the process in America's favor.

Some take this line of argument a step further and insist that even if the United States is opposed to certain provisions of an agreement, or a treaty as a whole, it is better to become a party to a bad treaty and try to make it "less bad" than it is to stay out of it entirely. It is the argument many liberals make regarding the International Criminal Court—that even though we don't agree with every detail, we would be better off allowing a few Americans to be tried before the court so that we can try to influence it and show the Europeans that despite what they read in the press, we're not isolationists after all.

But this line of thinking is, in diplomatic terms, pre-9/11. A similar mindset governed the FBI before September 11, 2001, when it perceived that its role in terrorism was to solve the crime after it occurred rather than to prevent the attack in the first place.

A similar strategy ought to rule our relationship with the United Nations. We need to prevent bad policy from making its way into the portfolio of U.S. treaties or American case law. The United Nations is the global parliament of anti-American public policy—let's shut it down instead of trying to improve the appearance of inherently flawed agreements. Instead of wasting time trying to make the United Nations a little less anti-American and a little less anti-Semitic, let's send the sponsors of such resolutions back to the rocks from under which they crawled.

We've identified and examined the problems.

• *The UN is anti-American to the core.* Attend any one of the United Nation's conferences and you will hear more denunciations of President George W. Bush than you would at the funeral of a prominent Democrat like Paul Wellstone or Coretta Scott King. There is more anti-American sentiment than you could have found in the old Soviet Politburo.

Though the United States has done more to protect and provide for the needs of most UN members than any other country on earth, it is not appreciated. There is no gratitude, only hostility. The irrelevant nations of the world have banded together to capture the General Assembly and turn it into a hotbed of hostility to the most generous people on earth. And instead of pulling the plug on this international megaphone of malice, the American taxpayers are asked to fund it, and fund it, and fund it some more. The only thing more sickening than the garbage that is spewed at America in the halls of the General Assembly is the willingness of the Congress and the executive branch to continue to cut checks to the craven collection of corruption.

• *The United Nations adversely affects American national security.* By convincing the United States to participate in UN peacekeeping missions where we have no vital national security interests, the UN is holding sway over U.S. policy and the lives of American servicemen. In other cases, when American security interests are engaged, as they were in Iraq, the United Nations forced delays in U.S. action that could have been deadly. It is a travesty that U.S. lawmakers are increasingly turning to the United Nations to advise and consent on matters that affect the lives and safety of American citizens.

• *The United Nations undermines America's national sovereignty.* From national security to trade, the United Nations is making decisions that affect American commerce and foreign policy. Members of Congress are now forced to write trade laws that comport with WTO demands. State laws and federal regulations are overturned or rewritten to accommodate the demands of WTO judges. Liberal jurists sitting on America's courts are trying their best to conform their decisions with the UN Charter and the dictates of international institutions.

• *The United Nations undermines the national sovereignty of other nations.* Just as the UN undermines U.S. sovereignty, it does the same to other countries, in some cases, in much more dramatic fashion. This only encourages these countries to become dependent upon the United Nations—which means the U.S. taxpayers support a third-world country that should learn to be self-sufficient. The United States cannot carry the world on its back. Our own society is becoming more socialistic; we are providing for the defense of Europe, trying to democratize the Middle East, and providing humanitarian and economic aid to the third world. Something has got to give. The nation-state must survive the attacks of the UN.

• *The U.S. government has surrendered certain constitutional authority to the United Nations.* By creating the WTO, the members of the U.S. Congress have abdicated their role to regulate commerce with foreign nations and have sold out the constituents whom they are supposed to represent. Trade policy no longer has "the consent of the governed." Through the Arms Trade Treaty and other international agreements, the U.S. Constitution is under attack. It is no longer just the federal courts in the United States that are re-writing that fine document, but international institutions of all stripes are adding their two cents to the legacy left to us by our Founding Fathers.

• *A growing number of Americans are giving their allegiance to the United Nations.* Unfortunately, there are American citizens who are willing to put their faith and trust in a corrupt and unaccountable institution rather than in their own government—simply because it is lead by a man they despise. They speak ill of their country and help the United Nations tear it down. When there is dissatisfaction with the ruling party in the United States, responsible citizenship requires reasoned dialogue and legitimate avenues of change. But by giving allegiance to the United Nations, some Americans are advocating a different form of government to replace our own.

• *The UN is corrupt and a waste of U.S. tax dollars.* The United States is the largest contributor to the United Nations and its peacekeeping efforts. The UN's handling of the Oil-for-Food program should tell us all we need to know about how the corrupt bureaucrats at the UN steward American generosity. The investigation into the program revealed bribes, payoffs, mismanagement, and corruption, for starters. When these faults were exposed, Kofi Annan and his minions stalled, obfuscated, and shifted the blame.

The Oil-for-Food program is only one of dozens of agencies and hundreds of programs at the United Nations that are managed by individuals from countries where governmental corruption is norm. The United Nations is a bureaucracy that gets bigger and more expensive each year, and the burden for its funding falls on the American middle class. It is time to stop throwing U.S. tax dollars into an international sink hole.

• *The United Nations legitimizes illegitimate regimes.* The UN has no standards, no moral authority. Responsible democracies and dictatorships are treated the same in Turtle Bay. There is no incentive for bad regimes to mend their ways when the red carpet is continually rolled out for them at the UN. America's most vocal critics and the world's worst dictators are provided prominent speaking roles and committee assignments at the United Nations. The UN tolerates evil, expects corruption, and rewards incompetence.

The "dots" have now been connected. It is time for American lawmakers to get their heads out of the sand and realize that further participation will only eat away at American sovereignty like a cancer and further injure our national pride. Let us show confidence in our own government and our countrymen to engage the world on America's terms. We do not want to withdraw from the world—only from the United Nations. But those who think the UN is vital to American policy and who place their faith in the false promises of utopian ideals must come to grips with the reality that the UN is contrary to America's best interests. They must realize that it is time for America to end her love affair with the United Nations.

Notes

Introduction

[1] Bob Barr, "International Organizations Continue Threats to our Republic," press release, 12 October 2002.

[2] Patrick J. Buchanan, "Nationalism versus Globalism," speech to the Boston World Affairs Council, 6 January 2000.

[3] Robert Wright, "Continental Drift: World government is coming. Deal with it," *The New Republic*, 17 January 2000.

[4] "Powell heckled at Earth Summit," *CNN.com*, 4 September 2002, http://cnnstudentnews.cnn.com/2002/fyi/news/09/04/earth.lastday.glb/.

[5] "Russia warns of veto on Iraq," BBC, 2 September 2002, http://news.bbc.co.uk/1/hi/world/middle_east/2231483.stm.

Chapter One

[1] White House Office of the Press Secretary, "Remarks by President Bush and Senator John Kerry in First 2004 Presidential Debate," 1 October 2004.

[2] Ibid.

[3] Evan Thomas et al., "Talking the Talk," *Newsweek*, 15 November 2004, 50.

[4] "Remarks by President Bush and Senator John Kerry in First 2004 Presidential Debate."

[5] White House Office of the Press Secretary, "President's Remarks at Victory 2004 Rally in Allentown, Pennsylvania," 1 October 2004.

[6] Political Advertising Resource Center, "Ad analysis," http://www.umdparc.org/AdAnalysisGlobalTest.htm.

[7] Samuel Goldhaber, "John Kerry: A Navy Dove Runs for Congress," *Harvard Crimson*, 18 February 1970.

[8] John Kerry, speech on floor of U.S. Senate, 9 October 2002, S10171.

[9] Ibid., S10174.

[10] Ibid., S10173.

[11] Ibid.

[12] Ibid., S10175.

[13] The 2004 Democratic National Platform for America, "Strong at Home, Respected in the World," 27 July 2004.

[14] Bill Gertz, "2 Russian generals given awards in Iraq on war eve," *Washington Times*, 30 October 2004.

[15] Francois-Xavier Ngoubeyou, UN Security Council, 4701st meeting, 5 February 2003.

[16] Ibid.

[17] Press release, "Hayworth Condemns Mexican Government Sponsorship of Illegal Immigration," 5 January 2005.

[18] Kofi Annan, address to the General Assembly, 12 September 2002.

[19] Charles Krauthammer, "Is This the Way to Decide on Iraq?," *Jewish World Review*, 20 September 2002.

[20] *Congressional Record*, 9 October 2002, S10191.

[21] Ibid.

[22] Ibid.

[23] Ibid., S10192-10193.

[24] Edward Kennedy, *Congressional Record*, 13 March 2003, S3702.

[25] Ibid.

[26] John Edward, "The Right Way in Iraq," *Washington Post*, 13 November, 2005.

[27] Ibid.

[28] Chris Dodd, *Congressional Record*, 9 October 2002.

[29] *Congressional Record*, 8 October 2002, S10077.

[30] Ibid., S10079.

[31] *Congressional Record*, 10 October 2002, H7740.

[32] Ibid., H7742.

[33] Ibid., H7743.

[34] Ibid., H7759.

[35] Ibid., H7759-7760.

[36] Ibid., H7756.

[37] Ibid., H7764.

[38] James Inhofe, *Congressional Record*, 9 October 2002, S10215.

[39] Charles Krauthammer, "The Myth of UN Support," *Washington Post*, 4 October 2002.

[40] Richard Wolffe and Daniel Klaidman, "Judging the Case," *Newsweek*, 17 February 2003.

[41] "Powell Distances Himself from President," *Newsmax.com*, 18 May 2004.

[42] Transcript, "U.S. Secretary of State Colin Powell Addresses the UN Security Council," 5 February 2003. http://www.whitehouse.gov/news/releases/2003/02/20030205-1.html

[43] Dana Priest, "Telling Secret: Not Just What, But How," *Washington Post*, 6 February 2003.

[44] Ibid.

[45] Fred Kaplan, "The Goods on Saddam," *Slate.com*, 31 January 2003.

[46] Ibid.

[47] Bill Nichols, "Powell shares intel on Iraq," *USA Today*, 6 February 2003.

[48] Patrick Radden Keefe, *Chatter: Dispatches from the Secret World of Global Eavesdropping* (New York: Random House, 2005), 210.

[49] Transcript, "U.S. Secretary of State Colin Powell Addresses the UN Security Council," 5 February 2003.

[50] Greg Miller, "U.S. Takes a Risk in Showing Spy Methods," *Los Angeles Times*, 6 February 2003, found at www.globalsecurity.org/org/news/2003/030206-unpowell04.htm.

[51] Transcript, "U.S. Secretary of State Colin Powell Addresses the UN Security Council."

[52] Tim Reid, "No place to hide from hi-tech spies in the sky," *Times of London*, 7 February 2003, found at www.globalsecurity.org/org/news/2003/030207-spies01.htm.

[53] Ibid.

[54] Kenneth Timmerman, *The French Betrayal of America* (New York: Three Rivers Press, 2004), 18.

Chapter Two

[1] John Keegan, "Bad law is making a Just War so much harder to fight," *Daily Telegraph*, 2 June 2005.

[2] Senator Dick Durbin, floor statement on Guantanamo Bay, 14 June 2005.

[3] "US Senator stands by Nazi remark," *AlJazeera.net*, 16 June 2005.

[4] Senator Jesse Helms, press release on Clinton signature, 31 December 2000.

[5] Senator Jesse Helms, *Here's Where I Stand* (New York: Random House, 2005).

[6] Ibid.

[7] Press release, Freedom Alliance, "No Mandate for Flawed Global Court," 15 October 2002.

[8] John Anderson, quarterly newsletter of the World Federalist Association (Spring 2002).

[9] Hans-Peter Kaul, statement before the Prepatory Commission, 27 November 2000.

[10] Fact Sheet: International Criminal Court, U.S. Department of State, 2 August 2002.

[11] Statement of John Bolton, hearings before the Committee on International Relations, House of Representatives, 25 July 2000.

[12] The Ethical Funds Company, "Canadian Energy and Mining Companies—Navigating International Humanitarian Law in the 21st Century," *Sustainability Perspectives*, June 2005.

[13] John Bolton, remarks to the Federalist Society, 14 November 2002.

[14] Ambassador David Scheffer, testimony before the Committee on Foreign Relations of the U.S. Senate, 23 July 1998.

[15] Kofi Annan, letter to Secretary of State Colin Powell, 2 July 2002.

[16] BBC News, "Annan slams war crime exemption," 18 June 2004.

[17] *The National Defense Strategy of the United States of America*, March 2005, 5. http://www.defenselink.mil/news/Mar2005/d20050318nds1.pdf.

[18] "The Pentagon and 'lawfare'," *Washington Times*, 24 March 2005.

[19] *National Defense Strategy*, March 2005, 20.

[20] John Lumpkin, "Legal Challenges, Terrorism Threaten U.S.," *Associated Press*, 18 March 2005.

[21] Criminal indictment against the United States' Secretary of Defense Donald Rumsfeld et al., Center for Constitutional Rights, November 2004.

[22] Amnesty International 2005 Annual Report, www.amnesty.org.

[23] Irene Khan, speech at Foreign Press Association, 25 May 2005.

[24] Press release, Amnesty International, "Selective U.S. Prosecutions in Torture Scandal Underscore International Obligation to Investigate U.S. Officials," 25 May 2005.

[25] Ibid.

[26] "The Dutch Back Down: Bush Sighs with Relief," *Der Spiegel*, 6 May 2005.

[27] *Financial Review*, "Dutch court refuses to jail Bush," 5 May 2005.

[28] Mike Wendling, "Belgium to Change War Crimes Law After US Threats," *CNSNews.com*, 23 June 2003.

[29] Bill Sammon, "Bush tells soldiers international court not for them," *Washington Times*, 20 July 2002, A2.

[30] Ibid.

[31] Harry Dunphy, "US Pulls Out of International Court Treaty," *Associated Press*, 6 May 2002.

[32] Senator Chris Dodd, speech on floor of United States Senate, 13 May 2002.

[33] "Can U.S. 'unsign' a treaty?" *Milwaukee Journal Sentinel*, 29 April 2002.

[34] Ibid.

[35] Glenn Kessler and Colum Lynch, "Critic of U.N. Named Envoy," *Washington Post*, 8 March 2005.

[36] Foreign Press Center Briefing, Pierre-Richard Prosper, U.S. Ambassador for War Crimes Issues, 6 May 2002.

[37] Daily Press Briefing, Richard Boucher, spokesman, U.S. Department of State, 6 May 2002.

[38] Press release, Majority Whip Tom DeLay, "DeLay Calls ICC 'Threat to America's Soldiers and Leaders,'" 6 May 2002.

[39] Ibid.

[40] Statement of Foreign Secretary Robin Cook, "Government to Introduce International Criminal Court Bill," Foreign & Commonwealth Office, 6 December 2000.

[41] Ibid.

[42] Senator Patrick Leahy, speech on floor of United States Senate, 15 December 2000.

[43] Linda Fasulo, *An Insider's Guide to the UN* (New Haven and London: Yale University Press, 2004), 101.

[44] Bruce Anderson, "Blair has let lawyers loose on our armed forces," *Sunday Scotsman*, 24 July 2005.

[45] "Tank chasers," *Daily Telegraph*, 24 July 2005.

[46] Ibid.

[47] Lord Bramall, speech to the House of Lords, 14 July 2005.

[48] Neil Tweedie, "Uproar over 'war crimes' trials," *Daily Telegraph*, 21 July 2005.

[49] Lt. Col. Tim Collins, speech to the 1st Battalion of the Royal Irish Regiment, 19 March 2003.

[50] "We can't brand these soldiers war criminals," *Daily Telegraph*, 21 July 2005.

[51] Lord Inge, speech to the House of Lords, 14 July 2005.

[52] Lord Hoyle, speech to the House of Lords, 14 July 2005.

[53] Julian Brazier, House of Commons Debates, 14 July 2005.

[54] Ibid.

[55] Lt. Col. Tim Collins, "They'll destroy the qualities that made our Forces great," *Daily Telegraph*, 21 July 2005.

[56] Author's interview with Jed Babbin, 8 September 2005.

[57] http://www.issues2000.org/2004/Wesley_Clark_Foreign_Policy.htm.

[58] Ibid.

[59] *Congressional Record*, 26 January 1994, S123.

[60] Ibid., S123.

[61] Ibid., S121.

[62] Dennis Kucinich, "The U.S. Administration and the ICC," *Common Dreams*, 9 December 2004, http://www.globalpolicy.org/intljustice/icc/2004/1209kucinich.htm.

[63] Senator Hillary Rodham Clinton, speech to the Munich Conference on Security Policy, 13 February 2005.

[64] Fox News Sunday, 21 March 2004, transcript #032101cb.

[65] Citizens for Global Solutions, http://www.iccnow.org/pressroom/member-mediastatements/2005/CGS_McCainpr_28Jan05.pdf.

Chapter Three

[1] *Marketplace*, American Public Media, news archives, 18 January 1996, http://marketplace.publicradio.org/shows/1996/01/18_mpp.html.

[2] Transcript, *NewsHour* with Jim Lehrer, 6 December 1999.

[3] Walter Jones, *Congressional Record*, 9 June 2005, H4304.

[4] Paul K. McMasters, national president, Society of Professional Journalists et al., letter to President William Jefferson Clinton, 14 September 1994.

[5] Newt Gingrich, quoted by Congressman Ron Paul, *Congressional Record*, 9 June 2005, H4305.

[6] Dana Rohrabacher, *Congressional Record*, 9 June 2005, H4312.

[7] United States Trade Representative, "State Sovereignty and Trade Agreements: The Facts," 14 April 2005.

[8] Jim Kolbe, *Congressional Record*, 9 June 2005, H4306.

[9] William Hawkins, "Risky WTO Trade-offs," *Washington Times*, 15 April, 2005.

[10] Ibid.

[11] Ileana Ros-Lehtinen, *Congressional Record*, 23 July 1998, H6189.

[12] Greg Wright, "WTO orders U.S. to stop unfair-trade relief to firms," *Gannett News Service*, 17 January 2003.

[13] John Skorburg, "House Passes Pro-Growth Tax Reforms," *Budget & Tax News*, 1 August 2004.

[14] Jeffrey Sparshott, "WTO derides U.S. tax breaks," *Washington Times*, 1 October 2005.

[15] Alan Beattie, "Boxed in: protectionism is again afoot but tight rules are keeping a lid on trade wars," *Financial Times*, 7 June 2005.

[16] Peter Ford, "Sparks still flying in transatlantic trade dispute," *Christian Science Monitor*, 8 December 2003.

[17] Press release, Public Citizen, 9 June 2005.

[18] Ibid.

[19] Peter Visclosky, *Congressional Record*, 9 June 2005, H4310.

[20] Federal Register, "Regulation of Fuels and Fuel Additives: Baseline Requirements for Gasoline Produced by Foreign Refiners," 6 May 1997, vol. 62, no. 87, p. 24775, http://www.epa.gov/fedrgstr/EPA-AIR/1997/May/Day-06/a11629.htm.

[21] Philip Crane, *Congressional Record*, 1 February 1996, E174.

[22] World Trade Organization, Dispute Settlement DS285, United States— Measures Affecting the Cross-Border Supply of Gambling and Betting Services, summary to date at 1 June 2005.

[23] Sam Cage, "U.S. Can Keep Some Restrictions in Internet Gambling, WTO Rules," *Associated Press*, 8 April 2005.

[24] Lee Davidson, "Outside Pressure: Will international deals force gambling on Utah?" *Deseret Morning News*, 30 June 2005.

[25] Press Release, "U.S. Byrd Amendment: WTO Says Eight WTO Members May Retaliate Against the U.S.—Joint Press Statement by Brazil, Canada, Chile, The EU, India, Japan, Korea, and Mexico," 31 August 2004.

[26] *NewsHour*, "WTO Approves Record Sanctions Against U.S.," 30 August 2002.

[27] Charles Grassley, *Congressional Record*, 24 February 2000, S775.

[28] *NewsHour*, "WTO Rules Against American Cotton Subsidies, U.S. Vows Appeal," 18 June 2004.

[29] *NewsHour*, "WTO Rules Against U.S. Cotton Subsidies," 27 April 2004.

[30] *NewsHour*, "WTO Rules EU Can Retaliate Against U.S. in Trade Dispute," 24 February 2004.

[31] Issue Brief, U.S. Business and Industrial Council, undated, http://www.usbusiness.org/i4a/pages/index.cfm?pageid=16.

[32] International Trade Administration, http://www.ita.doc.gov/td/industry/otea/usfth/aggregate/H04t01.html.

[33] Dick Nanto and Thomas Lum, U.S. International Trade: Data and Forecasts, Congressional Research Service, 16 August 2005.

[34] Jim Kolbe, *Congressional Record*, 9 June 2005, H4306.

[35] Joel Popkin and Company, "Securing America's Future: The Case for a Strong Manufacturing Base," National Association of Manufacturers, June 2003.

[36] Pat Choate, "Bootleg Kingdom of Asia," *International Herald Tribune*, 13 May 2005.

[37] Pat Choate, "The U.S. China Economic and Security Review Commission," Hoover Institution, April 2005.

[38] Lindsey Graham, *Congressional Record*, 27 April 2004, S4424.

Chapter Four

[1] George W. Bush, address to a joint session of Congress, 20 September 2001.

[2] Department of State, "Patterns of Global Terrorism 2003," April 2004. http://www.state.gov/s/ct/rls/pgtrpt/2003/31880.htm

[3] Kofi Annan, "Fighting Terrorism on a Global Front," *New York Times*, 21 September 2001.

[4] "American Jews Slam Kofi Annan's Visit to Arafat Grave," IsraelNationalNews.com, 18 March 2005.

[5] Yassir Arafat, address to the General Assembly, 13 November 1974.

[6] Ibid.

[7] Ibid.

[8] Fidel Castro, address to the General Assembly, 26 September 1960.

[9] "Fidel Castro on the United States: Selected Statements, 1958–2003," foreword by Jaime Suchlicki, February 2003.

[10] Department of State, "Country Reports on Terrorism 2004," April 2005.

[11] Arnold Beichman, "Assignment UN," *Washington Times*, 19 November 2004.

[12] "Country Reports on Terrorism 2004."

[13] Gareth Smyth, "Wipe Israel from map, says Iran's president," *Financial Times*, 26 October 2005.

[14] Ibid.

[15] Report of the International Independent Investigation Commission Established Pursuant to Security Council Resolution 1595, October 2005.

[16] Ibid.

[17] Contributions from Member States to the United Nations regular budget for the year 2003, www.runic-europe.org/swedish/FNsOrganMedlemmar/Budget/ST.ADM.SER.B.597.pdf.

[18] State Department, "Voting Practices in the United Nations 2004." http://www.state.gov/p/io/rls/rpt/c14622.htm

[19] "State Department Official Touts Partnerships for Peace, Human Rights," 4 October 2004. http://usinfo.state.gov/dhr/Archive/2004/Oct/05-345946.html

[20] *Macmillan Dictionary of Political Quotations* (New York: Macmillan Publishing, 1992).

[21] Human Rights Watch, "Child Trafficking in Togo," April 2003.

[22] Department of State, "Country Reports on Human Rights Practices 2004," 28 February 2005.

[23] Brief historic overview of the Commission on Human Rights," http://www.ohchr.org/english/bodies/chr/docs/brief-historic.doc.

[24] Ibid.

[25] George Gedda, "U.S. blasts human rights panel selection," *Seattle Post Intelligencer*, 8 February 2005.

[26] "U.S. Suspected of Keeping Secret Prisoners on Warships: UN Official," *Agence France-Presse*, 29 June 2005.

[27] Ibid.

[28] "Report of the Special Rapporteur on the Adverse Effects of the Illicit Movement and Dumping of Toxic and Dangerous Products and Wastes on the Enjoyment of Human Rights on her Mission to the United States of America," 10 January 2003.

[29] Report of the secretary-general, "In larger freedom: towards development, security and human rights for all," March 2005.

[30] Colum Lynch, "U.N. Official Quits in Harassment Case," *Washington Post*, 21 February 2005.

[31] Richard Waddington, "U.N. official quits amid harass case," *Washington Times*, 21 February 2005.

[32] John Zarocostas, "Refugees report more sex abuse," *Washington Times*, 24 October 2003.

[33] Colum Lynch, "Report Cites Mismanagement in UN Elections Office," *Washington Post*, 31 March 2005.

[34] Philip Pullella, "Mugabe calls Bush, Blair 'terrorists,'" *Washington Times*, 18 October 2005.

[35] Ariel David, "Mugabe, Chavez blame U.S., other rich nations for world's woes," *Associated Press*, 18 October 2005.

[36] Charles Lawrence and Philip Sherwell, "Annan talks of 'lynch mob' determined to destroy him," *Daily Telegraph*, 1 May 2005.

[37] http://www.theinterpretermovie.com.

[38] United Nations Educational, Scientific, and Cultural Organization, Approved Programme and Budget 2000–2001, http://unesdoc.unesco.org/images/0012/001206/120679e.pdf.

[39] Press release, "World Meteorological Day, 23 March 2005: Weather, climate, water and sustainable development," 23 March 2005.

[40] Press release, "Governance and administrative innovations to be recognized on Public Service Day," 21 June 2005, http://unpan1.un.org/intradoc/groups/public/documents/un/unpan020571.pdf

[41] UNESCO, Declaration of Principles on Tolerance, 16 November 1995.

Chapter Five

[1] Kofi Annan, address at the International Women's Forum, 27 May 1997, from *The Quotable Kofi Annan: Selections from Speeches and Statements by the Secretary-General* (New York: United Nations Department of Public Information, 1998).

[2] Kofi Annan, address to the World Economic Forum, 31 January 1998, from *The Quotable Kofi Annan.*

[3] *Macmillan Dictionary of Political Quotations* (New York: Macmillan Publishing, 1992).

[4] Ibid.

[5] World Commission on the Social Dimension of Globalization, "A Fair Globalization: Creating Opportunities for All," February 2004, paragraph 537. http://www.ilo.org/public/english/wcsdg/docs/report.pdf

[6] Ibid., paragraph 335.

[7] Ibid. paragraph 29.

[8] Richard Rahn, "Drift to World Government?" *Washington Times*, 31 May 2005.

[9] Gordon Brown, Conference on Corporate Social Responsibility, 22 January 2003.

[10] Press release, "UNDP Chief welcomes Gordon Brown's 'bold' new proposal for financing investment in developing nations," 22 January 2003.

[11] Report of the High-level Panel on Financing for Development, Principal Recommendations, June 2001, 22.

[12] Ibid.

[13] Kofi Annan, press conference, 21 March 2005.

[14] The UK Proposal for an International Finance Facility, April 2004, paragraph 4.3.

[15] Ibid., paragraph 3.7.

[16] Ibid., paragraph 3.9.

[17] Henry Hyde, "This is how America would tackle Africa," *Daily Telegraph*, 26 June 2005.

[18] Tobin Tax Network Position Paper on the International Finance Facility, Fall 2003.

[19] *Congressional Record*, 22 January 1996, S278.

[20] Mark Malloch Brown, letter to David Welch, assistant secretary of state for International Organization Affairs, 16 July 1999.

[21] World Commission on the Social Dimension of Globalization, "A Fair Globalization," paragraph 465.

[22] Ibid., 469.

[23] Report of the High-level Panel, June 2001, 26.

[24] Jacques Chirac, address to the UN World Summit on Sustainable Development, 2 September 2002.

[25] Irwin Arief, "Missing signature mars launch of war on hunger," *Reuters*, 22 September 2004.

[26] Ibid.

[27] Letter from the secretary-general to the president of the General Assembly, 25 June 2001.

[28] Report of the High-level Panel, June 2001, 28.

[29] Ibid., 65.

[30] Ibid., 9.

[31] Dan Mitchell, "A one-world taxing authority?" *Washington Times*, 21 August 2001.

[32] Report of the High-level Panel, June 2001, 28.

[33] Ibid., 66.

[34] Ibid.

[35] Ibid.

[36] Ibid., 5.

[37] *Macmillan Dictionary of Political Quotations*.

[38] Eduard Shevardnaze, address to the General Assembly, 7 September 2000.

[39] Compilation of quotes found at www.france.diplomatie.fr/frmonde/onue-en/onue66.html.

[40] Countries with the highest emissions of organic water pollutants, www.aneki.com/water_pollution.html.

[41] Marc Morano, "Eskimo Filing Against U.S. Just Tip of Legal Iceberg," *Cybercast News Service*, 17 December 2004.

[42] Report of the Working Group on Internet Governance, June 2005, 12.

[43] CircleID, "Interview with United Nations Secretariat of WGIG," 30 July 2004.

[44] Ibid., 13.

[45] Interview with Richard Lessner on Rightalk.com, 11 October 2005.

[46] Ibid.

[47] Carl Bildt, "Keep the Internet Free," *International Herald Tribune*, 11 October 2005.

[48] Transcript, press conference by the secretary-general, 21 March 2005. http://www.un.org/News/Press/docs/2005/sgsm9772.doc.htm.

Chapter Six

1 "Iraq says it will fire at planes in no-fly zones," CNN, 26 December 1998, www.cnn.com/WORLD/meast/9812/26/iraq.02/.

2 General Anthony Zinni, DoD News briefing, 25 January 1999.

3 Ibid.

4 Charles Duelfer, "Comprehensive Report of the Special Advisor to the DCI on Iraq's WMD," Regime Finance and Procurement, 30 September 2004, 3.

5 "The Saddam Oil Bribes: The Complete al-Mada List," 25 January 2004, found at www.globalpolicy.org/security/sanction/iraq1/oilforfood/2004/0125almadalist.htm.

6 *Macmillan Dictionary of Political Quotations* (New York: Macmillan Publishing, 1992).

7 "The Saddam Oil Bribes."

8 Ibid.

9 "Inside the Oil-for-Food Scandal w/Eric Shawn," Foxnews.com, 17 September 2004.

10 Christopher Shays, statement in House of Representatives, *Congressional Record*, 13 July 2004, H5627.

11 Robert Novak, "Oil for Graft At the U.N.," *Washington Post*, 15 November 2004.

12 Press release, "Kucinich, 20 Members of Congress, Send Letter of Support for UN Secretary-General Annan," office of Congressman Dennis Kucinich, 8 December 2004.

13 News release, "Serrano: Let Paul Volcker Do His Job," office of Congressman Jose Serrano, 3 December 2004.

14 David Sands and Katherine Clad, "Inspector saw 'holes' in oil-for-food," *Washington Times*, 18 March 2005.

15 Duelfer, "Comprehensive Report of the Special Advisor: Regime Finance and Procurement," 21.

[16] Ibid.

[17] Resolution 986, UN Security Council, 14 April 1995.

[18] Ibid.

[19] Duelfer, "Comprehensive Report of the Special Adviser: Regime Finance and Procurement," 22.

[20] Ibid.

[21] Resolution 986, UN Security Council, 14 April 1995.

[22] Paul Volcker, Independent Inquiry Committee, interim report, 3 February 2005.

[23] Michael Soussan, testimony before the House International Relations Committee, 28 April 2004.

[24] Volcker, IIC, interim report.

[25] Ibid.

[26] Betsy Pisik, "Annan fires oil-for-food staffer," *Washington Times*, 2 June 2005.

[27] Paul Volcker, Independent Inquiry Committee, third interim report, 8 August 2005.

[28] Volcker, IIC, interim report.

[29] Ibid.

[30] Volcker, IIC, third interim report.

[31] Ibid.

[32] Ibid.

[33] "U.N. Warns Oil-for-Food Companies on Documents," Fox News, 6 May 2004.

[34] Volcker, IIC, interim report.

[35] Dale McFeatters, "Clueless Kofi Annan," *Washington Times*, 2 April 2005.

[36] Paul Volcker, Independent Inquiry Committee, second interim report, 29 March 2005.

[37] Colum Lynch, "Annan's Contacts with Firm Probed," *Washington Post*, 24 March 2005.

[38] "Kofi's Accountability," *Wall Street Journal*, 30 March 2005.

[39] Yochi Dreazen, "Kofi Annan Calls Volcker Report An 'Exoneration,'" *Wall Street Journal*, 30 March 2005.

[40] Colum Lynch, "Kofi Annan Cleared in Corruption Probe," *Washington Post*, 30 March 2005.

[41] Bronwen Maddox, "Oil-for-Food fiasco could be repeated much too easily," *Times Online*, 31 March 2005.

[42] "US and UK blamed for oil scandal," BBC News, 15 April 2005.

[43] Colum Lynch, "Panel is Revisiting Annan Ties to Firm," *Washington Post*, 15 June 2005.

[44] Volcker, IIC, second interim report.

[45] Ibid.

[46] Ibid.

[47] Ibid.

[48] Jeff Johnson and Kathleen Rhodes, "UN Oil for Food: Conflicts of Interest and Institutional Corruption," *CNSNews.com*, 16 December 2004.

[49] Ibid.

[50] Volcker, IIC, interim report.

[51] United Nations Association of the United States of America, "Annual Report," 2000–2001.

[52] Nile Gardiner, "Kofi's Hour Is Up," *National Review*, 13 December 2004.

[53] Maggie Farley, "U.N. Oil-for-Food Inquiry Findings Surprised Volcker," *Los Angeles Times*, 28 October 2005.

[54] Desmond Butler, "Investigator decries oil-for-food probe," *Associated Press*, 23 April 2005.

[55] "Danforth: Volcker Doesn't Have Right Tools," Fox News, 8 January 2004.

[56] Paul Volcker, Independent Inquiry Committee, "The Management of the United Nations Oil-for-Food Programme," vol. 1, 7 September 2005.

Chapter Seven

[1] From Niccolo Machiavelli's *The Prince*, as found in *Macmillan Dictionary of Political Quotations* (New York: Macmillan Publishing, 1992).

[2] George W. Bush, remarks by the president on National Missile Defense, 13 December 2001.

[3] Bill Clinton, address to the General Assembly, 22 September 1997.

[4] Institute for Agriculture and Trade Policy, Treaty Database Online, http://www.iatp.org/global/tdb_execsummary.cfm.

[5] Tom Lantos, *Congressional Record*, 23 June 2004, H4788.

[6] Ibid., H4787.

[7] Phyllis Schlafly, "Kyoto's Goal = Kick the U.S.," *The Phyllis Schlafly Report*, July 2001.

[8] "Reality Check: Straight Talk About the Kyoto Protocol," U.S. Chamber of Commerce, undated.

[9] Bill Clinton, address to the General Assembly, 22 September 1997.

[10] United Nations Convention on the Law of the Sea, 10 December 1982, preamble.

[11] Frank Gaffney, "Freedom at sea, too," *Washington Times*, 25 January 2005.

[12] United Nations Convention on the Law of the Sea, preamble.

[13] Ibid., Article 144, paragraph 2.

[14] Phyllis Schlafly, "Defeat the UN Law of the Sea Treaty," *The Phyllis Schlafly Report*, February 2005.

[15] Ibid.

[16] Oliver North, "The Trojan Horse on America's Shores," *Military.com*, 31 March 2005.

[17] Doug Bandow, "Don't Resurrect the Law of the Sea Treaty," CATO Institute Policy Analysis, 13 October 2005.

[18] The Great UN Gun Debate with Rebecca Peters (IANSA) and Wayne LaPierre (NRA) from King's College, London, England, 12 October 2004.

[19] Ibid.

[20] United Nations Conference on the Illicit Trade in Small Arms and Light Weapons in All Its Aspects, July 2001, www.un.org/Depts/dda/CAB/smallarms/brochure.htm.

[21] Ibid.

[22] The Great UN Gun Debate.

[23] Control Arms Briefing Paper, "Toward an Arms Trade Treaty," June 2005.

[24] Ibid.

[25] Ibid.

[26] Founding Document of IANSA, www.iansa.org/mission/m1.htm.

[27] The Great UN Gun Debate.

[28] Ibid.

[29] UN General Assembly, Recommendation of Brazil, Mali, the Netherlands, and the United Kingdom of Great Britain and Northern Ireland, 10 April 2001.

[30] Ibid.

[31] Ibid.

[32] Ibid.

[33] Framework Convention on Tobacco Control, Article 3.

[34] Ibid., Article 4, paragraph 1.

[35] Ibid., Article 6, paragraph 2(a).

[36] Ibid., Article 11, paragraph 1(b).

[37] Ibid., Article 11, paragraphs 1(b)(iii), (iv), (v).

[38] Ibid., Article 13, paragraph 2.

[39] Ibid., Article 13, paragraph 3.

[40] "The Death Penalty in 2003: Year End Report," Death Penalty Information Center, December 2003.

[41] Jeffrey Toobin, "How Anthony Kennedy's passion for foreign law could change the Supreme Court," *The New Yorker*, 12 September 2005.

[42] Letter to Members of Congress, July 2000, quoted in "How the Death Penalty Weakens U.S. International Interests," ACLU, December 2004.

[43] John Paul Stevens, *Atkins v. Virginia*, majority opinion, decided 20 June 2002.

[44] Ibid., footnote 21.

[45] William Rehnquist, *Atkins v. Virginia*, dissenting opinion, decided 20 June 2002.

[46] Ibid.

[47] Antonin Scalia, *Atkins v. Virginia*, dissenting opinion, decided 20 June 2002.

[48] Ibid.

[49] William Brennan, *Stanford v. Kentucky*, dissenting opinion, decided 26 June 1989.

[50] Anthony Kennedy, *Lawrence v. Texas*, majority opinion, decided 26 June 2003.

[51] Ibid.

[52] Ibid.

[53] Ibid.

[54] Antonin Scalia, *Lawrence v. Texas*, dissenting opinion, decided 26 June 2003.

[55] Ruth Bader Ginsburg, *Grutter v. Bollinger*, concurring opinion, decided 23 June 2003.

Chapter Eight

[1] Rowan Scarborough, "Venezuela seeks nuclear technology," *Washington Times*, 17 October 2005.

[2] Mahmoud Ahmadinejad, statement before the General Assembly, 14 September 2005.

[3] Mahmoud Ahmadinejad, address before the General Assembly, 17 September 2005.

[4] "United Nations Conferences: What have they Accomplished?" www.un.org/News/facts/confercs.htm.

[5] Ibid.

[6] Jacques Chirac, address to the General Assembly, 6 September 2000.

[7] Wim Kok, address to the General Assembly, 6 September 2000.

[8] Qaboos bin Ali bin Faisal Al-Said, Sultan of Oman, prepared statement to the General Assembly, 6 September 2000.

[9] Marc Morano, "Bush Blamed for 'Devastating Consequences of Global Warming,'" *CNSNews.com*, 15 December 2004.

[10] Press Conference by UNAIDS at the World Summit on Sustainable Development, 30 August 2002.

[11] Transcript, "NOW with Bill Moyers," 30 August 2002. http://www.pbs.org/now/transcript/transcript132_full.html

[12] Tony Blair, Address to the General Assembly, September 6, 2000.

[13] President Richard Nixon, address to the 25th anniversary session of the General Assembly of the United Nations, 23 October 1970.

[14] UN Resolution 2626, paragraph 43, 24 October 1970.

[15] Press Release SG/SM/7406, "Secretary-General, Receiving Doctorate of Laws, Gives Commencement Address at Notre Dame," 19 May 2000.

[16] Kofi Annan, address to the International Conference on Financing for Development, 19 March 2002.

[17] George W. Bush, remarks by the president at the United Nations Financing for Development Conference, 22 March 2002.

[18] George W. Bush, remarks by the president on global development, 14 March 2002.

[19] Glenn Kessler and Jon Jeter, "Powell Jeered at Development Summit," *Washington Post*, 5 September 2002.

[20] Marc Morano, "American Environmentalist: 'I'm Ashamed for My Country,'" *CNSNews.com*, 5 September 2002.

[21] Heartland Institute, "Critics of U.S. confined to Johannesburg sidelines," 1 October 2002.

[22] Press release, "Chirac Goes Wild in Johannesburg," Freedom Alliance, 2 September 2002.

[23] Mary Robinson, United Nations press release, 18 January 2001.

[24] U.S. State Department, Country Reports on Human Rights Practices, 4 March 2002.

[25] Ibid.

[26] Tom Lantos, "The Durban Debacle: An Insider's View of the World Racism Conference at Durban," Fletcher Forum of World Affairs, Winter/Spring 2002.

[27] Remarks by the President and Secretary Rumsfeld in Announcement of Chairman and Vice-Chairman of the Joint Chiefs of Staff, 24 August 2001.

[28] CNN, "U.S. stance on U.N. racism conference debated," 29 August 2001.

[29] Lantos, "Durban Debacle."

Chapter Nine

[1] Gregory Jaynes, "Coming to America: A Somali Bantu refugee family leaves 19th-century travails behind in Africa to take up life in 21st-century Phoenix," *Smithsonian Magazine*, January 2004.

[2] Ibid.

[3] Jonah Goldberg, "Hollywood Fools," *National Review*, 18 September 2000.

[4] Michael Medved, "War Films, Hollywood, and Popular Culture," *Imprimis*, May 2005.

[5] CNN, "Annan courts celebrity support in L.A. visit." *CNN.com*, 22 April 1998.

[6] Kofi Annan, "The Humanitarian Challenge Today," address to the Los Angeles World Affairs Council, 21 April 1998.

[7] CNN, "Annan courts celebrity support in L.A. visit," *CNN.com*, 22 April 1998.

[8] UN Press Release SG/SM/8277, "Secretary-General Urges Goodwill Ambassadors 'To Help Us Make the World a Better Place,'" 18 June 2002.

[9] CNN, "Larry King Live," 15 October 2002, http://www.blackcommentator.com/14_belafonte_pr.html.

[10] Joseph Farah, "Belafonte, Glover trash U.S. in Cuba," *WorldNetDaily.com,* 16 December 2002.

[11] Ibid.

[12] Harry Belafonte, address at the 2004 Global Exchange Human Rights Awards Ceremony, 10 June 2004.

[13] Ibid.

[14] UN Newsservice, "Messengers of Peace, Goodwill Ambassadors to meet for first time at UN," undated, found at Foreign Policy Association, http://www.fpa.org/topics_info2414/topics_info_show.htm?doc_id=37807.

[15] Belafonte, address at the 2004 Global Exchange Human Rights Awards Ceremony.

[16] Ibid.

[17] Ibid.

[18] UN Press Release SG/SM/8277, "Secretary-General Urges Goodwill Ambassadors 'To Help Us Make The World A Better Place.'"

[19] Belafonte, address at the 2004 Global Exchange Human Rights Awards Ceremony.

[20] Ibid.

[21] *Tavis Smiley Show,* PBS, 4 February 2004.

[22] "Belafonte Says U.S. Leaders 'Possessed of Evil,'" *Reuters,* 4 March 2003.

[23] *Roll Call,* 9 March 2005.

[24] *Boston Globe,* 8 March 2005.

[25] *Reuters,* 7 March 2005.

[26] Media Research Center, "Actor Danny Glover Calls Bush a 'Racist,'" *Cyberalert,* 12 February 2003.

[27] Dave Sommers, "Lethal Lesson," *The Trentonian,* 16 November 2001, http://www.zwire.com/site/Danny_Glover.html.

[28] Ibid.

[30] Michael Medved, *Hollywood vs. America* (New York: Harper Collins, 1992), 216.

[31] Media Research Center, "Sarandon's Anti-War Rant," *Cyberalert,* 29 October 2002.

[32] Ibid.

[33] Ibid.

[34] "Sarandon attacks Oscars control," BBC News, 27 May 2003.

[35] United Nations, "Press Conference on 'Artists for the UN,'" 5 February 2004, www.un.org/News/briefings/docs/2004/artistsPC.doc.htm.

[36] "Drew Barrymore named 'Friend of the UN,'" Reuters, http://www.chron-watch.com/content/contentDisplay.asp?aid=5862.

[37] www.theinterpretermovie.com.

[38] Ibid.

[39] Ibid.

[40] Walter Cronkite, "United Nations, national sovereignty and the future of the world," address upon receiving the Norman Cousins Global Governance Award, 19 October 1999.

[41] Ibid.

[42] Ibid.

[43] Ibid.

[44] Walter Cronkite, "New hope for the UN," *Denver Post*, 29 July 2004, http://web.radicalparty.org/pressreview/print_right.php?func=detail&par=10628.

[45] Strobe Talbott, "The Birth of a Global Nation," *Time*, 20 July 1992.

[46] Ibid.

[47] Ibid.

[48] "Harvard Professor Condemns U.S. Policies in Johannesburg," Freedom Alliance, 29 August 2002.

[49] Jeffrey Sachs, "Africa's Suffering is Bush's Shame," *Los Angeles Times*, 12 June 2005.

[50] Jeffrey Sachs, *The End of Poverty* (New York: Penguin Press, 2005), 281.

[51] Jeffrey Sachs, "The March to Barbarism," *Project Syndicate*, May 2004.

[52] Ibid.

[53] Ibid.

[54] Ibid.

[55] Ibid.

[56] Jeffrey Sachs, "Globalization and the United Nations," *Project Syndicate*, November 2001.

[57] John Harris, "Bill Clinton Takes Spot on Global Stage," *Washington Post*, 1 June 2005.

[58] Bill Clinton, address to the UN General Assembly, 27 September 1993.

[59] Eddie Bernice Johnson et al., letter to UN secretary-general Kofi Annan, 1 July 2004.

[60] Ibid.

[61] Shelia Jackson Lee, *Congressional Record*, 21 September 2004, 7321.

[62] Steve Buyer, *Congressional Record*, 15 July 2004, H5862.

[63] "US lawmakers ask for poll observers," *Al Jazeera*, 2 July 2004.

[64] Corrine Brown, *Congressional Record*, 15 July 2004, 5865.

[65] Eddie Bernice Johnson et al., letter to UN Secretary-General Kofi Annan, 1 July 2004.

[66] Eddie Bernice Johnson, press release, "Congresswoman Johnson Gains Assurance from State Department that Observers will Monitor Upcoming Election," 4 August 2004.

[67] Press release, "Global Exchange Plans to Host at least 28 Independent Monitors to Observe U.S. Elections," undated, http://www.fairelection.us/PressRoom/pr_gx1.htm.

[68] Dick Gephardt, swearing in of Speaker Newt Gingrich, 4 January 1995, http://lab.pava.purdue.edu/pol101/Exercises/Ex33/Speeches/Speech8.html.

[69] OSCE/ODIHR Needs Assessment Mission Report, 7-10 September 2004.

[70] Ibid.

[71] Ibid.

[72] Ibid.